D0152587

Graham and Anna Ritchie

SCOTLAND
Archaeology and early history

WITH 149 ILLUSTRATIONS

THAMES AND HUDSON

Ancient Peoples and Places
GENERAL EDITOR: GLYN DANIEL

First published in the USA in 1981 by Thames and Hudson, Inc., 500 Fifth Avenue, New York, New York 10110

Library of Congress Catalog Card Number 80-52043

Printed in Spain

D.L.TO – 985–80

Contents

Acknowledgments

We would like to thank the Royal Commission on the Ancient and Historical Monuments of Scotland, the Scottish Development Department and the National Museum of Antiquities of Scotland for permission to use a number of Crown Copyright photographs and drawings, and also the many people and institutions who have made photographs available and have given permission to publish them, including material relating to SDD financed excavations now held by the National Monuments Record of Scotland. Details will be found in the List of Illustrations.

Several friends have given permission for the use of photographs of their as yet unpublished excavations and have provided us with information about the sites; we are particularly grateful to John Barber, Michael Brooks, Trevor Cowie, John Hedges, Peter Hill and Trevor Watkins for their assistance. Betty Naggar and Rupert Roddam have kindly made available a number of photographs for incorporation in this volume.

The line drawings have been prepared by Ian G. Scott and we are much indebted to him for his collaboration and skill.

We are specially grateful to colleagues who have read and commented upon our manuscript, in particular David Breeze, Joanna Close-Brooks, Alastair MacLaren, Jack Stevenson and W. F. Ritchie, and we are very grateful for the patience and skill of Elizabeth Glass who typed it.

Graham and Anna Ritchie

The Watch Stone and the Stone of Odin, with the Ring of Brodgar in the background, Orkney. The Stone of Odin was felled and broken to pieces in 1814

1 Map of Scotland showing administrative regions and districts

BORDERS REGION
1 Berwickshire
2 Ettrick and Lauderdale
3 Roxburgh
4 Tweeddale

CENTRAL REGION
5 Clackmannan
6 Falkirk
7 Stirling

DUMFRIES AND GALLOWAY REGION
8 Annandale and Eskdale
9 Nithsdale
10 Stewartry
11 Wigtown

FIFE REGION
12 Dunfermline
13 Kirkcaldy
14 North-East Fife

GRAMPIAN REGION
15 Aberdeen
16 Banff and Buchan
17 Gordon
18 Kincardine and Deeside
19 Moray

HIGHLAND REGION
20 Badenoch and Strathspey
21 Caithness
22 Inverness
23 Lochaber
24 Nairn
25 Ross and Cromarty
26 Skye and Lochalsh
27 Sutherland

LOTHIAN REGION
28 East Lothian
29 Edinburgh
30 Midlothian
31 West Lothian

STRATHCLYDE REGION
32 Argyll and Bute
33 Bearsden and Milngavie
34 Clydebank
35 Cumbernauld and Kilsyth
36 Cumnock and Doon Valley
37 Cunninghame
38 Dumbarton
39 East Kilbride
40 Eastwood
41 Glasgow
42 Hamilton
43 Inverclyde
44 Kilmarnock and Loudoun
45 Kyle and Carrick
46 Lanark
47 Monklands
48 Motherwell
49 Renfrew
50 Strathkelvin

TAYSIDE REGION
51 Angus
52 Dundee
53 Perth and Kinross

Preface

'The zeal for Archaeological investigation which has recently manifested itself in nearly every country of Europe, has been traced, not without reason, to the impulse which proceeded from Abbotsford.' In 1851, Daniel Wilson, in *The Archaeology and Prehistoric Annals of Scotland*, looked back to the writings of Sir Walter Scott for the beginnings of archaeology as a popular subject. The study of Scotland's past had been embraced within the wide interests of such seventeenth- and eighteenth-century scholars as Sir Robert Sibbald, Alexander Gordon and Sir John Clerk of Penicuik. The standing stones, brochs and Roman remains of the Scottish countryside had been included by travellers such as Edward Lhwyd, Thomas Pennant, Richard Pococke and Sir Joseph Banks in accounts of their northern tours. Daniel Wilson, however, set out the theoretical basis on which the study of archaeology in Scotland was to proceed, within a 'consistent and comprehensive system', introducing for the first time the term 'prehistoric' to the English language.

Scottish archaeology from the middle of the nineteenth century till World War I embraced two main scholarly traditions: the first, collecting, cataloguing and publishing material primarily, though not exclusively, within a Scottish context; the second, seeking to place aspects of the archaeological record into a wider framework, either from the point of view of European archaeology as a whole, or from the point of view of practical ethnology. Joseph Anderson, who was in charge of the collections of the Society of Antiquaries of Scotland, and thus of the National Museum of Antiquities of Scotland, from 1870 to 1913, set new standards in the study of prehistoric and historical material in Scotland, often using a recent discovery or a series of finds to classify a whole range of existing material. Anderson's masterly survey of the archaeology of Scotland was undertaken as the Rhind lectures of the Society of Antiquaries of Scotland between 1879 and 1882, and published as *Scotland in Early Christian Times* (1881) and *Scotland in Pagan Times* (1883 and 1886); Gordon Childe's assessment of Anderson's achievement, in the introduction to his own *Prehistory of Scotland*, was that he 'had sketched the essential outlines of Scottish prehistory in a comprehensive and scientific survey such as then existed in no other country'. Robert Munro and the Hon. John Abercromby presented Scottish discoveries in broader European contexts. Sir Arthur Mitchell, on the other hand, saw the importance of modern ethnography in illuminating ancient remains.

Scottish archaeology in the 1920s and 1930s seems to have suffered from over-zealous excavations with at best rudimentary recording systems, but there were also more meticulous workers such as H. E. Kilbride-Jones, whose important excavations of the stone circles of Cullerlie and Loanhead of Daviot, in Aberdeenshire, were published in 1935. Gordon Childe, holder of the Abercromby Chair of Archaeology at the University of Edinburgh from 1927 to 1945, worked energetically in Scotland, undertaking excavations at Skara Brae and Rinyo in Orkney, and fieldwork in many areas of the country at the beginning of World War II. He produced two general accounts, *The Prehistory of Scotland* in 1935 and *Scotland Before the Scots*, the latter being the Rhind Lectures for 1944, in which he adopted a Marxist stance to explain the changes in prehistory in 'strictly historical action'. Stuart Piggott, holder of the Abercromby Chair from 1946 to 1977, directed excavations on many important sites, including Cairnpapple, West Lothian and Dalladies, Kincardineshire; Childe and Piggott saw Scottish archaeology within a British and European context.

The chronological framework of this study of early Scotland is provided by a large number of radiocarbon determinations, a method that has revolutionized our approach to the past. All living things contain a small quantity of radioactive carbon which is lost through radioactive decay but which, in life, is replenished by cosmic radiation and thus remains a constant amount. On death, however, the radioactive carbon (carbon-14) decays at a fixed rate. The principle of the radiocarbon dating method is to measure the remaining proportion of radioactive carbon to inactive carbon (carbon-12) in the sample of bone, wood or charcoal and thus to calculate how long the process has been under way. The 'date' calculated in this way is a statement of probability, and is thus expressed along with a standard deviation of the statistical error; so for a date of 5460 bc±80 there is a two to one chance that the actual date will fall between 5540 bc and 5380 bc. But there is a further complication; by comparing radiocarbon dates with tree-ring dates, it has been discovered that there are discrepancies in the results, which may be caused by differing amounts of radioactivity in the atmosphere at different periods. Thus radiocarbon 'dates' are not calendar dates, but an indication of radiocarbon 'years' – and they are expressed with bc or ad as a suffix or prefix to differentiate them from calendar years (BC or AD). Correction tables allow us to calibrate radiocarbon dates and to indicate their 'true' age; there is little fluctuation back to about 500 BC, but earlier dates are too young, for example a radiocarbon date of 1500 bc indicates a calendar date between about 1700 and 1900 BC and 4500 bc is in reality between about 5300 and 5500 BC. We have made the necessary corrections in general indications of the date or span of archaeological events, but we have quoted individual radiocarbon dates in an unaltered form together with their laboratory reference number. It has become fashionable to write about prehistory in terms of radiocarbon years alone, and to expect the reader to make the necessary alterations himself by using the best correction tables available at the time. In a book such as this, that spans prehistory and early history, we should be guilty of using two different time scales – radiocarbon years for Chapters I to V and calendar years for Chapters VI to VIII. The early antiquity of man, and our conception of the length of time covered by the early periods of the archaeology of Scotland, would, we believe, be obscured by the use of uncalibrated dates.

We have tried to keep to the minimum of archaeological jargon, but some is inevitable; 'Mesolithic' describes hunting and gathering communities (Middle Stone Age), 'Neolithic' describes farming communities, with stone but not metal tools (New Stone Age), with 'Bronze Age' and 'Iron Age' providing useful labels for two subsequent periods. The use of such labels does not, however, imply sudden cultural or social differences, any more than does the division of later British history into the Georgian, Victorian and Edwardian periods.

Modern Scotland comprises that part of Britain which lies to the north of the Cheviot Hills. It is an area that possesses complex landforms and geomorphology, to the extent that variety of scenery is one of Scotland's greatest natural assets. There are strong contrasts between the east and west coasts, but the basic divisions of the mainland of Scotland are the geological fault-lines which run southwest-northeast; these form the Southern Uplands, most of which is hill country, the Central Lowlands which, although they include some striking ranges of hills, are marked by such low-lying areas as Strathmore and the Forth and Clyde valleys, and the Highlands. The latter area is divided by the Great Glen, along which runs the modern Caledonian Canal, and it includes the Hebridean islands off the west coast and the Northern Isles of Orkney and Shetland. The Highlands show great contrasts of landscape, from the sand-dune pastures (*machair*) of the Outer Hebrides, through the mainland mountain belt to the eastern lowlands of Caithness and Buchan.

Sea-level changes in post-glacial times have affected Scottish coasts in different ways, and their effects are important for the surviving distribution patterns of archaeological material. As the last ice-sheet melted, the level of the land rose as the weight of the ice was removed (known as 'isostatic recovery'), and sea level also rose with the addition of melt-water; in consequence, there are raised beaches along much of the coast of eastern and south-western Scotland, which increase in altitude towards the main area of glacial accumulation around Rannoch Moor, but, in peripheral areas such as Orkney and Shetland, the rise in sea level exceeded isostatic recovery, with the result that land has been submerged. Continuing coastal erosion is probably the greatest single threat to the survival of archaeological sites in Scotland.

The end of the Ice Age with its accompanying rise in temperature wrought considerable changes in flora and fauna. Open grasslands were replaced by dense woodland, and reindeer were replaced by roe deer, red deer, elk and aurochs (wild cattle). This was the environment encountered by the earliest human visitors to Scotland, and it was initially exploited as hunting grounds and latterly adjusted by forest clearance to meet the needs of farming communities. In coastal areas, the destruction of tree-cover brought its own problems in the form of sand-blow, and it is thought that here the effects of a rising sea may have been at work, as well as the human factor, causing not only submergence but also erosion of woodland by salt-spray. Coastal pastures were nevertheless very attractive to animal and human communities; good grass, seaweed and light soils for easy cultivation, together with exploitation of the sea as a food resource, accounts for the concentration of human settlement in such areas. Favourite inland environments from Mesolithic times onwards were river valleys, for ease of movement as well as for their hunting and fishing potential, and the development of mixed farming in Neolithic times made the fertile soils of such areas as Orkney, Aberdeenshire, Angus and central Perthshire attractive to settlers. Relatively little of Scotland is suited to cereal cultivation, however, without intensive drainage, and pastoralism is likely always to have played the major role in the economy.

In early times, the combination of highland terrain, dense woodland and boggy moorlands made internal communication very difficult, and the sea remained the primary means of access. For this reason, the early colonization of Scotland and subsequent movements of people, artefacts and ideas tended to follow two main routes: up the east coast from England or from north-west Europe, and a west coast route from Ireland or western England.

Following local government reorganization in Scotland in 1975 counties were abandoned in favour of a two-tier system based on regions and districts. In the text we have used the old county names as they still provide readily understood geographical divisions; in the index we have added the modern administrative district, where appropriate, as a number, and the map on page 8 bears the numbers with a key alongside.

1

Hunters and Fishermen

The great variety of the natural habitats, the interplay of sea, mountain, river and forest, provided many different environments for the hunting-gathering-fishing communities who made their way into Scotland from the south from about 7000 BC. The coasts of the west offered calm fjords and sheltered bays with good fishing, a rich shoreline and a forested hinterland with abundant deer and boar. Skilled navigation and sturdy skin boats would be necessary for some sea crossings, but sea travel would be the highway to many hunting grounds – not least for seals on outlying skerries.

On the island of Jura a recent series of excavations by John Mercer has allowed a detailed artefact sequence to be built up for the first time in Scotland, a sequence that has been confirmed by a number of radiocarbon dates. While the remains of camp-sites are sparse, three con- 2
joined stone rings on a terrace above the River Lussa, on the east coast of Jura, may be the remains of the earliest stone-built setting so far recorded in Scotland; the stone rings, each about 1.5m in overall diameter, were at the centre of a broad scoop, indicating perhaps the outline of a tented site. Radiocarbon dates of 6244 bc±350 (SRR-160) and 6013 bc±200 (SRR-159) were obtained from charcoal at the bottom of the rings, and with the charcoal were found hazelnuts, red ochre, bones and limpet shells. The flints included small trapeze-shaped and triangular tools. The flint-work suggests a community involved in hunting and in the preparation and use of skins as well as bone and wood; tiny flint implements (microliths) may also have been hafted to assist in the gathering and preparation of vegetable foodstuffs. From the beginning of the sixth millennium BC there is a wider range of flint implements, including burins and chisels. Because of the 3

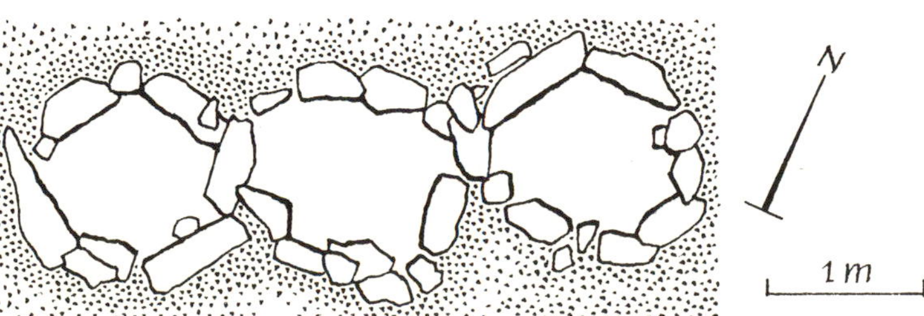

2 Stone rings, Lussa Wood, Jura, Argyll

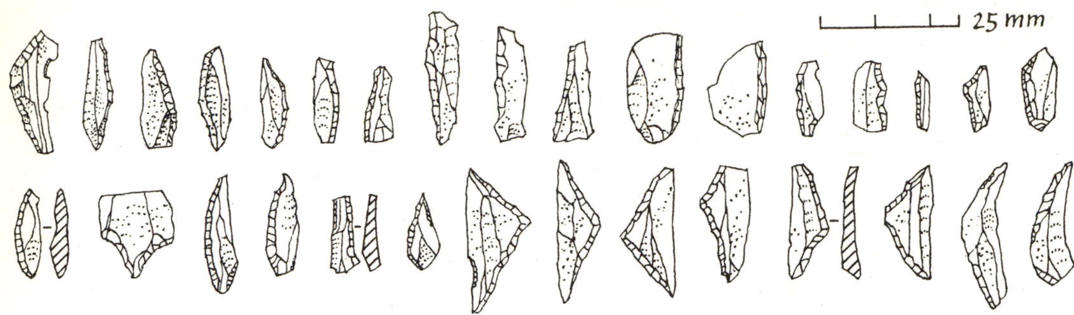

3 Flint microliths, Lussa Bay, Jura, Argyll

acidity of the Jura soil, however, other aspects of the archaeological record, bone-work particularly, are lacking. The second phase of the Jura sequence took place at about the time of the greatest incursions of the post-glacial sea level along the Atlantic coastline; a radiocarbon date of 5464 bc±80 (SRR-161), for example, comes from the beginning of the occupation at North Carn, on the north-east coast of Jura. The tool types of the third of Jura's main phases, belonging to a time when the sea level was already falling in relation to the shore, are less well developed, including flint tools for bone-working and hammer-stones, which also have been found in Mesolithic levels on the nearby island of Oronsay.

Jura is a long mountainous island rising steeply from the sea with a barren hinterland of moors and lochs; the rocky bays and river terraces clearly attracted Mesolithic settlers, while the plentiful game of the interior would have provided an important supply of food and skins. The island of Oronsay contrasts both in habitat and economy; separated from adjacent Colonsay just by a tidal strand, it has a fringe of hills only on the north-west, most of the rest of the island being flat *machair* and undulating sand-dunes. The shell-middens of Oronsay have been well known since the late nineteenth century when trenches were driven into them. Six shell-mounds of varying size are known, the most famous being Caisteal-nan-Gillean and Cnoc Sligeach, which measure about 30m in diameter and 3.5m in height and some 25m in diameter and 2.5m in height respectively. They are composed of layers of shell-midden with blown sand, and are formed by the accumulated debris of many years. The mounds lie on or slightly above the maximum extent of the high post-glacial sea levels; indeed the presence of raised-beach deposits within the lowest levels of Cnoc Sligeach indicates high sea levels at the time of the beginning of the formation of the mound, though most of it must have built up after the falling of the ocean level. The available land in Oronsay would thus be considerably reduced, with much of the island under water.

The artefacts from Oronsay include hammer-stones, stones with ground ends, sometimes called 'limpet hammers', antler and bone
4 implements, including mattocks, fish-hooks and awls. Perhaps the most remarkable are the bone 'harpoon-heads' from Caisteal-nan-Gillean; these are closely comparable to 'harpoon-heads' from other sites on the west coast, including the island of Risga in Loch Sunart

and a series of caves or middens round Oban Bay; others come from Shewalton in Ayrshire and Whitburn, Co. Durham. Only two examples, from MacArthur Cave in Oban and Whitburn, have a perforated base and may thus properly be termed harpoons. Recent excavations on Oronsay by Paul Mellars have concentrated on the environmental and chronological evidence that might be obtained from the sites. A series of radiocarbon dates indicates that the main period of the exploitation of the island's resources by Mesolithic communities was taking place about the middle of the fifth millennium BC, though several of the analyses also suggest a rather more recent date for such occupation. The mass of shellfish debris has in the past given an unbalanced picture of the economy of the Mesolithic communities of Oronsay; fishing too was an important source of food, with saithe or coalfish being the predominant species. Crab and bird bones hint at some culinary variety.

In the south-west important Mesolithic deposits have been found at the head of Campbeltown Loch in Kintyre, round Luce Bay and Wigtown Bay in Galloway. The settlement-site at Low Clone in Wigtownshire well illustrates the sort of position favoured by the coastal Mesolithic communities; it is situated on the top of the low cliff, the base of which marks the greatest extent of the post-glacial sea, and just beside the ravine through which the Clone burn falls to the shore. A large scooped area, measuring 13.7m by 5.5m, was associated with a light stake-built structure, with two fire areas just

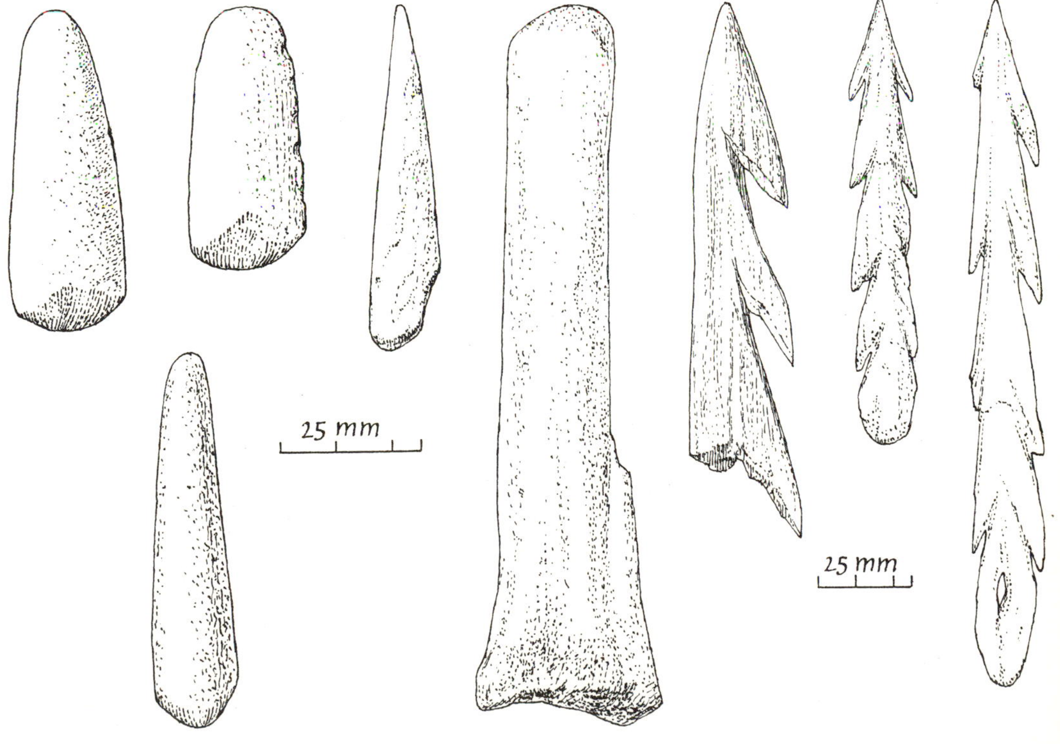

4 Left: three stone 'limpet-hammers', Caisteal-nan-Gillean, Oronsay, Argyll
Centre: two bone implements, MacArthur Cave, Oban, Argyll
Right: harpoons, Druimvargie Rock-shelter and MacArthur Cave, Oban, Argyll

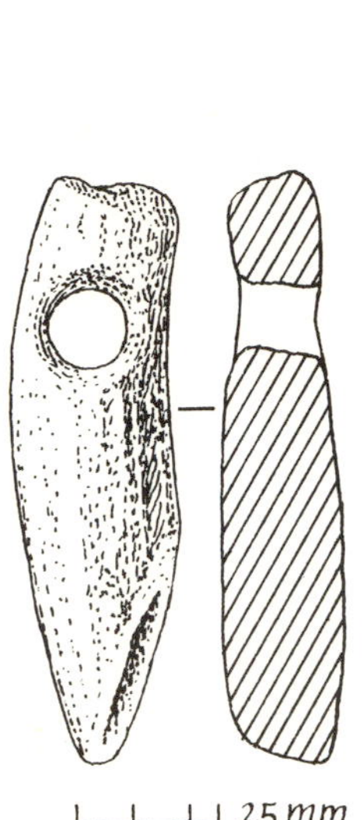

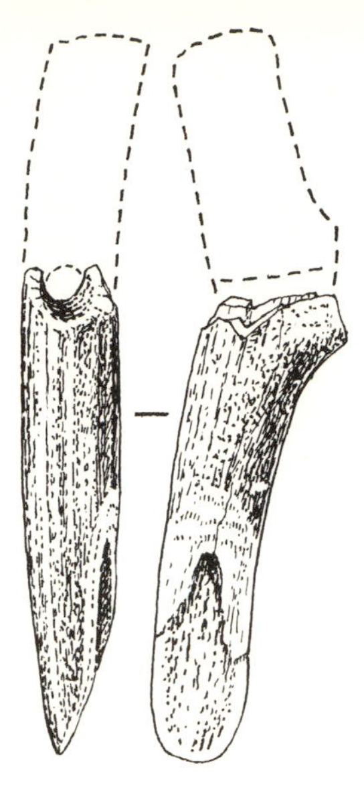

5 Mattock-heads of stag antler, from Risga, Loch Sunart and Cnoc Sligeach, Oronsay, Argyll

outside it. Many flints were found, including microliths of several types, burins, backed blades, scrapers, awls and cores. A radiocarbon date for a hearth at the comparable site at Barsalloch, Wigtownshire, suggests a date early in the fifth millennium BC for such activities.

On the east coast of Scotland, flints of Mesolithic date occur in the Tweed Valley, Tentsmuir in Fife, Deeside and the Aberdeenshire coast among other areas. The hunting and fishing resources of the Tweed allowed Mesolithic communities to settle at least seasonally along its banks, with the best-known finds at Dryburgh Mains in Berwickshire, and Rink Farm in Selkirkshire. Scatters of microlithic tools, broken implements and the large quantities of waste flakes indicate camp-sites, but no area excavation has been undertaken to discover the traces of hearths or temporary shelters.

Extensive shell-midden deposits in the Forth Valley at Inveravon and Polmonthill show the abundance of oysters, mussels, winkles, cockles and whelks at the disposal of the Mesolithic peoples. Several hearths have been discovered within the middens, an indication either of a cooking place or of the presence of a temporary camp-site. The remains of stranded whales have been discovered further up the Forth Valley, particularly near Dunmore and Stirling; the carcasses would have been a source not only of meat and oil to the Mesolithic peoples
5 but also whalebone. Antler mattocks with wooden hafts were employed
to cut up the carcasses; those from Meiklewood and Blair Drummond still had the remains of their handles when they were discovered in the last century.

6 At Morton, on Tentsmuir in Fife, excavation has uncovered the foundation of light timber huts, hearths associated with midden material, working floors and large quantities of flints. The midden deposits showed that shellfish had formed an important aspect of the diet, but that this had been supplemented by fish and seabirds.

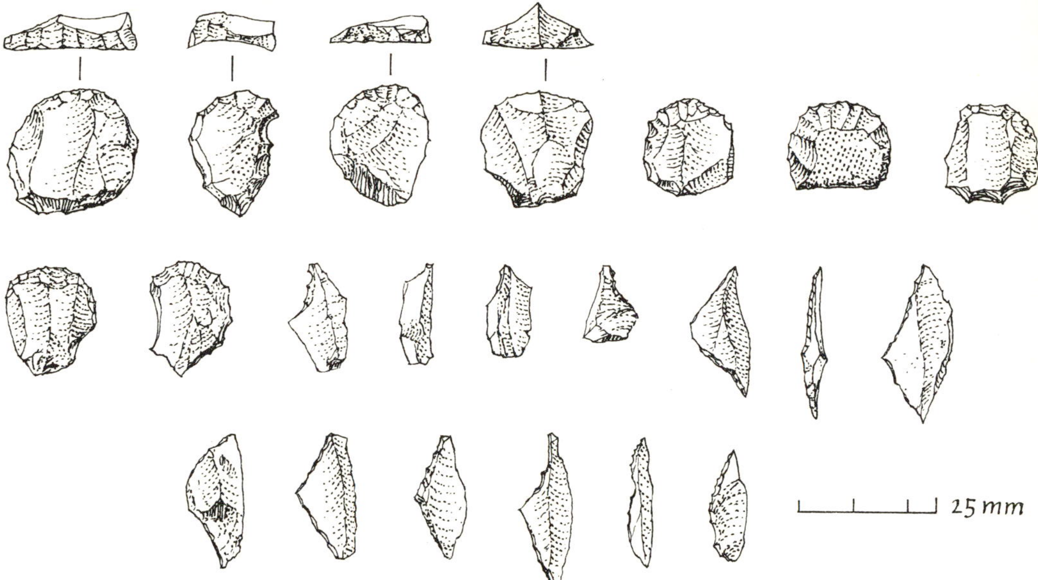

6 Edge tools and microliths, Morton, Tentsmuir, Fife

At Birkwood on Deeside there are the remains of a camp-site, but all the other discoveries of microliths in north-east Scotland are without associated settlement; they may represent hunting bands following the rivers in search of deer and the fruits of the inland forests, and, in the autumn and winter perhaps, supplementing hunting with river and estuarine fishing. Local flint was employed for microlithic tools including obliquely-blunted points and triangular and rod-shaped implements. Scrapers, presumably for working wood and skin, have also been discovered.

It is possible that too much stress has, in the past, been laid on animal hunting as the main activity of Mesolithic societies, for the eating of meat may well have played a secondary role in the diet, with plant food, fish, and shellfish having a more important part to play. Deer hunting would certainly have provided skins, antler and bone for making tools, as well as venison, but it is unlikely that the earliest peoples of Scotland were predominantly meat-eaters.

The various Mesolithic groups are not now given the cultural labels of earlier studies, 'Obanian' or 'Larnian', as it is clear that the tool types found in one place may be the response to seasonal activities, and that the same people may have used a separate artefact-assemblage in another area at another time of year; the material from Oban and Oronsay, for example, may represent the same groups as the hunters on Jura, at different seasons and in different habitats. It is all too easy to emphasize the squalor and uncertainty of the Mesolithic way of life, and to contrast it unfavourably with that of Early Neolithic communities. But it is possible that, the problem of seasonal movement apart, the needs of such groups may be more readily met than those of the first farmers, leaving perhaps more time for leisure. 'Hunters keep banker's hours', was one assessment of the hunting and gathering communities of the 'original affluent society'.

2
Early Farming Communities

The Neolithic settlement of Scotland, as elsewhere, created a new world. Whatever the impact of the hunting and gathering communities upon their natural environment may have been, it was no more than a distant foreshadowing of the changes to be made under fully established Neolithic management, although aspects of the lifestyle of the earliest agriculturalists may have been little different from that of the existing Mesolithic population. With the gradual clearance of woodland and the establishment of arable and grazing areas, a mode of subsistence was developed (based on mixed farming, together with fishing and hunting where appropriate or necessary) that was to remain little changed in many parts of Scotland till comparatively recent times. The earliest Neolithic colonization took place in coastal areas, the western and northern isles and along the fertile lowland plain of eastern Scotland. Analysis of molluscan faunas in the sand-dune areas of the Outer Hebrides and Orkney has demonstrated the clearance of woodland in Neolithic times prior to the deposition of sand, and it is in these areas that the post-glacial rise in sea level is likely to have destroyed much of the evidence of Neolithic settlement that would strengthen the overall impression of sea-borne colonization. Conditions for sea voyages were good, for a climatic optimum had been reached, and by 3000 BC temperatures equalled the present-day range, while there were fewer storms and less strong winds than in earlier times.

Burial monuments, particularly stone chambered tombs, are by far the most numerous class of structure surviving from Neolithic times, and it is the form of the tombs, and to a lesser extent their contents, that provide information about the immediate origins of the settlers. Tomb typology indicates clearly a primary movement of people up the west coast from the Irish sea area, while earthen long barrows and pottery evidence combine to demonstrate a contemporary or perhaps slightly earlier movement of people from Yorkshire and north-east England. The earliest radiocarbon dates come from earthen long barrows, stone chambered tombs and domestic settlements; the dates cluster between about 3250 bc and 2800 bc, thus indicating that the Neolithic settlement of Scotland as far north as the Northern Isles was well established early in the fourth millennium BC.

Chambered tombs

The funerary monuments of the earliest agricultural communities belong to the only class of field monument in Scotland to have been comprehensively studied: Audrey Henshall's *The Chambered Tombs of Scotland* published in 1963 and 1972. Perhaps the most important aspects of recent discussion concern the composite nature of many of the tombs and the realization that the burials and grave-goods require cautious analysis, particularly with regard to their value as dating evidence. Until the last two decades, excavators concentrated on the stone chambers – the burial vaults – and on the area immediately outside them, without examining in detail the structure of the cairns or barrows themselves. This resulted in the collection of a large amount of pottery and some skeletal material; no information about the building sequence could, however, be recovered. Radiocarbon analysis of material from within the chamber, taken from bone or charcoal, would provide a date only for the use of the tomb, and not for its construction. In a series of brilliant excavations, John Corcoran was able to demonstrate that the cairn material itself could provide the evidence of various structural phases. At Tulach an t-Sionnaich, Caithness, he was able to show that a small passage-grave enclosed within a round cairn had been modified with the addition of a 'heel-shaped' platform, to which a lower long cairn had subsequently been added. A structural sequence has also been shown at Tulloch of Assery, Caithness,
Balvraid, Inverness-shire, Mid Gleniron, Wigtownshire, Glenvoidean, 7
on Bute, and Achnacreebeag, Argyll, where a passage-grave was added
to one side of a round cairn covering a simple closed chamber built of 8
massive stones. Such building phases have not only been found within

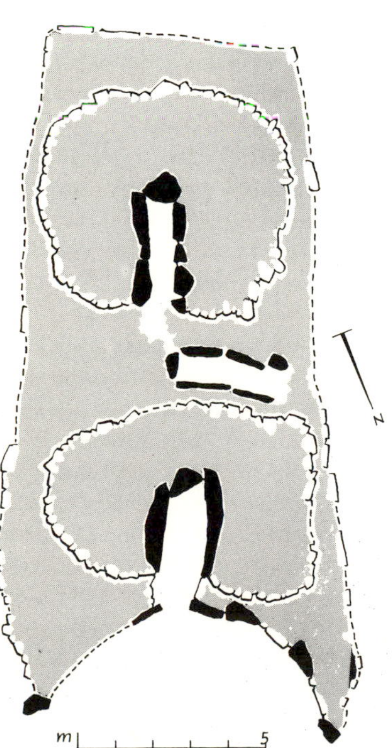

7 Chambered cairn, Mid Gleniron I, Wigtownshire

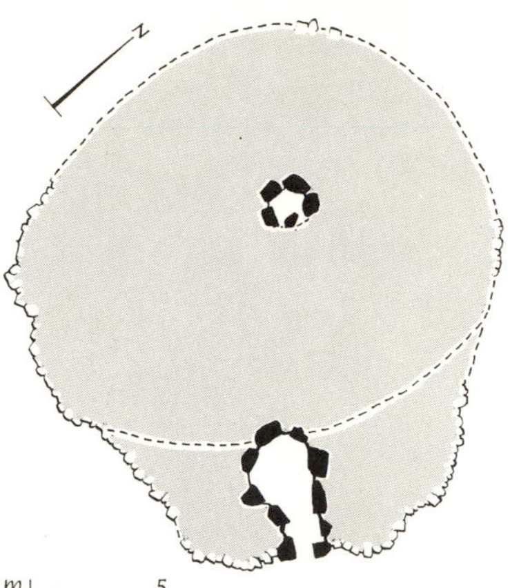

8 Chambered cairn, Achnacreebeag, Lorn, Argyll

the Neolithic use of chambered tombs; excavation has also shown periods of remodelling in the second millennium BC at, among others, Ardnacross II and Dalineun, both in Argyll. The use of chambered tombs over a longer time-span than was previously thought, allowing for the reconstruction and enlarging now demonstrated by excavation, is underlined by a series of radiocarbon dates; before the advent of this dating method, most archaeological schemes allowed only a short time-span for the Neolithic period, but now a longer time-scale is necessary to accommodate the available radiocarbon analyses, and we must envisage the building of some chambered tombs as early as the fourth millennium BC.

The structural phases of a chambered cairn or long barrow can be shown by excavation to cover a considerable period, and the deposits within the tombs have become increasingly difficult to interpret by any single model. The burials in the chambered tomb of Midhowe on the island of Rousay, Orkney, provide an example of one of the ways in which 'collective burial' may have taken place: this is a long rectangular chamber belonging to the Orkney-Cromarty group, divided by a series of upright slabs projecting from the side-walls into twelve compartments, seven of which are provided with slab-shelves a little above floor level. The remains of twenty-five individuals were discovered; all but one of the side-shelves had from two to four burials, several of which survived as crouched skeletons with their backs to the side-wall of the chamber and their heads laid next to the upright stones. Several of the skeletons had been gathered into heaps in the centre of the shelf, and further bones were found under the shelves. It may be suggested that the earlier burials were swept aside or bundled under the shelves to make way for more recent interments. Sherds of pottery were recovered, but one of the most interesting features is the range of animal and bird bones associated with the burials, including ox and sheep; skua, cormorant, guillemot, buzzard, eagle, gannet and carrion-crow; an egg-shell, and bones of bream and wrasse. Such an array cannot easily be explained as the result of funerary feasting and some may represent talismans or tribal emblems.

It is clear that continued access to the chambers allows not only for the clearing aside of earlier burials, but also for the wholesale removal of burials and grave-goods in order to make way for later deposits. At West Kennet, Wiltshire, there is no doubt that skulls and long bones were removed in the period between the original deposition and the final blocking of the chambers. In 1900 T. H. Bryce undertook a series of excavations in the chambers of several cairns on the island of Arran in order to further his study of early anatomy; at Torlin, for example, he found skulls in the corners of the chambers with long bones along the side, but complete skeletons could not be accounted for. A further possibility to explain the partial nature of the skeletal material in some tombs is that, when the bones were finally deposited in the chambers, they had already been laid out or exposed for a time elsewhere, possibly in a timber 'mortuary house' or on a raised 'mortuary platform'. At Isbister, South Ronaldsay, Orkney, the stalled burial chamber had 9
three small side-cells opening off it; along the walls of the main chamber were found many skulls, each with a pile of disarticulated bones, though in no case was a complete skeleton represented. Animal and bird bones were discovered on the floor of the chamber, as well as quantities of eagles' talons. In two of the small side-cells there were groups of skulls, which, in John Hedges' vivid phrase, were 'lying on the floor as if they had been bowled in'. Enough has been said to indicate that no single interpretation can account for the variety of rituals encountered during excavation. It should be stressed, however, that the burials and grave-goods recovered need not represent the original use of the tomb, and thus to think of 'primary burial-deposits' can be misleading; pottery and skeletal remains found in a tomb are more likely to represent the latest rather than the earliest funerary deposits.

9 Chambered cairn, Isbister, South Ronaldsay, Orkney; entrance to side cell and burial deposits at the side of the main chamber (scale in 10 cm divisions)

After each act of deposition, or even ritual 'clearing' of the site, it is assumed that the tomb was resealed with stones or dry-stone walling; at the end of the use of the tomb, however, this might take a more permanent form, including the filling of the chamber with rubble and earth and the concealment of the outside of the entrance with large boulders. Again, this deliberate sealing-up of a chamber has been shown to have taken place on different occasions at several sites. At Achnacreebeag, in the Lorn area of Argyll, the chamber and passage were filled with boulders, covering an earlier deposit of Neolithic pottery and scattered throughout the stones in the chamber were fragments of beaker ware, flint, and jet disc-beads; carefully laid boulders outside the chamber were built up in order to mask the entrance. Several chambers in Orkney, including Midhowe and Knowe of Yarso, seem to have been deliberately filled, and the entrance passages of four of the Rousay tombs were sealed by well-set stones.

Study of the chambered tombs in Scotland has concentrated on their morphology and five main groups can be identified: *Clyde* tombs in Argyll and Arran with outliers in the Hebrides, Perthshire and the south-west; passage-graves of Orkney-Cromarty-Hebridean type, a name that also identifies their geographical spread in the north and north-west; the *Maes Howe* type of passage-grave forms a distinct group only found in Orkney; passage-graves of the Bargrennan group are found in south-west Scotland; *Clava* passage-graves and ring-cairns are situated in Inverness-shire and adjoining counties. Long cairns and barrows, often apparently unchambered, are now known to contain, in some examples at least, mortuary structures of timber and stone; the geographical distribution of this class falls in the eastern and southern parts of Scotland. The following discussion provides an outline of the main architectural features of each group, but it is a sobering thought that these are the tangible remains of beliefs about which we know next to nothing.

Clyde cairns

The distinctive chambers of this class of cairn are rectangular on plan with massive slabs forming the parallel side-walls and the end-walls, with lower slabs dividing the chambers into several compartments. The number of compartments varies: single-compartment chambers are known; those with only two compartments may be constructed of very massive stones, for example Dalineun in Argyll; chambers with five compartments, for example Clettraval in North Uist, are complex constructions not unlike an elongated 'house of cards'. Very few chambers are roofed by their original capstones, and in some cases tall dividing slabs between the compartments imply either that the height of the chambers was increased by dry-stone walling, or, less likely, that subsequent access was obtained by removing some of the capstones.
10 At Nether Largie South in Mid Argyll, dry-stone walling adds to the height of the chamber and provides a more level support for the capstones of the roof.

10 Chambered cairn, Nether Largie South, Mid Argyll; interior of chamber (scale in feet)

J. G. Scott has suggested that the chambers of the *Clyde* group follow a developmental series beginning with simple chambers of one compartment, 'closed chambers', to which an outer element was built,

and thus by process of elaboration, chambers with five compartments might be envisaged.

The existence of simple chambers at Mid Gleniron I, and inferred at Cairnholy I and II, to which more complex chamber arrangements, façades and cairns have been added, means that the typological similarities with tombs outside Scotland, which were formerly thought to be the antecedents of the *Clyde* tombs, are no longer helpful in providing an origin for the class as a whole. The *Clyde* tombs are a local response to the widespread burial traditions outlined earlier; Scott has suggested that a simple timber structure was translated into stone and subsequently elaborated; while this has met with general agreement as a working concept, the simple closed stone chambers he cites are more difficult to prove as a first phase. Be that as it may, there is no reason to doubt that Mid Gleniron I and probably the first phase of Cairnholy I were early in the sequence. Subsequent elaboration attests not only to the vitality of the cult but also to its receptiveness to ideas from outside Scotland, at least as shown by the architectural evidence. Features which appear to indicate such influences include the use of cairns with a trapezoidal ground-plan and a flat façade, often employing upright slabs with dry-stone walling between; these structural elements can be paralleled among the Cotswold-Severn tombs. Influence from Ireland has also been detected in the use of concave façades in the later phases of Mid Gleniron I and Cairnholy I. 11

Grave-goods found in *Clyde* cairns include a number of round-based vessels – carinated bowls, lugged-bowls and simple cups. More highly decorated sub-groups of this widespread pottery family, including Achnacree bowls and Beacharra bowls, are also present, the former from Glenvoidean, on Bute, for example, and the latter from Beacharra, in Argyll, and Clettraval on North Uist. Flint knives and other artefacts were also deposited in the tombs, notably on Arran.

Radiocarbon analyses of material from *Clyde* tombs have tended to confirm the early date of this class, the earliest being from charcoal from a hearth under the forecourt blocking at Monamore, Arran, of 3160 bc$\pm$110 (Q–675), indicating a date as early as 4000 BC. A comparable analysis from an early phase of the multi-period tomb at Glenvoidean, on Bute, 2910 bc$\pm$115 (I–5974), is in calendar terms only three centuries later. We must thus envisage the use of many *Clyde* tombs from 4000 BC to 2500 BC at least and remember that they might remain the focus for interment for several centuries thereafter.

Passage-graves: Orkney – Cromarty – Hebridean tombs

This broad class includes a number of variations of ground-plan, some of which were determined by local geology, others the result of continuous adaptation of building traditions. At their simplest the tombs have a small chamber, which is entered by a short passage as at Achnacreebeag, Argyll, or Unival in North Uist; in ground-plan such sites find parallels in other areas of Atlantic Europe and it is to the south that we should probably seek the origin of this group. The intractable granite erratics which form the side-walls at Achnacreebeag underline the difficulties that the builders must have encountered. In Caithness and Orkney the use of flagstone enabled bolder concepts 12

11 Chambered cairn, Cairnholy I, Kirkcudbrightshire; façade

12 Chambered cairn, Achnacreebeag, Lorn, Argyll; passage grave from above (scale in feet)

13 Chambered cairn, Camster, Caithness; round cairn, showing forecourt

14 Chambered tomb, Unstan, Orkney; interior of chamber showing upright partitions

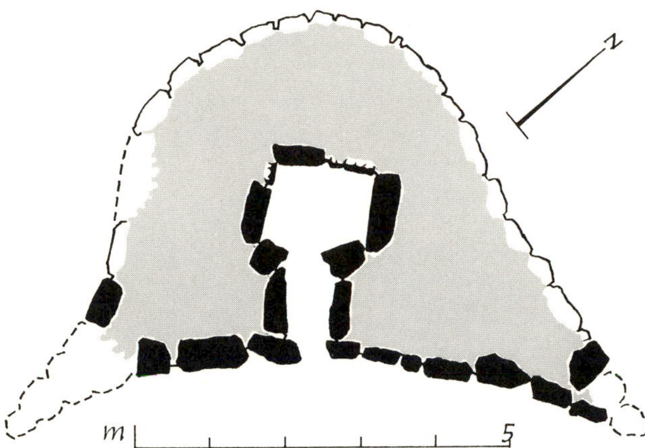

15 Chambered tomb, Islesburgh, Shetland

to be tested, and larger chambers divided into compartments by upright slabs projecting from the side-walls were constructed, as at 13
Camster, and Tulloch of Assery, Caithness. In Orkney there are two broad groups: those tombs in which the complex chamber is on the same axis as the passage and secondly a number of tombs where the passage is at right angles to the elongated central chamber. Two of the latter group, Unstan and Isbister, have small additional side-cells, one 14
at the former site and three at the latter. In Shetland the chambers are less regularly laid out and many of the cairns are heel-shaped, several 15
having low boulder façades, as at Islesburgh.

There are few radiocarbon dates for simple passage-graves but from Embo, in Sutherland, analysis of animal bones from a context contemporary with the building of the passage-grave has provided a date of 1920 bc±100 (BM-442) indicating a date between 2500 and 2250 BC. Embo is also a good example of a site where the sanctity of the cairn was remembered by later peoples whose burial traditions had radically altered from wholly Neolithic burial ideals, with the insertion of two short cists into the mound, one containing an adult female and an infant, and the other a child and an infant. Radiocarbon dates have recently been obtained from three tombs on the Orkney island of Rousay that were excavated in the 1930s: the Knowes (mounds) of Ramsay, Rowiegar and Yarso. The interpretation of these dates is fraught with the same problems as that of other small finds; we do not know at what point the bones were inserted into the tombs, but the dates do seem to indicate the period of its use, though not necessarily its construction. The dates from the three sites range from 2055 bc±60 to 2390 bc±65 (Q-1227 and 1223), a range in calendar years of between about 2500 and 3000 BC; coupled with that from Embo, the dates show that both simple tombs and chambers with fourteen compartments, with all the ritual complexities described from Midhowe, were

16 Chambered tomb, Maes Howe, Orkney; interior of chamber

being used in the first half of the third millennium BC. The deposits recorded at the Knowe of Ramsay, one of the largest tombs of this class, are in some ways comparable to those from the tomb of Quanterness on the Orkney mainland: animal and human bones were intermixed, many of the former being charred. Like the collection already quoted from Isbister, South Ronaldsay, the bones recovered from the Knowe of Ramsay imply rituals far beyond 'simple' burial, for they included sea eagle, bittern, curlew, great auk, conger eel and swan.

Grave-goods include Achnacree bowls from Rudh' an Dunain on Skye, Beacharra bowls from Unival and Achnacreebeag and Unstan ware from Midhowe, Isbister, and from Unstan itself in Orkney. Flint objects were also deposited with burials at a number of sites including leaf-shaped arrowheads and plano-convex knives.

Maes Howe tombs

The tombs of this small class in Orkney are among the most impressive achievements of the Neolithic architects in Scotland; at Maes Howe 16
the chamber is entered along a narrow passage which incorporates several massive slabs of stone. The square central chamber has three side-cells, one opposite the entrance passage and two others in the side-walls; the cells would originally have been sealed by large rectangular blocks, but sadly, when the tomb was opened in 1861, the excavators found that the cells were empty. The tomb had been explored by parties of Norsemen in the twelfth century who had carved a series of runic inscriptions recounting their exploits. One of these mentions the existence of 'treasure' within the tomb, but it seems unlikely that this can refer to the original Neolithic grave-goods. Stone and bone artefacts discovered during excavations in 1952 by Gordon Childe in the tomb of Quoyness, on Sanday, indicated that the use of this class of tomb, though not necessarily their building, was contemporary with the settlement of Skara Brae. Excavations by Colin Renfrew at Quanterness have confirmed the use of such tombs by the makers of a style of pottery known as grooved ware, which is also found at Skara Brae, and have also provided a series of radiocarbon dates within the early third millennium BC. Dates for a burial early in the use of the tomb show that it was already built by about 3000 BC (2220 bc±75, Q-1479 and 2410 bc±50, SRR-754); a pair of dates for a late interment shows that the tomb was still in use some six hundred years later (1955 bc±70, Q-1480 and 1920 bc±55, SRR-755). It has been suggested that the construction of Maes Howe itself is rather later than Quanterness, perhaps about 2800 BC, from the evidence of a radiocarbon determination from basal peat in the surrounding ditch. Maes Howe is thus the culmination of a local passage-grave tradition rather than being the earliest in the sequence, but such elaborate and eccentric tombs as Holm of Papa Westray are rather later. The ground-plan of Maes Howe is comparable to that of the spectacular chambered tomb at Newgrange, Co. Meath, Ireland, which is of similar, or perhaps slightly earlier, date (2475 bc±45, GrN-5462-C; 2465 bc±40, GrN-5463; 2585 bc±105, UB-361), and it is an interesting possibility that there may have been contact between this part of Ireland and the Orkney mainland at this period.

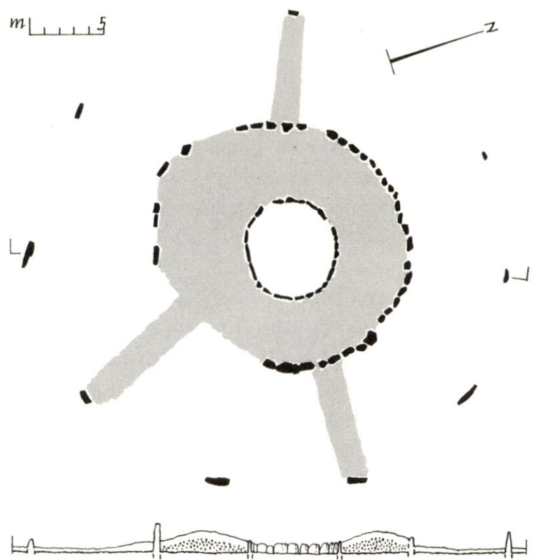

17 Ring-cairn, Balnuaran of Clava, Inverness-shire

At Quanterness, where over 150 burials were found, the practice of 'excarnation' has been clearly demonstrated, and, as none of the bones exhibited gnaw marks, the bodies were clearly protected from carnivorous animals and birds, perhaps by burial in the sand-dunes. Exposure on a 'mortuary platform' can thus be ruled out in this case. During and after translation to the chambered tomb, the bones were broken up into small pieces; it seems likely that fires were burnt within the chamber at this stage, and to judge from the bones of sheep, cattle, fish and birds, feasting for the mourners or at least the deposition of food for the dead, accompanied these rituals. The bones of a dog, scattered over the central chamber at Quanterness may well represent a sacrificial offering.

A small group of burials set in a pit and in a cist dug into the floor of the central chamber are probably among the earliest burials; the pit contained the crouched burial of an adult male to which two further, fragmentary, deposits were subsequently added. The cist contained the poorly preserved remains of a crouched adult inhumation. It is interesting to note that a cist set within the floor of the tomb of Quoyness revealed the fragmentary remains of at least ten adults and four or five children.

Clava passage-graves and ring-cairns

There are only eleven passage-graves of *Clava* type, all of which are situated in the vicinity of Inverness or in the Spey valley; they have round chambers at the centre of substantial circular cairns with long passages leading to them. Ten cairns have concentric circles of standing stones. Unlike the majority of passage-graves, where an easterly alignment is preferred, the *Clava* tombs face the south-west; this is well illustrated at Balnuaran of Clava, Inverness-shire, where the two

passage-graves are aligned on exactly the same south-west axis, a line that also points to the mid-winter sunset. Between the two passage-graves there is a well-preserved ring-cairn, but only a few flint flakes 17
were found when it was excavated in 1857 and a layer of cremated bone when it was re-examined in 1953. Three unusual cobbled areas shown on the plan link three standing stones to the skirts of the cairn, but their purpose is not known. Provided with massive inner- and outer-kerb-stones, ring-cairns did not have roofed central chambers and there was thus no need for a passage. About a dozen of these distinctive sites are known, most with a surrounding setting of standing stones. In many cases the stones of the circles and the kerb-stones of the cairns are graded in height, with the largest on the south-west, an axis that they share with the recumbent stone-circles of Aberdeenshire. Audrey Henshall has suggested that the *Clava* passage-graves are a locally evolved group and has put forward an ancestry within henge monuments, stone circles and ring-cairns; she rightly points out the absence of any hint of multi-period construction, the presence of stones graded in height and of cup-markings – all features alien to the mainstream of passage-grave tradition. Excavations have produced little in the way of dating evidence, and the chronological position of the Clava sites is not at all clear.

Bargrennan tombs

The dozen tombs of this small group in south-west Scotland, are named after the cairn at Bargrennan in Wigtownshire, which was excavated in 1949 by Stuart Piggott and T. G. E. Powell; they have simple chambers with access by means of a passage, structural elements akin both to early *Clyde* cairns and to passage-graves. Bargrennan tombs appear to be a local variation adopting features of both main groups. A date early in the third millennium BC is considered likely on typological grounds, but there is little dating evidence from the tombs themselves.

Long barrows and long cairns

Long barrows and long cairns, the distribution of which stretches from the north-east to the south-west, formed, until two recent excavations, one of the most enigmatic groups of Neolithic monuments. It could be inferred from the evidence of examples in the south and east of England that complex settings of timber and stone might be found beneath them, but in the absence of any excavations in Scotland, almost nothing was known about their internal construction or about their date. As a result of recent work at Lochhill, in Kirkcudbright, 18
and Dalladies in Kincardineshire, information has been recovered not only about the variety of the internal arrangements of such sites but also about their early chronological position in the Scottish Neolithic period.

At Lochhill, Lionel Masters has found a timber mortuary structure within a trapezoidal cairn; measuring about 7.5m in length, the timber setting had been built of massive split-timbers at each end, and between them two smaller posts in a single post-hole. The two sides and one end of this structure were formed of large granite boulders;

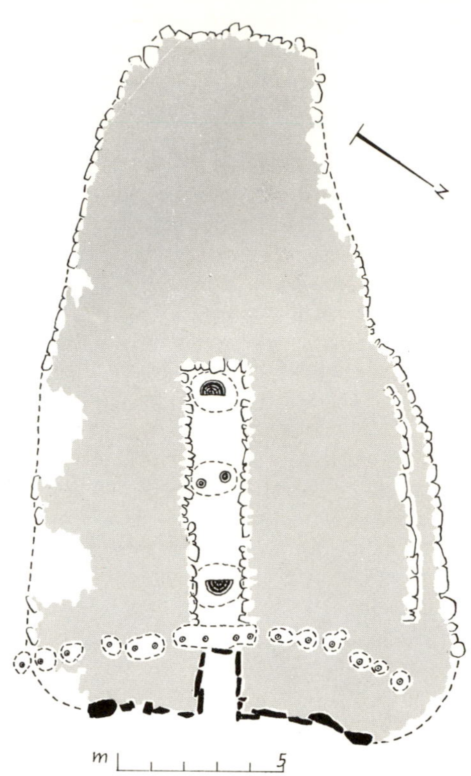

18 Long cairn, Lochhill, Kirkcudbrightshire

the presence of a wooden floor was indicated by burnt oak planks between two of the posts. At one end of the mortuary structure, the remains of what may be interpreted as a timber façade were discovered; sixteen upright timbers had been set in post-holes at right angles to the mortuary structure and at the centre of this concave façade, and on the same axis as that of the massive posts behind it, was a stone porch constructed of two pairs of upright slabs. Human bones were deposited in the mortuary structure and at a subsequent stage the timbers were set alight. At a still later date the trapezoidal long cairn was built to cover the remains, further stones were added to the porch to form a small stone chamber, and a stone façade was constructed at the front of the finished cairn. The chamber had been partly robbed, but sherds of Neolithic pottery were found within it. After the final deposits, the chamber and façade had been carefully sealed. Sherds of beaker pottery from the top of the cairn, presumably accompanying a later burial, complete the sequence and demonstrate the continuing sanctity of the site. Radiocarbon analysis of a plank in the mortuary structure has provided a date of 3120 bc ± 105 (I-6409).

A barrow at Dalladies, in Kincardineshire, excavated by Stuart Piggott in advance of its destruction by quarrying, was almost twice as long as the cairn at Lochhill and has revealed a mortuary structure with a complex sequence of timber and stone phases. The barrow was aligned east and west with a shallow crescentic façade at the east end;

the mortuary structure was at the north-east end, but it opened on to the side of the mound rather than on to the façade. In its earliest phase, it was composed primarily of timber uprights, which seem to have decayed in position before the construction of a wood and stone setting within which there was a light timber building roofed with birch bark; a plano-convex flint knife and a cup-marked slab were found inside along with a fragment of skull. The building was subsequently burnt. Radiocarbon dates for this phase include one of 3240 bc±105 (I-6113), comparable to that from Lochhill, and others of 2710 bc±50 (SRR-289) and 2585 bc±55 (SRR-290), which are considered to be rather more reliable. The mound was made up of horizontal layers of turf and top soil rather than material obtained from adjacent quarry-ditches. As at Lochhill, the barrow was used for later burials in cists and small stone settings, including one accompanied by a fine beaker vessel.

The timber mortuary structures of the Dalladies and Lochhill long mounds show clear affinities with long barrows of eastern England, such as Willerby Wold in Yorkshire, and in southern England at Wayland's Smithy, Lambourn and Fussell's Lodge in Wessex. Lochhill also has close parallels with Doey's Cairn, Dunloy, in Co. Antrim. There can be little doubt that the Scottish long cairns and barrows represent local reactions to widespread rituals of collective burial, involving deposition in some kind of mortuary structure, coupled with the subsequent building of a long mound, and that the northern examples result from contact with Neolithic groups further south.

Settlements

The best known of the Scottish Neolithic settlements is, of course, Skara Brae in Orkney, but there are others, and Skara Brae is not the earliest among them. Traces have been found of only a dozen or so settlements in Scotland, datable to the third and fourth millennia BC, and in most cases their surviving record is very incomplete; none can claim to be typical in terms of house-plans and building tradition. The best-preserved sites are the three Orcadian settlements at Skara Brae, Rinyo and Knap of Howar, where the houses were not only built of stone but also, in the case of Skara Brae and Knap of Howar, were enveloped in a protective covering of sand soon after their abandonment. Their walls stand to heights of 2m or more, and the architectural details thus preserved mirror the sophisticated stone-work of many chambered tombs. The site currently under excavation at Balbridie, Kincardineshire, appears to be a version of the aisled timber long-house that is familiar from early Neolithic settlements in Holland and Germany; radiocarbon dates indicate occupation around 3600 BC in corrected calendar years. The evidence from Balbridie supports the possibility that rectangular timber-built houses may have existed elsewhere, particularly in the forest areas of north-east Scotland. Traces of occupation contemporary with Balbridie have been uncovered beneath a burial mound at Fochabers in Moray. There a domestic Neolithic midden had been established on a sandy knoll in an oak forest, but it had been levelled by the builders of the burial mound and only stake-holes, hollows and hearths survived to indicate the presence

19 Knap of Howar, Papa Westray, Orkney, doorway to house 1 (scales in 50 cm divisions)

of structures associated with the midden. There was some evidence to suggest that slash-and-burn clearance of the forest had taken place.

In order to gain a detailed impression of Neolithic domestic settlement, one must turn to the Northern Isles. Until recently, the early settlers of the Orkney Isles could be identified only from their burial tombs and not from the homes they occupied while they were alive. There were hints that there might be links between the settlements at Skara Brae and Rinyo and the Maes Howe type of chambered tomb: the strange spiked stone objects at Skara Brae had also been found in the tomb at Quoyness, and Skaill stone knives, so familiar from Skara Brae and Rinyo, had been found in the platform built around the Quoyness tomb. Grooved ware has recently been discovered at Quanterness, and radiocarbon dates for this tomb show that its use was broadly contemporary with the two settlements.

Knap of Howar

19–22 On Papa Westray, one of the most northerly of the Orkney islands, there is a domestic site that was first uncovered in the early 1930s. It consists of two stone-built houses, lying side by side, and, in the absence of distinctive finds, it was thought probably to be Iron Age in date. Further excavations by Anna Ritchie in 1973 and 1975 yielded not only artefacts but also radiocarbon dates showing that the houses were built and inhabited by the users of Unstan pottery, who buried their dead in the stalled cairns of the Orkney-Cromarty group. This was the first Unstan ware settlement to be identified in the Orkneys – and probably the earliest known domestic settlement in the Orkneys – and its associated artefacts have extended the range of objects known from tomb-finds to be part of the Unstan cultural assemblage.

20 Knap of Howar, Papa Westray, Orkney; interior of house 1 (scales in 50 cm divisions)

21 Knap of Howar, Papa Westray, Orkney; interior of house 1 showing wall construction (scales in 50 cm divisions)

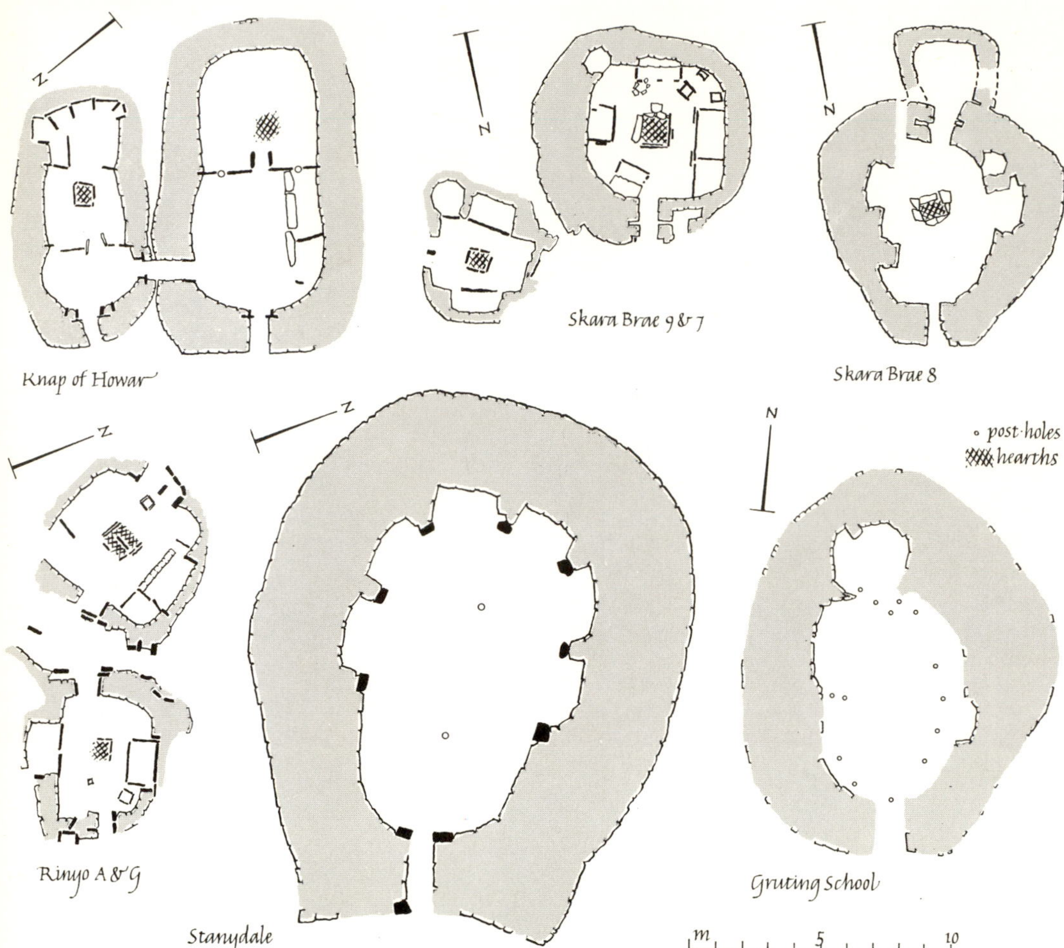

22 Knap of Howar, Papa Westray, Orkney; Skara Brae, Orkney, houses 7 and 9; Rinyo, Rousay, Orkney, houses A and G; Stanydale, Shetland; Gruting School, Shetland

Knap of Howar lies, at the present day, on the west coast of the immensely fertile island of Papa Westray, but to judge by the molluscan and soil evidence found during the recent excavations, at the time of its occupation in the later fourth millennium BC the site lay not directly on the coastline but well back from the sea, behind sand-dunes. It is even possible that Papa Westray and its neighbouring island of Westray were still joined together at that time, and that the site lay beyond a sheltered bay suitable for the oysters and other sandy foreshore species of marine mollusca that were abundant in the Knap of Howar middens. The present-day exposed and rocky shore could certainly not support oyster colonies.

There are two stratigraphically very distinct phases of occupation at Knap of Howar, although in cultural terms both belong to a uniform period of Early Neolithic settlement characterized by Unstan ware. The two surviving stone houses were built immediately on top of an earlier domestic midden; in fact the internal areas of both houses were

cleared of the primary midden down to the boulder clay subsoil, and the midden material itself was used as core for the hollow stone walls of the houses. No structures belonging to the primary occupation survived in the excavated area, apart from incomplete stone paving. The two extant houses are rectilinear with rounded ends, in plan-form totally unlike the houses at Skara Brae and Rinyo; internally house 1 22
measures about 9.5m by 4.5m, and house 2 measures about 7.5m by 3m. Both are divided internally into two and three rooms respectively by upright stone slabs, a device familiar from stalled cairns with their individual burial compartments separated in exactly the same way. Another link with tomb architecture is the way in which the paving of the entrance passages into both houses was overlapped on either side by the basal wall-courses; this was a very practical way of minimizing the shifting effect of continual traffic over the paving, just as the long entrance passage with the door set at the inner end was a most necessary means of cutting down the draught inside the houses from the strong Orcadian winds. The door itself, probably wooden or wood-framed with a skin covering, was closed against a slab-check with a bar set into the holes that survived on either side of the doorway.

Although no trace survived of the roofs of the two houses, it is likely that here, as at Skara Brae, the inner stone wall-facing was corbelled inwards slightly, and a timber-framed roof, perhaps supporting stone flags or simply turf, rested on the wall-tops. The discovery of tilting slabs inside one of the houses at Rinyo suggests the use there of a flagstone roof.

House 2 appears to have been designed as a storage and working unit, with cupboards lining the westernmost of the three rooms and specialized working tools concentrated in the central room where the hearth lay. The two houses are connected by a low passage through their conjoining walls. Although coastal erosion may have destroyed other minor structures, it is unlikely that there were more houses, and Knap of Howar must be seen as a small, compact farmstead, the home of perhaps one large family. Only a few grains of barley were recovered, but soil conditions were not suitable for the survival of plant material and no pollen remained in the midden deposits. Some cultivation is likely, but the economy of the farmstead depended primarily upon rearing cattle and sheep, and upon the exploitation of the sea for both fish and shellfish. Among the bird bones were found remains of the great auk, an extinct flightless bird of which the last breeding pair in Scotland was recorded on Papa Westray in 1813.

The Unstan pottery found at Knap of Howar includes not only the fine decorated bowls found as grave-goods in chambered tombs but also a range of plain coarsely-made pots designed for domestic use as storage jars. Several vessels have holes drilled below the rim after the pot was fired, as a means either to repair cracks or to fasten leather covers or lids. Pottery manufacture was carried out on the site itself, as was bone- and stone-working for tools. A small polished stone axe was made from local fine-grained dolomite. The tool assemblage includes three new types which are at present unique to Knap of Howar: a dimpled bone gouge, a multifunctional stone grinder and a stone borer. Whalebone was used for several implements, including

23 Skara Brae, Orkney; general view

spatulas and mallet-heads. Unstan ware has also been found on domestic sites in the west of Scotland, at Eilean-an-Tighe in North Uist and at Northton in Harris, but in both cases there was virtually no structural evidence of houses. It is clear from radiocarbon dates that the period during which Unstan ware was fashionable in Orkney overlapped in its later part with the use of grooved ware, but there is as yet no instance of any site, domestic, ceremonial or funerary, on which both types of pottery have been found. The users of Unstan ware and the users of grooved ware were apparently distinct and separate communities, each with its own material equipment and style of tomb.

Skara Brae

On the west coast of the mainland of Orkney there is a large sheltered bay known as Skaill Bay; constant erosion of the sand-dunes behind the bay led, after a particularly violent storm around 1850, to the discovery of the Neolithic settlement of Skara Brae. This site has become one of Britain's most famous archaeological monuments, and it has now been excavated no less than six times. The major excavation was that undertaken by Gordon Childe in 1928–30, but his mandate was to supervise the archaeological aspects of opening up the site for public view, and the archaeological results of his work were correspondingly limited. Opinions about the date and significance of Skara Brae were 22–24

24 Skara Brae, Orkney; interior of house 1

modified over the years: throughout the late nineteenth and early twentieth centuries experts veered between about 500 BC and 500 AD as the most probable date, and Childe in his monograph published in 1931 favoured 500 BC, though he hedged his bet by subtitling the book 'A Pictish Village in Orkney'. Then in 1936, Stuart Piggott identified the pottery from Skara Brae as Late Neolithic ware, now known as grooved ware, and placed the settlement in its true cultural context. Radiocarbon analyses of animal bones found during recent research excavations by David V. Clarke indicate that the settlement was occupied over a period between about 3100 BC and 2450 BC in calendar years; the thirteen radiocarbon dates range between 2480 bc ± 100 and 1830 bc ± 110 (Birm.-637 and 437).

During that period, individual houses were built, dismantled, rebuilt or modified, in a continuous sequence of occupation. Little structural trace survives of the earliest settlement, which was built partly on sand-dunes and partly on bare rock; like Knap of Howar, Skara Brae was not originally as close to the seashore as it is today. At least six new houses were built on top of this early level and, although they in turn were dismantled to floor level to make room for later houses, their ground-plans survive in part. They were square or rectilinear, one-room houses with central hearths and flanking bed-alcoves built into the walls. The best-preserved houses are those of the later phases of the settlement, which were inhabited just before the site was abandoned and blanketed with sand. It was this wind-blown sand, together with the habit of allowing domestic rubbish to accumulate around the houses, that preserved the site so well: the later houses and passage-ways survive virtually intact to eaves-level. There is a remarkable uniformity about these houses, with the exception of house 8 on the perimeter of the settlement, which may be quite separate and later in date than the rest. The basic house in its final form is a one-room, single-storey model, built to last with walls 2m thick. It measures between about 4m and 7m internally, with a central kerbed hearth and a slab-built box-bed against the wall on either side (projecting into the room rather than recessed into the walls as in the earlier houses). Shelves or cupboards are built into the walls, and against the far wall opposite the entrance is a massive stone-built version of the old farmhouse dresser. The pottery found throughout the levels of the settlement is grooved ware, and the flat bases of the jars would be ideally suited to use on such dressers. Additional storage is provided by stone-lined and clay-luted tanks let into the floor, which were perhaps used for storing live limpets as fish-bait, and by cells built into the walls. Storage was clearly an important factor: amongst the pottery are sherds of jars up to 0.6m in diameter. The recent excavations yielded much carbonized grain, and this may have been one of the commodities requiring dry storage.

It is likely that the inhabitants of Skara Brae were cultivating cereal crops rather than importing the grain, and they were certainly breeding cattle, sheep and pigs, fishing and collecting shellfish, as well as utilizing stranded whales and hunting occasionally.

An exciting aspect of the recent excavations is the retrieval of organic material such as wood, heather rope, puff-balls and other plant remains from waterlogged levels of the midden deposits. This material, currently being studied, should add much to the reconstruction of Neolithic domestic activities, for its survival is a rare occurrence. There is a wide range of artefacts made of flint, stone, bone, ivory and antler, many of which have affinities with material found in Ireland and on sites belonging to grooved ware communities in England.

The only local source of flint in the Orkneys is the beach, where nodules are washed up from marine deposits, and the flint assemblage from Skara Brae is limited, consisting mostly of scrapers and flakes. The more spectacular, apparently ceremonial artefacts, such as a macehead, carved balls and spiked objects were made of local stone, as were the axes and the pebble flakes known as Skaill knives. Extensive use was made of animal bone and whalebone for awls, needles, knives, pins, beads, adzes, shovels, small paint-pots and bowls, and eleven pins were made of ivory, including very large pins up to 240mm long, which are similar to examples found in the Boyne passage-graves in Ireland. A strong interest in art and design is evident not only from the decoration carved on pins, stone balls and spiked objects and the incised and plastic motifs on the pottery, but also from the decorated slabs incorporated into the houses and passageways. These simple designs are in the general tradition of passage-grave art, and traces of red pigment suggest that the motifs may originally have been picked out in colour, a device that would certainly have made a bold decorative effect.

Skara Brae is so remarkable a prehistoric monument that the existence of an almost identical site at Rinyo on the island of Rousay comes as an unmerited anticlimax. Rinyo was excavated in 1938 and 1946 by Gordon Childe and the landowner, Walter Grant and, although its state of preservation did not match conditions at Skara Brae, its house-plans and material culture were very closely comparable. The settlement was built on the lower slope of a hillside, and some quarrying was necessary in order to create level terraces on which houses might be built. The surviving houses belong to secondary phases of occupation, and material from the primary middens was used to help in levelling the terraces. Drainage problems were met by slab-built drains, some at least lined with hazel bark. The remains of eight stone-built houses were uncovered, of which only two or three were inhabited at any one time; the social unit involved was obviously small, even allowing for the possibility that the excavated area does not include the entire original site, but the settlement seems to have been occupied over a very long period. Soil conditions did not favour the preservation of bone, but a radiocarbon date of 1900 bc$\pm$70 (Q-1226) was obtained recently from the animal bone that remained.

The surviving walls were mostly only two or three courses high, but the design of the houses is clear: single rectilinear chambers, 4m to 5m by 5m to 6m in area, enclosed by solid walls about 1.2m thick and entered through passage-doorways furnished with jambs and door-checks at the outer end. The central square hearth is kerbed with stone slabs set on end, a dresser occupies the wall opposite the entrance, and there is a stone bed to left and right of the entrance. There is greater variation than at Skara Brae in whether the beds are wholly recessed into the wall, partially recessed or projecting entirely from the face of the wall. Each house has a stone-lined box with a stone lid, normally set entirely into the floor but in house G projecting well above floor level and luted with clay on the outside instead of inside. One of the most exciting structural features at Rinyo is the clay oven in house C; this is the only oven still in position, but the base-plates of dismantled ovens were reused as drain covers. The oven had been built alongside a hearth, and it consisted of clay walls resting on a large stone slab and outlining a 0.6m square oven interior, the area of which was also hollowed out (probably by heat action) on the base-plate. The clay walls survived only to a height of 0.2m, but it is likely that they would originally have risen to form a dome.

Evidence of the economy practised at Rinyo is lacking, but stock-breeding and fishing were probably of major importance. Many sherds of grooved ware were found, and the stone artefacts echo the Skara Brae range of tools: a polished flint knife, flint scrapers, stone axes, a stone macehead, plain stone balls and Skaill knives. Only a pin and a fabricator survived out of what must have been an extensive assemblage of bone tools, and pieces of grooved pumice indicate the former presence of awls.

Another grooved ware settlement has been identified in Orkney, at Links of Noltland on the northern island of Westray. Its excavation is still in progress, and it appears, from the spread of midden deposits, to cover an area four times the known size of Skara Brae. Finds of pottery, stone- and bone-work show close similarities to the assemblages from Skara Brae and Rinyo.

One of the most exciting Late Neolithic sites that have been excavated in recent years is at Meldon Bridge in Peeblesshire; it is such a unique site that it is difficult to class it either as domestic or ceremonial. A promontory extending over about twenty acres between two rivers was cut off by a massive timber barrier. Posts up to 0.6m in diameter were used, and a strong element of defence or outstanding prestige must have been involved in the design of the site. The interior is covered with pits, some of which were apparently domestic, while others contained cremation burials. Within the area excavated, only one possible timber house has been found in the form of a circle of post-holes about 9m in diameter.

Shetland

A tantalizing fact is that Shetland is remarkably rich in early prehistoric house-sites and yet their precise date and cultural affinities are for the most part extremely vague. The houses are normally oval in plan with very thick walls, and they consist of one room with side-cells of varying proportions recessed into the walls. The house-plan itself is no guide to date, because it appears to have been standard throughout the prehistoric and into the historic period, but in some cases there are links in a distinctly heel-shaped outline and in building technique with the chambered tombs of Shetland. In a few instances, houses and tombs are physically so close to one another and so isolated from other monuments as to suggest distinct units. There are also links in material culture between the houses and tombs, and it is clear that some at least of the surviving house-sites belong to the period of the Neolithic chambered tombs. In many cases the houses, either singly or in groups of up to four buildings, are associated with enclosed fields, and the excavation at Ness of Gruting yielded a large cache of barley, which has a radiocarbon date of 1564 bc±120 (BM-441). There is a remarkable amount of evidence for agriculture, not only the Ness of Gruting barley and the stone-walled fields but also many querns and stone bar-shares. These Shetland house-sites provide an obvious target for future research excavation, and the affinities of some of the Ness of Gruting pottery with Hebridean Neolithic wares indicates that the Shetland communities were not isolated and that it may be possible eventually to set them into a wider context. Excavations by Alasdair Whittle at Scord of Brouster on the west mainland of Shetland are exploring a typical complex of oval stone houses associated with enclosed fields and clearance cairns. Finds of stone mattock-heads and bar-shares, together with carbonized barley, underline the importance of agricultural activities, and a radiocarbon date of 2220 bc±

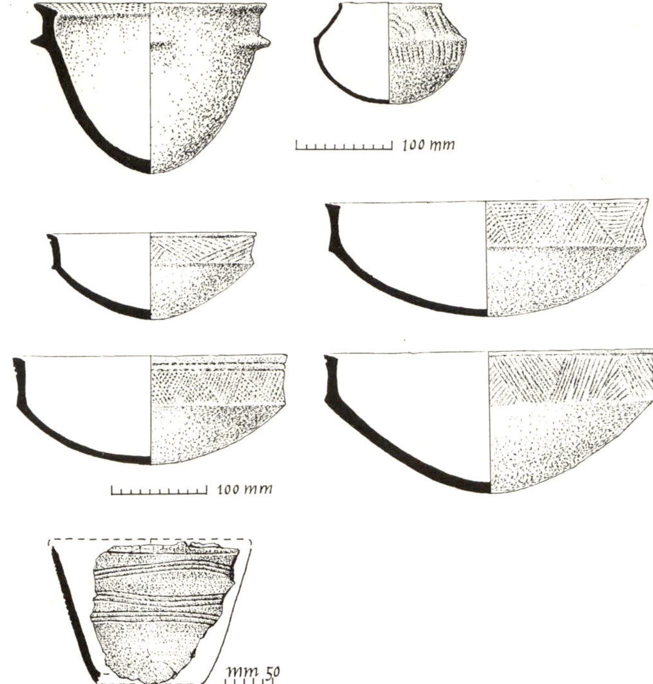

25 Top: Beacharra, Kintyre, Argyll. Centre: Unstan ware, Unstan, Orkney
Bottom: Grooved ware, Stones of Stenness, Orkney

80 (HAR-2413) from the interior of one of the houses, reinforced by pollen evidence for land clearance several centuries earlier, suggests that the Neolithic settlement of Shetland may have been well under way in the early third millennium BC.

Pottery

25 Most of the pottery found in chambered tombs takes the form of finely made, round-based bowls. The most distinctive, and those that show clear regional variation, are the decorated carinated bowls: along the west coast are found Achnacree bowls, which are characterized by heavy expanded rims and near vertical necks, with light fluting on the rim; Beacharra bowls show an inturned collar and sharp carination and are decorated with channelling, incision or stabbing, and their distribution is restricted to the west coast; Hebridean pottery, found on the islands, is characterized by highly decorated collared bowls, jars and flanged dishes, the motifs carried out by incision or stabbing. Unstan ware includes both plain and decorated bowls, the decoration confined to the collar and executed in incision or stab-and-drag (where a small implement is stabbed into the wet clay and then dragged along the surface a short way); most of this pottery has been found in Orkney, but it occurs also in north-east Scotland and in the Hebrides. Undecorated rounded bowls and cups are also common, and their forms, which include the use of lugs, indicate contacts with the Early Neolithic communities of Ireland, Wessex and Yorkshire.

The main types of pottery in use in Late Neolithic Scotland are the impressed wares, grooved ware and flat-rimmed ware, all of which are markedly different in form, fabric and decoration from earlier Neolithic pottery. The impressed wares are the equivalent of the contemporary Peterborough pottery of England and Wales, but there is greater variety and they cannot be classified neatly into regional and successive sub-styles. The fabric is uniformly coarse, and the decoration consists of impressed whipped cord or stab-and-drag, and bird-bone or stick impressions; there is considerable variety in forms, mostly shallow to deep round-based bowls.

Grooved ware pots are characteristically flat-based and profusely decorated jars, sometimes of considerable size – some of the jars from Skara Brae were more than 0.6m in diameter and must have been used primarily for storage. Fabric is coarse and gritty; decoration is carried out by grooving, incision or applied strips or pellets of clay, and it usually forms geometric designs based on triangles and lozenges. Plastic decoration was particularly fashionable at Skara Brae and Rinyo, where pots with scalloped rims have also been found. Radiocarbon dates associated with grooved ware are considerably earlier in Orkney than elsewhere, but the nature of the relationship between grooved ware communities living as far apart as Orkney and southern England is as yet barely understood. It may be noted that the only certain associations of stone maceheads with grooved ware are in Orkney, which is thought to have been where maceheads originally developed from antler prototypes.

One of the most distinct pottery styles is that represented by beakers, small, well-fired vessels, of reddish or sandy coloured ware, decorated with a great variety of motifs. Several of the groups of beakers have such close similarities to vessels found elsewhere in Europe, Spain and Portugal, western France and the Low Countries, that movement of people or a transfer of ideas may be inferred. As far as Scotland is concerned the most likely points of origin are Brittany and the Low Countries, though doubtless travellers made intermediate landfalls. The chronological span for the use of beaker ware, extended by recent radiocarbon determinations, now covers the period between about 2500 BC and 1500 BC, during which time a number of local styles of decoration developed, and these will be described later. Two of the earliest groups are known as All-over-cord ornamented beakers, which are shaped not unlike a hand-bell and are up to about 180mm tall, decorated with the impression of a twisted two-strand cord over the complete outer surface of the pot. Radiocarbon analysis from an inhumation at Sorisdale, on Coll, which was accompanied by such a vessel, has provided a date of 1934 bc±46 (BM-1413). European bell beakers are similar in shape but carry a wider range of motifs made by impressions of a short-toothed comb. Beakers of both groups occur widely in Scotland from the dunes of Luce Sands, Wigtownshire, Coll and Ardnamurchan as well as from east coast sites such as Tentsmuir, in Fife, Archerfield and Hedderwick, in East Lothian.

In general the makers of beaker pottery, particularly later styles, favoured individual inhumation in a cist or grave. At Cairnholy I, however, burials associated with fragmentary beakers, impressed ware, and a flint knife, were inserted before the final blocking of the tomb. Sherds of All-over-cord ornamented beakers have been found in the tombs of *Clyde* type at Cragabus, Islay, and Dalineun in Argyll; later styles were associated with the blocking of the passage-grave at Achnacreebeag. An All-over-cord ornamented beaker found in a cist at Salen, Mull, in 1882 was accompanied by two flint flakes and two fragments of arsenical copper, illustrating not only the new burial ritual but also the introduction of a knowledge of metals.

26 Carved stone ball, Towie, Aberdeenshire

Stone axes and carved stone balls

One of Neolithic man's most essential tools was the axe, vital for forest clearance. For geological reasons, most axes were in Scotland made of igneous rock rather than flint and, even in the case of imported axes, igneous stone was preferred. An Irish origin has been identified for more than sixty axes found in Scotland, predominantly in Aberdeenshire and around the Clyde estuary; these are made of porcellanite from sources in Co. Antrim. Local axe production has been recognized in Perthshire, Orkney and Shetland, though only in Perthshire and Shetland have the factory sites been found. The working-site near Killin in Perthshire produced axes made of a fine-grained grey-green stone, which is very similar to the greenstone from the Great Langdale axe-factory in the Lake District; it may be that some of the Scottish finds attributed to Great Langdale originated at Killin. Not only axes but knives of a distinctive oval form and other implements were made in Shetland, almost entirely for local consumption, of blue-grey felsite. In Orkney, axes made of local camptonite have been found, but no working-places have been identified; like felsite, camptonite occurs as intrusive dykes, which outcrop sporadically, in Orkney mostly around the coasts.

About 390 examples of carved stone balls have survived, a number that makes them a major type of prehistoric artefact in Scotland, and their size and treatment show remarkable uniformity: most are about
26 70mm in diameter, carved with knobs and sometimes decorated with incised spirals or concentric circles, the most remarkable being that from Towie, Aberdeenshire. The majority of provenanced balls has been found in east Scotland, between the Moray Firth and the River Tay, but they have inevitably become collector's items and relatively few, perhaps only half, can now be attributed securely to a findspot. Very few balls have been found on archaeological sites, but those from Skara Brae clearly demonstrate their use in Neolithic times. Old records of balls having been found in burial cists suggest that their reverence if not their manufacture continued into Bronze Age times, but, on the whole, it seems likely that they were a relatively short-lived and peculiarly Scottish phenomenon.

3

Henge Monuments and Stone Circles

The chambered tombs and long cairns of Scotland are part of a west European tradition of burial and ritual; found only in Britain, on the other hand, is a distinct group of circular earthworks known as 'henge monuments', consisting of a deep quarry ditch, a concentric outer bank and one or more entrance causeways across the ditch and through the bank. The internal area varies considerably in size, but two classes of henge have been distinguished using the number of entrance causeways as a criterion, Class I having a single entrance into the interior and those of Class II having two opposed entrances through the bank and ditch. Several henges are also accompanied by circles of standing stones. Henge monuments are scattered throughout the eastern part of Scotland with a few outliers elsewhere. Henges of Class I include Overhowden, Berwickshire, Balfarg, Fife, and the Stones of Stenness in Orkney; examples of Class II are more numerous, including Broadlee, Dumfriesshire, Normangill Rig, Lanarkshire, Cairnpapple Hill, West Lothian, Broomend of Crichie, Aberdeenshire and the Ring of Brodgar, in Orkney. A group of allied but 27–8
rather smaller earthworks has been found in Aberdeenshire and Ross and Cromarty; at Wormy Hillock, Aberdeenshire, the central platform is only 6m in diameter. The function of henge monuments is not known, but perhaps the most reasonable interpretation is that they were social or religious centres for the population of a wide area.

Only one Class I henge monument has been extensively examined in recent years, Balfarg, and Roger Mercer's work here has shown that an area of some 4,000 sq. m. was enclosed within a ditch 5m wide and 2.5m deep, and that a timber ring and probably two stone rings were set up within it. The remains of the timber circle of sixteen upright posts were well preserved, measuring about 25m in diameter, with deep post-sockets, within the packing of which were quantities of grooved ware sherds. On the south-west side, two outlying post-holes indicate the presence of a 'porch'. The stone circles, the sockets of which were not well preserved and the stones themselves long since removed, were clearly secondary to the ring of upright timbers. Within the circle there was a grave-pit containing an inhumation accompanied by a handled beaker and a flint knife. A series of radiocarbon dates indicates that the timber ring, and thus the henge ditch as the timbers are concentric to it, were constructed about 3000 BC. At the Stones of Stenness, Orkney, excavated by Graham Ritchie, the bank and ditch have a single entrance causeway giving access to a central plat-

form some 44m in diameter with the remains of a magnificent stone 29
circle; at the centre of the site, and presumably the focus for the ritual activity, there was a square stone setting associated with cremated bone, charcoal and pottery. This well-preserved feature can be compared to a central setting within the stone circle of Balbirnie, in 30
Fife, and perhaps to another, now removed, at Cairnpapple. Between the stone setting and the entrance causeway there were the remains of a small timber structure, which originally possessed upright portal stones, as well as a further setting of stones, which was reconstructed into a spurious 'dolmen' (or table-tomb) in the early years of this century. Some impression of the social complexity that such monuments imply may be gauged by the work-effort involved in their construction. At Stenness a figure of 20,000 man-hours has been suggested for the time taken to quarry the surrounding ditch out of the solid rock and to mound up the concentric bank – an estimate that may be compared with the 900,000 man-hours postulated for the Durrington Walls earthwork and 1,560,000 man-hours for the massive henge at Avebury (both in Wiltshire).

Deposits from the terminals of the rock-cut ditch included the bones of domestic ox and sheep as well as the bones of wolves and dogs; the remains of ox and sheep are for the most part mandibles and the extremities of limbs, in other words the debris left after removing the more succulent joints. Perhaps feasting or sacrificing animals had

27–8 Henge monument and stone circle, Ring of Brodgar, Orkney

29 Stone circle, Stones of Stenness, Orkney

some part to play in the ceremonial of such sites. A radiocarbon date of 2356 bc±65 (SRR-350) was obtained from analysis of the bones, and this indicates that the ditch had already been dug by the early third millennium BC. The central setting of stones is of comparable date – 2238 bc±70 (SRR-351). Ritchie suggested that, because of the difficulty of moving and erecting the stones of the circle after the ditch has been dug, they must have been set in position before or during this operation. Grooved ware pottery and radiocarbon dates from the Stones of Stenness indicate that it was being put up within the architectural milieu of the construction of Quanterness and the Maes Howe class of chambered tombs; the cruciform passage-grave of Newgrange, Co. Meath, has a number of similarities with the Orkney tombs, and it is interesting to note that its mound is surrounded by a carefully laid-out setting of standing stones, which, if contemporary with the construction of the tomb, is another early stone circle. One of the kerb-stones at Newgrange is decorated with a motif that finds an echo on a grooved ware sherd from Skara Brae. Of Scottish chambered cairns the only examples to have surrounding stone circles are the *Clava* tombs and the small passage-grave within the circle at Callanish on Lewis; it would, however, be unwise to see such a feature as forging any cultural connection in itself.

31 At Strathallan, Perthshire, a Class II henge monument revealed an internal ring of timber posts set in deep sockets. Evidence for timber settings, as at Balfarg and Strathallan, coupled with the early date for henge monuments with stone circles in those areas where timber was of poor quality, such as Orkney, show the importance of the henge tradition in the origin of freestanding stone circles, at least in Scotland.

As a result of excavations within a number of unusually large henge monuments in Wessex, in which substantial timber buildings have been discovered, it has been suggested first that such earthworks are secular rather than ceremonial; the large amount of bone refuse, together with pottery and stone objects, has been seen to argue against the wholly ritual nature of the Wessex sites. Geoffrey Wainwright

30 Stone circle, Stones of Stenness, Orkney; central setting (scale in 50 cm divisions)

31 Barrow and henge monument, Strathallan, Perthshire; aerial photograph showing inner circle of post-holes

envisaged such sites as Durrington Walls and Marden, in Wiltshire, and Mount Pleasant, Dorset, as secular centres with large public buildings. Euan MacKie, however, described the great henges of Wessex as the 'permanently inhabited ceremonial centres of a later Neolithic theocratic governing class' for whom grooved ware pottery was specially made. Skara Brae and Rinyo are described as perhaps 'the residences of some of these wise men and their families who were engaged in astronomical, ceremonial and magical work in the Orkney Islands?' On balance we feel that this is an unlikely interpretation of the archaeological evidence, though it is rarely possible to disprove any theory on the basis of the available material; there is no doubt that the users of grooved ware pottery were prodigious and exacting builders both in timber and in stone, and that some of their achievements can be given an astronomical interpretation. It may also be suggested, on the evidence of tomb contents for example, that there were two distinct groups in Orkney in the third millennium BC, but it is wrong to suppose that the archaeological evidence can show the dominance of the users of grooved ware over the makers of Unstan ware. Nor can the small number of settlements so far discovered in Scotland allow us to identify the occupation of the inhabitants of Skara Brae and Rinyo as anything other than farmers and fishermen. But then the excavation of a vicarage today would not perhaps identify its occupant, though that of a doctor's or dentist's residence might. Finally, as MacKie indeed noted, the location of Skara Brae and Rinyo far away from the great ceremonial monuments of Orkney, the Stones of Stenness and the Ring of Brodgar, seems to diminish the likelihood of any special social status for their inhabitants.

The Ring of Brodgar introduces two further aspects to this study of stone circles – the design of such sites on a precise mathematical basis and the implication that their purpose was to assist with astronomical calculations. The Ring of Brodgar occupies a commanding position on a narrow promontory between the Lochs of Stenness and Harray, with the smaller Class I henge about 1.5km to the south-west; the Class II henge of Brodgar, unusual in that it lacks any bank, has opposed entrances in the north-west and south-east quadrants. The henge ditch was as much as 3m in depth and 9m across and has, like Stenness, been cut into the underlying bed-rock; it may have involved as much as 80,000 man-hours' work. There were originally sixty stones in the circle set near the inner edge of the ditch, although only thirty-six survive either as uprights or broken stumps, but it is clear that they were put up six degrees apart. The identification of a unit of measurement, employed in the construction of many such sites, the 'megalithic yard' of 0.829m, and the realization that some apparent stone 'circles' are in fact 'flattened circles', 'egg-shaped circles' and ellipses, is the result of painstaking field survey by Alexander Thom, although aspects of his work have not gone unchallenged. The Ring of Brodgar has a diameter of 125 megalithic yards, and the surviving stones show how precisely they have been erected to ensure that the plan was completed accurately. The astronomy of the site involves the use of a number of barrows round about it and is rather more problematical; it has been inferred that the builders of the site in laying out the barrows have made possible the tracking of lunar movements by using a number of horizon points as markers. A date of between 1700 BC to 1400 BC has been calculated for the likely span of this activity, a rather later date than might have been suggested on archaeological grounds for the construction of the circle, although clearly possible for the barrows. This dilemma may help to demonstrate the difficulty many archaeologists have in coming to terms with the astronomical interpretation for such sites – an interpretation that demands detailed recording knowledge in a society that was non-literate. This is not to deny that such considerable engineering feats necessitated social organization and cohesion, mathematical skills, and an appreciation of broad principles of solar or lunar movements, but merely to express caution that astronomical observations should not be given too great a prominence in our appreciation of life in the third and second millennia BC, and that they ought not be used to imply a stratified society, a theocratic elite, or a gene pool of mathematically gifted people.

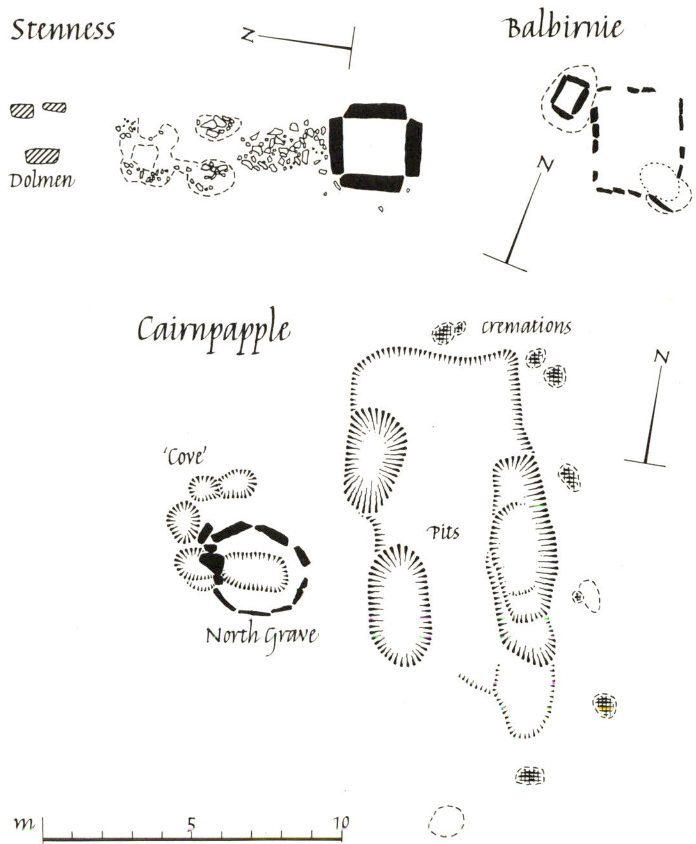

32 Central settings at the Stones of Stenness, Orkney; Balbirnie, Fife; Cairnpapple, West Lothian

Cairnpapple Hill

Excavations at the Stones of Stenness and Balfarg have provided much information about the internal arrangements of henge monuments; Stuart Piggott's work at Cairnpapple Hill, West Lothian, between 1947 and 1948, discovered a structural sequence of ritual and burial monuments spanning the years between about 2800 BC and the middle of the second millennium BC. Cairnpapple Hill is situated a little to the south of Linlithgow and commands extensive views in all directions including the summits of Schiehallion, in Perthshire, and Goatfell on the island of Arran. Piggott identified five periods of activity including, as the second phase, the building of a Class II henge monument. Period I consisted of an arc of seven small pits, six of which contained deposits of cremated bone, a further five cremations found on the old ground surface, and perhaps a setting of upright stones or 'Cove', represented only by their sockets, near the centre of the arc. Two fragmentary pins of antler or bone were found with the cremations. Fragments of Neolithic axes from 'factories' as far afield as Langdale, Westmorland, and Graig Lwyd, Caernarvonshire, imply perhaps that the site was a place for meeting or exchange. The construction of the henge monument would not have involved the same amount of effort as the Orcadian monuments; the ditch measures only about 3.5m in breadth and up to 1.3m in depth, but the outer bank would have helped

to increase its visual effect. The two entrance causeways, one to the north and the other to the south, gave access to an oval area measuring about 40m by 30m. In the interior there had been a setting of twenty-four standing stones, laid out to form one of Thom's 'egg-shaped rings', but the stones were taken down in a subsequent period. At the
32 centre of the site a series of pits may once have formed the sort of rectilinear setting that was found at the Stones of Stenness, but the contents of the pits were removed in the course of the remodelling of the site in a later phase; it is also possible that the stones of the 'Cove' may have been part of this setting rather than an earlier phase. One context for the reconstruction of part of the site is the building of a small free-standing cairn, with a standing stone at its west end, which was set up partly in one of the sockets of the 'Cove'. The central grave-pit, which was dug into the solid rock, revealed only the stain of an extended inhumation, and an oak object overlying the face of the burial; two pottery vessels of beaker ware, and a second object, possibly a club, were also found in the grave. Another, and indeed probably earlier burial associated with beaker pottery was discovered in a grave-pit near one of the sockets of the ring of standing stones.

The third of the periods of activity on the hill-top involved the construction of a large cairn some 13m in diameter, above two Bronze Age cist-burials, one an inhumation with an accompanying food vessel and the other a cremation deposit: the cairn also covered the small beaker cairn, and, as it overlay two of the stones of the stone circle, it must have necessitated the removal of at least some of the stones. In fact it is likely that these were removed to provide kerb-stones and building material for the cairn. Period IV involves the enlarging of the cairn to contain two burial deposits in cinerary urns; the final phase of activity includes four further burials, probably inhumations, the date of which is not known.

In this chapter we are concerned primarily with the henge monument of the second period; when the excavation was published the henge and the beaker burials were thought to belong to a single period, but it seems permissible, at a time when longer chronologies are fashionable, to divide this period into two or indeed three phases: first the construction of the henge, the possible central setting and the 'Cove'; secondly the beaker burial beside stone-hole no. 8; and thirdly the small free-standing cairn containing as it does two beakers of rather later style.

Stone circles

The larger henges, the great stone circles, such as Callanish, and the monumental recumbent stone circles of the north-east are the cathedrals of prehistoric Scotland, spanning many centuries of building or reconstruction. Massive pillars of stone make such an important contribution to the Scottish landscape that it is easy to forget we know so little about them. For example, there is sparse evidence from Scottish sites about the methods employed in raising standing stones, although some interesting experimental work was undertaken by H. E. Kilbride-Jones during the partial reconstruction of the recumbent stone circle at Old Keig in Aberdeenshire.

33 Stone circle, Lochbuie, Mull, Argyll

Stone circles are to be found in several distinct geographical areas of Scotland: the south-west, Arran, the Western Isles, the north-east and Perthshire, with outliers to all these groups. There are very few, however, in the midland belt, Angus or Argyll. In the south-west Torhousekie, Wigtownshire, is a well-preserved example of a 'flattened circle' of large boulders rather than thin slabs. A central setting with one small stone flanked by two larger boulders may be reminiscent of some of the recumbent stone circles of the north-east, but the presence of a central stone is a feature of a number of the circles in the south-west. On the west coast of Arran there is a remarkable group of circles, both of boulders and of tall slabs on Machrie Moor, which was undoubtedly the cult centre for the immediate area. Cists containing burials have been discovered in several of the circles, with food-vessel pottery and flint objects as accompanying grave-goods; it is possible that the circles were put up several centuries earlier than the burials and that these were inserted into a site considered to be sacred. On
Bute and on Mull there are isolated circles standing at the heads of 33
fertile bays at Kilchattan and Lochbuie respectively.

Callanish

The supreme achievement of the architects of stone circles is at 34
Callanish, on Lewis; here on a ridge overlooking East Loch Roag, a site that, like the Ring of Brodgar, offers a shimmering interplay of sky, sea and land, stands a cross-shaped setting of stones radiating from a central circle, in fact one of Thom's 'flattened circles'. A massive
upright at the centre of the circle standing about 4.7m in height pro- 35
vides an impressive focus for the site. Occupying much of the eastern half of the circle there is a small, and now much ruined, passage-grave;

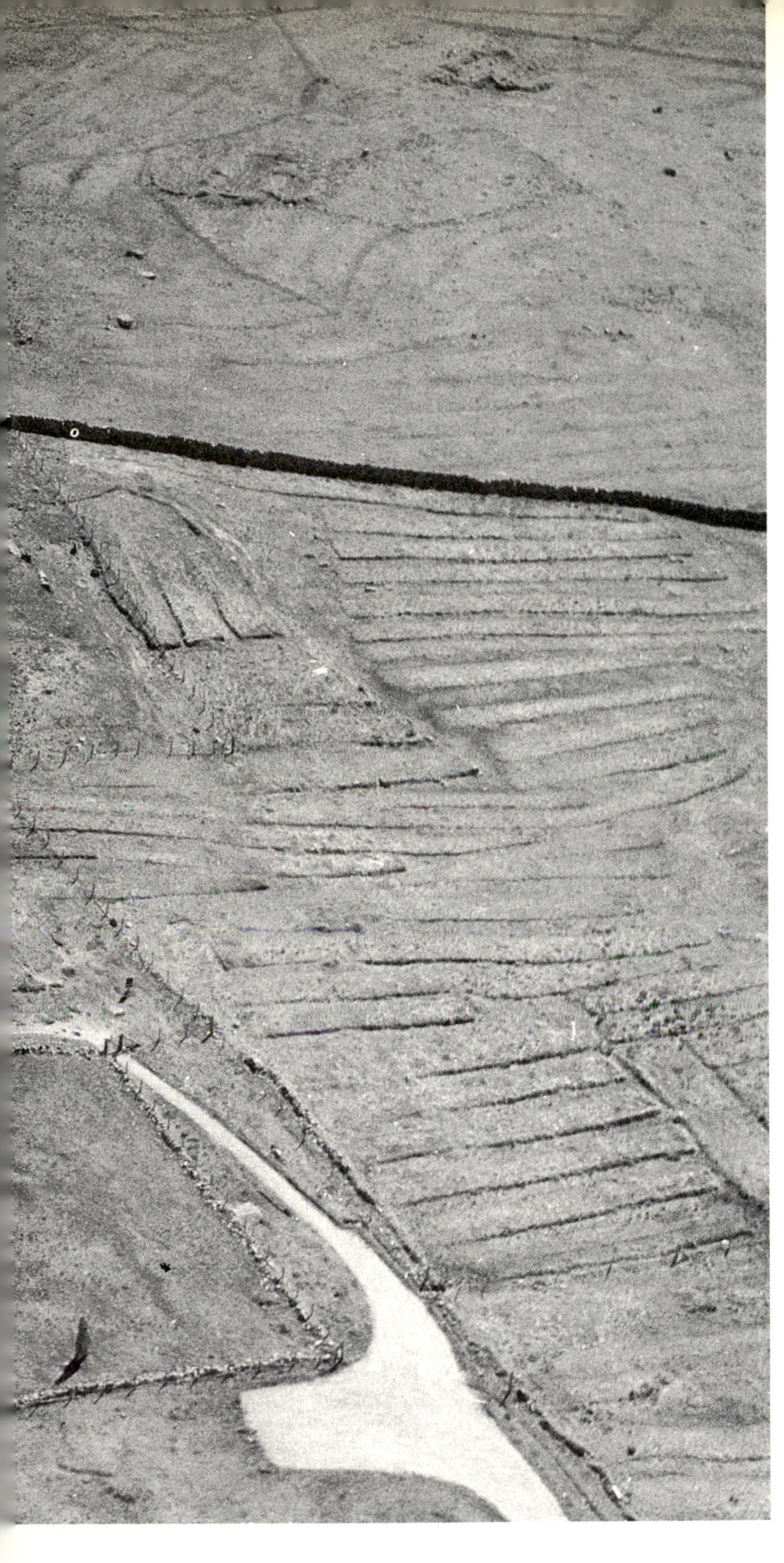

34 Stone circle and alignments, Callanish, Lewis

35 Stone circle, Callanish, Lewis

the central stone acts as a kerb-stone of the cairn and is situated immediately to the back of the chamber, which is entered between two of the stones of the circle, one of them doubling as a portal-stone. An avenue of stones leads to the NNE, the remains of what may have been a comparable avenue exist to the south, and single alignments radiate to the east and west.

The circle and the adjacent stones were, until 1857, embedded in
36 peat to a depth of about 1.5m, but at this date the peat was cleared and the chambered tomb discovered. Excavation revealed only a small quantity of cremated bone and 'a black unctuous substance, in which these fragments were contained'. The position of the chambered cairn within the sequence of building of the circle has been the subject of much speculation. In general, archaeological opinion has preferred the suggestion that the tomb was added to an existing monument.

Recumbent stone circles

The recumbent stone circles of central Aberdeenshire, generally situated in conspicuous positions, are among the most impressive megalithic monuments in the country. The geographical distribution is markedly inland, in the foothills of the Grampians, with concentrations between the rivers Dee, Don and Deveron; there is a small isolated group in Buchan. They take their name from the presence of a large prostrate slab ('the recumbent') which is often flanked by the

36 Stone circle, Callanish, Lewis; chambered cairn

two tallest uprights of the circle; this grouping is frequently in the south-west quadrant of the circle, an axis also favoured by the builders of the *Clava* monuments. A further link with these sites is the presence of a low ring-cairn either joining the stones or set within the circle. At Old Keig the recumbent stone weighs about fifty tons and would have needed several hundred men to move it. Many circles have been excavated in the past, but we have reliable information about very few of them. At Loanhead of Daviot, however, H. E. Kilbride-Jones uncovered the plan of a well-preserved circle and ring-cairn, with 37 adjacent to it an enclosed cemetery of cremation burials. Loanhead has eight individual stones, together with the recumbent boulder and its flanking uprights, laid out in a circle of some 20m. The ring-cairn had been constructed inside the circle and it covered almost the entire central area. Kilbride-Jones demonstrated that the earliest period comprised the stone circle and a number of small 'cairns' around the bases of the stones, some of which contained beaker pottery and one yielded a cremation deposit in an undecorated urn. A hollow in the centre of the circle revealed patches of burning, pottery, including beaker ware, and cremations. Associated with the secondary ring-cairn were further cremation burials. One of the stones of the circle has five cup-marks. Several recumbent stones bear cup-marks including Sunhoney, Aberdeenshire, and Rothiemay, Banff, which, with 119 cup-marks, is the most extensively decorated of the group.

37 Recumbent stone circle, Loanhead of Daviot, Aberdeenshire

The origin of these distinctive circles is uncertain. No convincing prototypes outside the north-east can be adduced; similarities with aspects of the *Clava* monuments have been used to suggest a derivation from this group, but this is not altogether convincing. A developmental series has been put forward, in which such sites as Sunhoney, Old Keig, and Loanhead of Daviot, in Aberdeenshire, appear to be early, and less regular sites as Garrol Wood, Kincardineshire, are late, but there are few radiocarbon dates and little pottery has been found in sealed contexts. Excavations at Berrybrae, Aberdeenshire, on a circle thought to be late in the series have provided two radiocarbon dates from charcoal associated with a beaker vessel found in a pit filled with clay: 1500 bc±80 and 1360 bc±90 (HAR-1849 and 1893). The dates appear to be from a late phase in the use of the circle.

A small group of ring-cairns in Aberdeenshire and Kincardineshire shares with recumbent stone circles an elusive link with the cairns of the *Clava* group; certainly at Raedykes, Kincardineshire, where two of the ring-cairns are surrounded by stone circles, the similarities with the *Clava* monuments are valid. At other sites, such as Sundayswells and Sands of Forvie, it is possible that the local ring-cairn tradition is in fact the dominant influence. An All-over-cord ornamented beaker was discovered at the centre of Sundayswells, in the late nineteenth century, but it cannot in itself provide a date for the construction of the site. Pottery comparable to that recovered from Loanhead of Daviot has, however, been found in a little ring-cairn in the Sands of Forvie; at its centre, a square area was demarcated by four upright stones at the corners, with cremated bone, white quartz pebbles and charcoal within it. At Cullerlie, Aberdeenshire, a circle of eight boulders contains within it eight small cairns with well-defined kerbs, six of them containing deposits of cremated bone. Together with recumbent stone circles, however, these sites illustrate the variety of ritual and burial monuments employed in the north-east between about 2500 and 1700 BC.

Several types of stone circle are represented in Perthshire, and a number have been excavated in recent years, including Croft Moraig, Fortingall, Moncrieffe and Sandy Road, Scone. One group of circles with six stones shows a consistent pattern with the largest stone to the south-west quadrant. Yet another group, the 'four-posters', are small rectangular stone settings with outlying examples elsewhere in eastern Scotland, Arran and Islay; what little dating evidence there is suggests that 'four-posters' come late in the circle tradition. At Croft Moraig, excavation demonstrated the existence of three main phases with an initial timber horse-shoe setting which was later replaced by two stone phases. Two styles of pottery were found at Croft Moraig: well-fired and finely tempered Neolithic wares, as well as fragments of more coarsely-made bucket-shaped vessels with rounded or flattened rims, comparable to sherds from, for example, Loanhead of Daviot. The latter style had formerly been assigned to the latest phases of the Scottish Bronze Age, but can now be shown to be present in much earlier contexts. From Culbin Sands, Morayshire, there is a radiocarbon date from a layer stratified between two midden deposits containing 'flat-rimmed ware' of 1259 bc±75 (Q-990).

At Sandy Road, Scone, a circle of seven boulders had at its centre an upright cinerary urn with a small and presumably token cremation deposit and quantities of charcoal; analysis of the charcoal produced a radiocarbon date of 1200 bc±150 (GaK-787), a similar date to that just quoted from Culbin Sands.

The excavation by Graham Ritchie of the small stone circle at 38
Balbirnie, Fife, illustrates the problems of disentangling the various phases of activity within such sites; here ten stones had been erected in an ellipse with a low rectangular setting of stones at the centre.

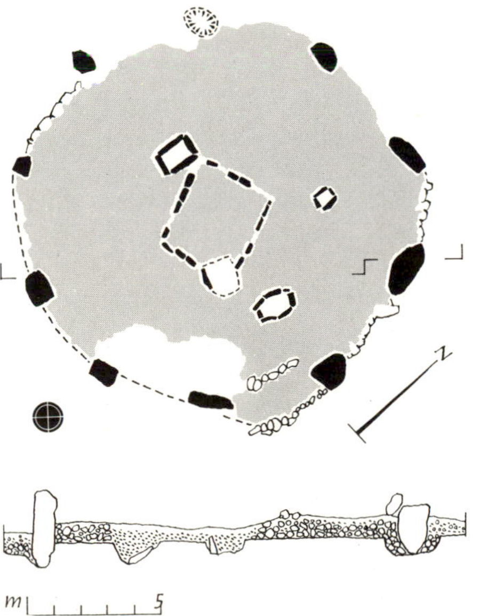

38 Stone circle and cairn, Balbirnie, Fife

39 Food vessel, Balbirnie, Fife

40 Cup and ring marked stone in cist I, Balbirnie, Fife

Cremated bones had been deposited into the sockets of four of the uprights, but, apart from two sherds that may be akin to grooved ware, there was no dating evidence for this period. In the second period, several cists were inserted within the circle, containing among other
39 grave-goods a food vessel and a small bone toggle, and all were covered by a large cairn of stones. Two stones decorated with cup-
40 marks and cup-and-ring marks were reused as packing or as a side-slab for two of these cists; Ritchie suggested tentatively that the stones had originally formed part of the central setting and drew a parallel with small structures interpreted as 'grave-houses' or 'temples' in Denmark. Finally at least sixteen cremation burials, some associated with cinerary urns, were deposited within the cairn.

Our discussion of henge monuments, stone circles and some allied monuments highlights many of the problems encountered by archaeologists when faced with a class of field-monument or artefact the function of which is not known. With, for example, chambered tombs or hillforts we assume, perhaps wrongly, that we understand the function, and thus the monuments; with stone circles we are at a loss, although anthropological parallels may help to suggest possible uses for similar settings of upright timbers or stones, both in secular and religious terms. It must be admitted that the information at our disposal is scanty and partial, that past excavations have raised more problems of interpretation than they have solved, and that we are dealing with functions that can probably never be recovered by archaeological means. It can be shown, however, that timber and stone circles within henge monuments were being put up early in the third millennium BC, at the same time as the use of chambered cairns, and that the building and rebuilding of stone circles continued at least into the mid-second millennium BC. Burial plays an important part in many sites and a rudimentary interest in astronomical happenings is not ruled out. Local architectural traditions developed, including recumbent stone circles and 'four-posters'; by the first millennium BC, however, the communal effort implied by such public works was channelled into the building of defensive structures such as hillforts.

4

The First Metalworkers

Pottery and burials

The fashion for barrow-digging in Wiltshire, Dorset and Yorkshire in the nineteenth century has coloured our picture of the archaeological remains dating broadly to the second millennium BC and has given them an essentially funereal aspect. The grave furniture from cists, cairns and barrows, along with chance finds of bronzes, either singly or in hoards, provided for many years a chronology based on the typology of objects. In 1902, beaker pottery, for example, was set out in a typological sequence by Abercromby, with each type representing a certain period of time, and all the types imagined as parallel columns of different lengths, 'beginning at different altitudes and terminating for the most part at different levels'. The inclusion in graves of exotic artefacts such as faience beads, which were thought to have their origin in Egypt between about 1600 BC and 1300 BC, helped to link British chronological schemes to the literate societies of the eastern Mediterranean. With the advent of radiocarbon dates, however, an independent and more reliable scheme can be constructed. We have already seen that introduction of beaker pottery must be considered to have taken place within the Neolithic period, but the use of such vessels may have gone on for as much as a thousand years to judge from recent radiocarbon dates. For example, radiocarbon dates associated with beakers from Sorisdale, Coll, of 1934 bc±46 (BM-1413) and from Balbirnie, Fife, of 1330 bc±90 (GaK-3425) indicate a span of between about 2500 BC and 1600 BC in calendar years.

Several typologies for beaker pottery have been proposed but the most recent sees the vessels in a series of broad regional steps, with All-over-cord ornamented beakers and European bell beakers occurring early in the sequence (within steps one and two). We have already seen that these have been discovered in such chambered tombs as Cairnholy, Kirkcudbrightshire, and accompanying individual inhumations as at Sorisdale, on Coll. Beakers of step three are of more slender proportions and display a much greater variety of decorative motifs, while step four vessels are characterized by a definite neck, possibly emphasized by a sharper bend or by contrasting decoration. A fine
beaker with bands of horizontal tooth-comb impressions found with 41
an inhumation in a cist at Culduthel, Inverness-shire, in 1975, was

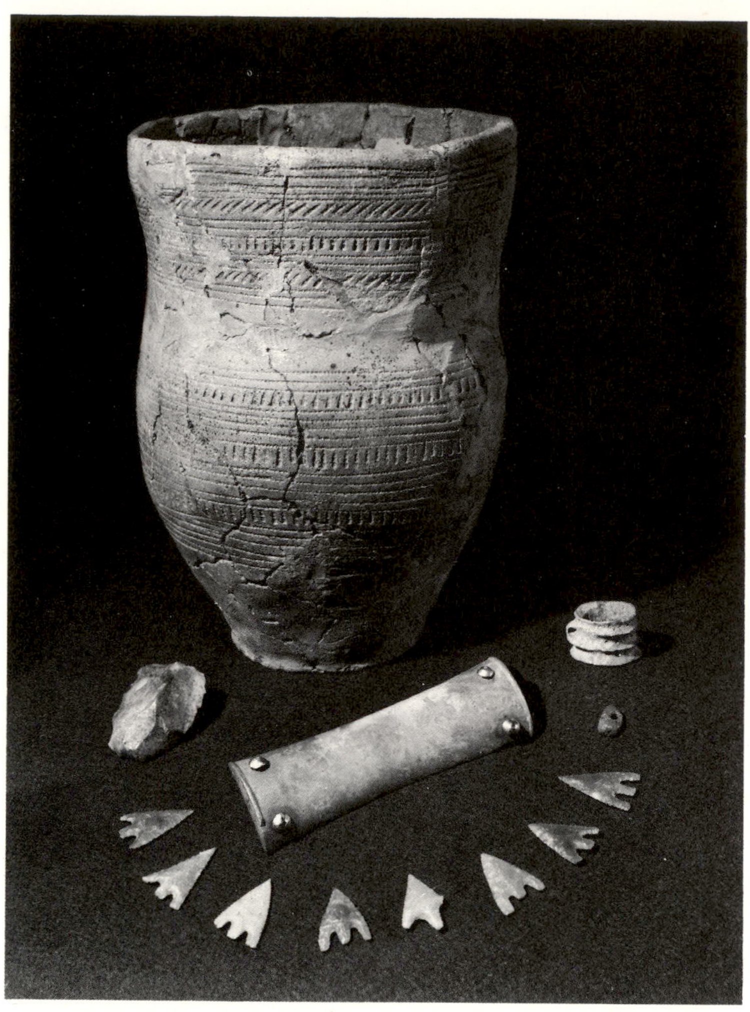

41 Grave group from Culduthel, Inverness-shire; beaker, gold-studded bracer, flint arrowheads and bone ring

accompanied by an archer's bracer with gold-capped rivets, an amber bead, a bone toggle, flint strike-a-light and eight barbed-and-tanged arrowheads. The arrowheads and the bracer (wrist-guard) are the
42 accoutrements of an archer. A tall vessel from Glebe Street, Campbeltown, Argyll, allows us to illustrate the techniques of decoration both of twisted cord and of impressions with a fine square-toothed comb.
43–4 A well-proportioned step four beaker from East Drums, Brechin, Angus, was found with an inhumation in a short cist accompanied by a number of flint implements and flakes; a unique aspect of this burial is the fact that the capstone of the cist had been carefully shaped around the edge of its under-surface, so that it fitted closely over the side and end slabs like a tightly sealed lid. Beakers of steps five to seven are characterized first by accentuated necks, then by a bipartite scheme of shape and decoration and finally by the absence of any division between these two areas with general patterning over a rather shapeless vessel.

42 Beaker, Glebe Street, Campbeltown, Kintyre, Argyll

43–4 Beaker and rebated cover slab, East Drums, Brechin, Angus

Students of beaker pottery have differed in their interpretation of this phenomenon. David L. Clarke saw several styles of beaker as indicating invasions from the continent; Lanting and van der Waals, whose 'steps' have been described above, see only All-over-cord ornamented vessels as indicating actual movements of people. There is some doubt about the transfer of Lanting and van der Waals's system to Scotland beyond the south-east part of the country. Thus the present writers prefer to see Scottish beakers developing in ways that satisfy both extremes of invasion and of local development. All-over-cord and European bell beakers do seem to indicate the arrival of new people; there is evidence that beaker users had a broader face and rather shorter skull formation than those of the builders of chambered cairns, and thus the introduction of new people seems likely. Stuart Piggott, following Margaret Stewart, noted the similarity of several vessels from the north-east to those from the Low Countries, and contact, and probably movement, of peoples seem most likely. The local development embodied in the later stages of both Clarke's scheme and that of Lanting and van der Waals shows how strong the fashion of making beakers had become.

The term 'food vessel' like that of 'beaker' has an antiquarian origin at a time when the grave-goods were thought to contain the food and drink for the journey to the next world. It has recently been suggested that the beaker from Ashgrove, Fife, contained a mead made from lime honey flavoured with flowers of meadow-sweet; food remains, however, have proved more elusive. Food vessels are for the most part bowls, squat in shape, with a profusion of ornamental motifs, some with decoration comparable to pots from Ireland and the north of England. These vessels accompany both inhumation and cremation burials in cists found under cairns and also without any apparent mound. Radiocarbon dates for burials associated with food vessels are

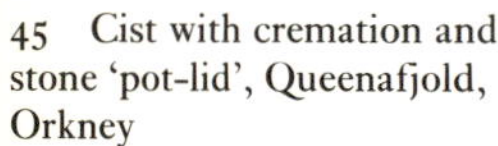
45 Cist with cremation and stone 'pot-lid', Queenafjold, Orkney

46 Enlarged food vessel, Ferniegair, Lanarkshire

clearly earlier than a number of beaker deposits elsewhere. At Aberdour Road, Dunfermline, Fife, a date of 1631 bc±40 (SRR-292) was obtained from a crouched burial in a cist accompanied by a flint knife, a flint strike-a-light and a nodule of iron ore; a cist-burial at Gairneybank, Kinross-shire has yielded a date of 1510 bc±70 (GU-1119). But food vessels have also been associated with burials of rather later date, including, for example, a crouched inhumation in a cist at Reswallie Mains, Rescobie, Angus which yielded a date of 1210 bc±70 (N-1238).

Individual inhumation in a short cist is still perhaps the most common burial tradition of the makers of beaker vessels, but it is not the only rite for which there is evidence; more careful analysis of the bones from such burials has in recent years shown that multiple inhumations are found and cremation burials are not unknown. Nor should we always assume that cist-burials are of Bronze Age date, for inhumations accompanied by iron objects show that this tradition continued to the early centuries AD. Unaccompanied burials or those with undatable objects like the stone pot-lid with a cremation burial from 45
Queenafjold, Orkney, are part of a burial practice that is of long duration.

The change from inhumation to cremation that appears to have taken place was also doubtless a gradual one, but cremation was clearly an important aspect of burial rituals from an early stage; the lighting of fires in chambered tombs shows that heat and flames were an aspect even of inhumation practices. Cremations within a complex mortuary structure under a round barrow at Pitnacree, Perthshire, may be mid-fourth millennium BC in date, for there is a radiocarbon date of 2860 bc±90 (GaK-601) for charcoal from the old land surface under the mound. A scattered cremation deposit with quantities of charcoal found in a standing stone socket on the top of this mound has a date of 2270 bc±90 (GaK-602).

The practice of cremating the dead has thus a long ancestry; the use of large cinerary urns, however, adds another dimension to the ceramic 46
styles of the Early Bronze Age and must in some areas at least have involved a deliberate change in burial practices. At Cairnpapple Hill, for example, the Period IV cairn was enlarged to receive two cremation

deposits in inverted cinerary urns. At Grandtully, Perthshire, a cordoned urn with cremation and charcoal yielded a radiocarbon date of 1270 bc±100 (GaK-603), a date comparable to that quoted earlier from the cremation deposit at Sandy Road, Scone, Perthshire. Several distinct styles of cinerary urn have been identified, their distribution falling in the east and south-west parts of Scotland, including collared urns, cordoned urns, encrusted urns and a final group, the profile and decoration of which are akin to food vessels but their size is comparable to that of cinerary urns. In a number of cases the deposits are so concentrated within a small area that they must be considered as cemeteries, with examples in the south-west at Misk Knowe, Ardeer Sands, Ayrshire, and Palmerston, Dumfriesshire; among the associated finds from Ardeer were segmented and star-shaped faience beads. Extensive cremation cemeteries on the gravel terraces of the River Clyde and in north-east Fife, must represent the burial places of farming communities living nearby, for which there are no other traces of settlement. Distribution maps of food vessels and cinerary urns show marked concentrations in the east and southern parts of Scotland, and this has led to the impression that the west and north were hardly occupied at this time. Such an impression was based partly on the fact that the pottery from the west cannot be given the convenient labels of the more coherent eastern styles and partly because many burials were not accompanied by funerary vessels at all (cremations in small kerb-cairns for example). Generalized attitudes to Scottish prehistory have tended to be formulated from a standpoint based on the museum collections of central Scotland.

Not all cremation burials of this period were deposited in cinerary urns; two cremation cemeteries, at Weird Law, Peeblesshire, and Whitestanes Moor, Dumfriesshire, are circular banks of stone with burials set in pits within the enclosed area. Radiocarbon dates of 1490 bc±90 (NPL-57) and 1360 bc±90 (GaK-461) indicate the chronological horizon for this class of cemetery. One of the burials from Whitestanes was accompanied by a perforated accessory vessel, flints and some pieces of leather or skin – perhaps the remains of a bag in which some carbonized wood and ash had been placed over the cremation. At least thirty-five individuals were buried within a cemetery adjacent to the recumbent stone circle of Loanhead of Daviot, in Aberdeenshire; marked out by two shallow ditches with causeways in the north-east and south-west, the central area contained burials in inverted cinerary urns and in grave-pits.

Cairns and standing stones

48 The round cairns and the standing stones of the Bronze Age play an important part in the Scottish landscape; cairns may on excavation have a complex structural history comparable to many chambered tombs, or they may be comparatively simple mounds covering only a single burial.

One group of cairns which rarely contain pottery has recently been identified, and because of their well-preserved kerb-stones have been termed kerb-cairns. Such cairns vary in size from about 3m to 5m and

47 Cairn and standing stone, Strontoiller, Lorn, Argyll (scale in 50 cm divisions)

they are of low drumlike appearance rather than being bowl-shaped mounds. Excavations in Argyll, at Strontoiller and Claggan for example, have shown that the choice of their kerb-stones is very largely determined by local geology; from Claggan there are radiocarbon dates of 1058 bc±50 and 975 bc±50 (SRR-285 and 284) from central cremation deposits. Such cairns may well be more common in highland areas of Scotland than was once expected, and comparable examples have been found at Logie Newton, in Aberdeenshire, and Monzie in Perthshire.

Several cairns appear to be associated with impressive standing stones. Very few excavations have been conducted round single stones and we are left with the same suggestions for their function as those put forward by antiquaries of a century ago: route- or territorial-markers, calendrical- or astronomical-gnomons, or memorial stones. Pairs of standing stones occur particularly in Perthshire and neighbouring counties, and some of these at least are memorial- or gravestones; a pair of stones at Orwell in Kinross-shire was clearly associated with a number of cremation-burials, and a two-storeyed stone setting within the stone socket of one of the uprights contained a

48 Cairn, Kilpatrick, Arran

double cremation deposit. Linear settings of stones are also known either as isolated alignments of spaced stones as at Dervaig, on Mull, or almost parallel alignments as at Ballymeanoch, in Mid Argyll. The series of monuments at Ballymeanoch is one of the most interesting in this key area of Argyll, comprising a small Class II henge, an internal mound with two cists (one containing a beaker burial), alignments of
49 impressive standing stones, some decorated with cup-marks, and a small kerb-cairn. An impression of the importance of this area may be gauged by the remarkable series of cairns and standing stones near Kilmartin village; the chambered cairn of *Clyde* type at Nether Largie South acted as the focus for a linear cemetery of Bronze Age cairns, a clear indication of continuity of tradition. The standing stones near Temple Wood have an unusual arrangement, two pairs and a single one in a line from north-east to south-west; the central stone has spectacular cup-and-ring and cup-mark decoration. Recent excavations at the nearby cairn or stone circle of Temple Wood are revealing a complex burial and ritual monument incorporating stone settings akin to kerb-cairns. On one of the upright stones there is a carefully pecked double spiral ornament.

Decorated stones

The translation of decorative motifs from pottery, woodwork or textiles on to stone may be seen in a small number of chambered cairns particularly in Orkney; at Holm of Papa Westray for example a series of eyebrow motifs, zigzag lines, conjoined ovals and concentric circles have been pecked on to the surface of the stones. This is a rare occurrence and we lack in Scotland the richness of passage-grave art in Ireland. The decorated stones incorporated in the settlement at Skara Brae show that such art, or at least artistic doodles, were an important cultural aspect of grooved ware traditions – lozenges, chevrons and triangles were incised or pecked in a number of combinations. Decoration by pecking out hollow depressions or cup-marks on to the surface of boulders has an early origin, for there is a slab with eight cup-marks on the floor of the mortuary structure in the long barrow of Dalladies, in Kincardineshire. Cup-marks, cup-and-ring markings and other forms of rock art are found on some of the standing stones and cist-slabs including the monoliths of Ballymeanoch and Temple Wood. Rock surfaces decorated with extensive areas of cup-and-ring marks are among the most enigmatic aspects of Bronze Age religion, be it sun worship or indeed associated with other forms of astronomical observation. Among the most impressive
50–1 examples are those from Achnabreck, in Mid Argyll, Greenland, in Dunbartonshire, or Drumtroddan, in Wigtownshire.

Some of the most interesting decoration occurs on stones that have been used as slabs or cover-stones for cists. The side-slab of a cist from
52 Badden, in Mid Argyll, is decorated with pecked multiple lozenges; this slab is also an example of the translation of the carpentry techniques to stone building, for two grooves at the ends of the stone have been pecked out to allow the end-slabs to be slotted into position. It has been convincingly suggested that the decoration may, by analogy

49 Standing stone decorated with cupmarks and cup and ring marks, Ballymeanoch, Mid Argyll

with tombs in the Salle valley in Germany, reflect textile wall-hangings of contemporary houses.

Stones decorated with naturalistic motifs include a small group in the Kilmartin cemetery, in Mid Argyll, with carvings of flat axes at the cairns of Nether Largie North and Ri Cruin.

50–1 Cup and ring-marked rocks, Greenland, Dunbartonshire (scales in feet)

52 Decorated slab, Badden, Mid Argyll

Bronze and gold objects

A knowledge of metalworking was introduced into Scotland before 2000 BC in the wake of the movements of makers of beaker pottery; but metallurgy is not wholly to be associated with this phenomenon for, although a few beaker graves contain metal objects, the vast majority do not. Ireland played an important role in the dissemination of the knowledge of the techniques of metalworking, not least because supplies of raw material are plentiful, and there is clear evidence there of an early tradition of metalworking.

The earliest flat axes are made of copper and have broad butts in relation to their length; later and more numerous examples in bronze have in general rather narrower butts. Metalwork studies are built up to a large extent by typology (or developmental sequences) and we must envisage considerable overlap as fashions or techniques of manufacture changed. Scottish flat axes and halberds (prestige weapons, hafted at right angles to a shaft) are part of wider traditions of metalworking and exchange. Axes with a variety of hammered decoration show close affinities to Irish examples. Although several hoards contain metalwork of Early Bronze Age date, there are few that are helpful in showing a range of contemporary objects deposited at one time; some hoards contain only axes (e.g. Ladyhill, Ross and Cromarty; Colleonard, Banffshire, where six axes, found in 1857, were deposited in a pottery vessel in a rough protective setting of stones) or only halberds (New Park, New Machar, Aberdeenshire; Auchingoul, Banffshire; Kingarth, Bute). A number of stone moulds for casting flat axes have been found in north-east Scotland, including two from Culbin Sands, Morayshire.

One hoard, however, which illustrates the range of early bronze-working in Scotland, is that from Migdale, in Sutherland, which also shows some central European influence; it comprises six bronze armlets with D-shaped or oval section, two moulded armlets, a flat axe, an ear-ring, tubular beads with a wooden core and a thin sheet-bronze covering, conical bronze objects (perhaps button covers) and six V-bored jet buttons. One D-sectioned armlet was found with a burial associated with a food vessel at Ratho, Midlothian, and two armlets were found with a similar vessel in a grave at Kineff, Kincardineshire. The range of date quoted already for the use of this class of vessel indicates the horizon of this phase of bronze-working. The conical button covers have clear parallels in central European bronze-working traditions.

It is an interesting reflection of the deliberate choice that is involved in the preparation of grave-goods that flat axes are almost unknown from burials, but that daggers and armlets were thought to be suitable gifts for the dead. Flat axes on the other hand are represented on decorated slabs such as those from Ri Cruin and Nether Largie North cairns, in Mid Argyll, but no dagger carving has so far been found in Scotland. One of the best-preserved daggers is that from Ashgrove, Fife, with a hilt made of plates of wood and horn tipped by an ivory

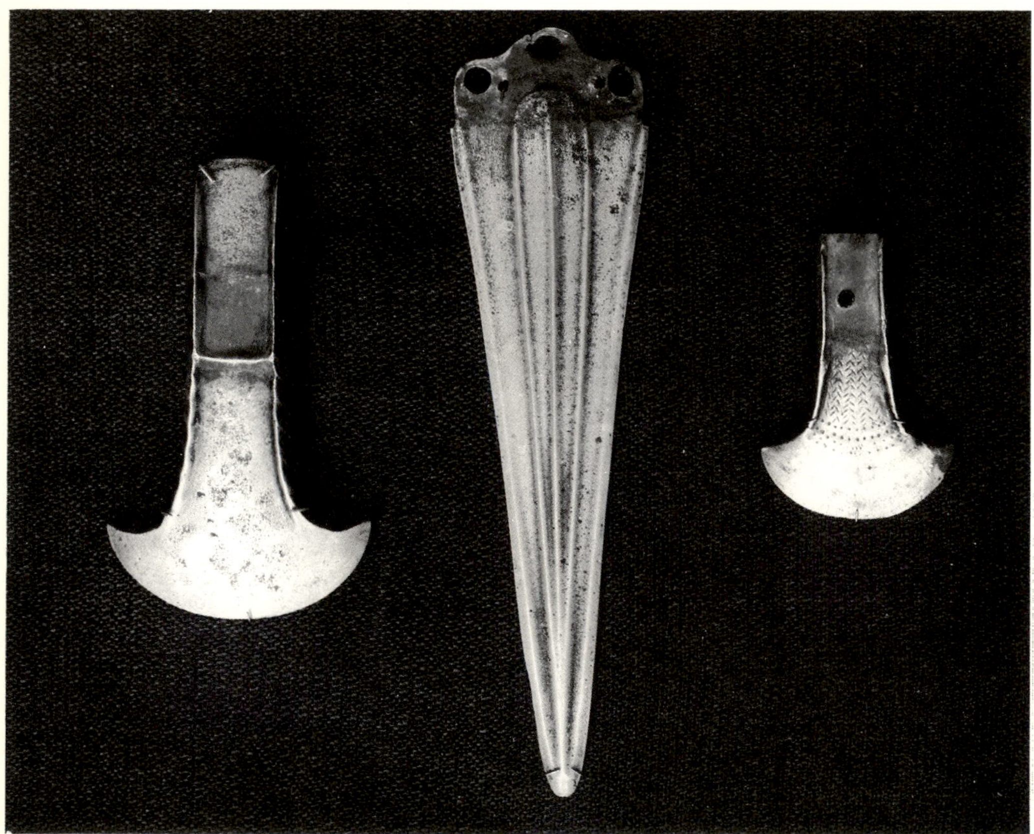

53 Bronze hoard, Gavel Moss, Renfrewshire

pommel. Parts of the hide sheath also survived. The beaker bore scored decoration; analysis of vegetable matter on the chest of the skeleton provided an unusually late radiocarbon date of 1000 bc±150 (Q-764). A small number of bronze daggers had gold hilt pommels, for example, Skateraw, East Lothian and Blackwaterfoot, Arran, both of which were associated with cist-burials under cairns. A ribbed dagger from Gavel Moss, Renfrewshire, similar to that from Blackwaterfoot, 53
was found along with two flanged axes, one of which is decorated with stacked chevron motifs; this hoard probably dates to about 1500–1600 BC. Two armlets of beaten bronze from a cist at Melfort, in the Lorn area of Argyll, were associated with a necklace of jet beads comprising fusiform (cigar-shaped) beads and spacer beads, which allowed the complex stringing to spread out. Two cist-burials from Fife illustrate the range of associations of such early metalwork; from Kirkcaldy, Gordon Childe recovered a tanged blade, an awl, a beaker, twelve V-bored buttons and a single bead of jet. From Masterton, Audrey Henshall excavated a burial associated with a dagger, two bronze armlets, like those from Melfort, and a jet necklace.

Splendid necklaces of jet beads are a feature of the Early Bronze Age in Scotland and have been found not only in cists at Campbeltown, Kintyre, Argyll, and Pitkennedy, Angus, but also with a food vessel in

54 Jet necklace, Pitkennedy, Aberlemno, Angus

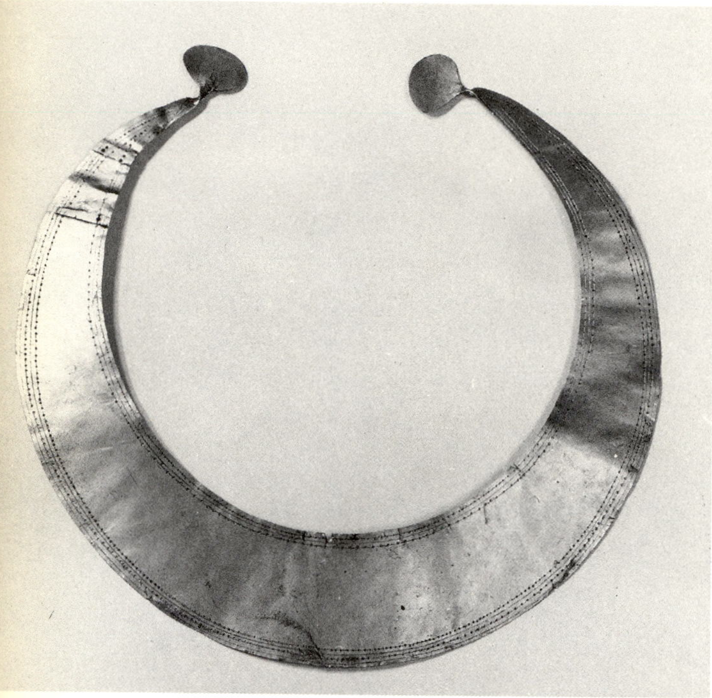

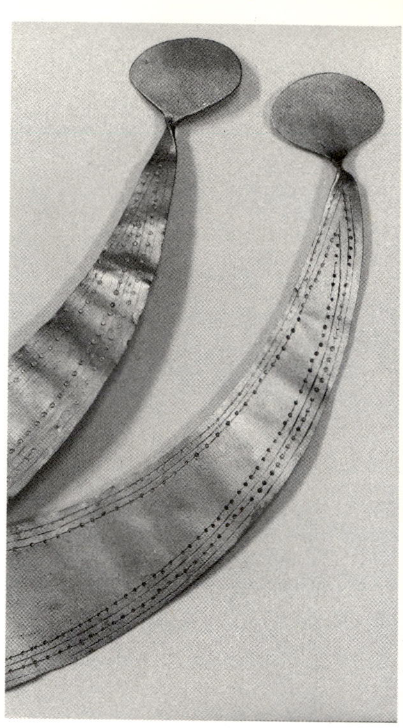

55–6 Gold lunulae, Southside, Peeblesshire; one of the pair and details of the terminal decoration of both lunulae

a secondary interment in a chambered tomb at Brackley, Kintyre, Argyll. Several beakers were associated with necklaces or beads of jet discs including late examples from Balbirnie, Fife (1330 bc±90; GaK-3425), and Stoneykirk, Wigtownshire. The intricate boring with a bow-drill through the thin spacer plates of necklaces like Pitkennedy
54 is a reminder of the skills of the Bronze Age craftsmen in materials that have not survived – particularly wood. The decoration on the spacer-plates contains motifs that may be found on comb-ornamented beaker ware.

Gold was also used to make jewellery, both in the form of crescent
55–6 shaped collars (lunulae), ear-rings and gold discs. Lunulae such as the pair from Southside, Peeblesshire, are among the most impressive achievements of ancient craftsmen in beaten gold and some almost certainly come from Irish workshops. They are often decorated with hammered ornament, particularly near the horns, using motifs from the beaker repertoire; the problem of the relationship of lunulae, jet spacer-plate necklaces and the amber spacer-plate necklaces of Wessex is not as yet clearly resolved, but current opinion suggests that lunulae are the earliest type. Gold discs, including those from Barnhill, Angus, and from one of the Knowes of Trotty, Orkney, also have similarities to examples from Wessex, and it is interesting that the Orcadian examples were found with amber beads including spacer-plate fragments. The only gold ear-rings from Scotland are the beautiful pair from a cist at Orbliston, Morayshire, although just one now survives.

57 Bronze axe, near Peebles, Peeblesshire

58 Steatite mould for a socketed axe, Sittenham, Rosskeen, Ross and Cromarty

The metalwork described above belongs to the period between
about 2000 BC and 1400 BC; objects of Middle Bronze Age date, from 57
1400 BC to about 900 BC, are marked by increasing sophistication of
both design and metalworking techniques. Closed moulds of two or 58
more pieces allowed socketed implements to be cast for the first time. Flanged axes were developed further to improve the stability of the hafting. Palstaves were produced; these are axes with side-flanges and a cross-bridge to receive a wooden haft. This cross-ridge or 'stop' was intended to prevent the butt from splitting the haft and its binding when the axe was used. In some cases the haft was additionally attached by tying the binding thong through a small bronze loop on the side of the blade.

Spearheads were also provided with loops, though some earlier examples are known, and dirks and rapiers appear for the first time. The rapier was the most important side-arm of the period and a range of types was produced. A hoard of a dozen rapiers found at Drumcoltran, Kirkcudbrightshire, in 1837, contained blades of three different sections, including one measuring over 0.6m in length. We have more information at this period about the tools of the bronze-smiths; chisels, punches, hammer-heads and anvils have all been discovered. At this time too there is evidence for shaving with the introduction of small bronze razors: Class I razors have a leaf-shaped blade and a tang, Class II have two 'wings' with a mid-rib and tang. Razors have often been found associated with burials and, as two were found with the Glentrool hoard, Kirkcudbrightshire, they form a useful link between bronze types and funerary pottery. A razor of Class I was found with a cremation in a cordoned urn in a cemetery at Magdalen Bridge, Edinburgh; another was discovered in a cinerary urn at Sandmill Farm, near Stranraer, Wigtownshire, along with a fine battle-axe and a fragment of a bone pin. Class II razors have been found with hoards of bronzes, as at Glentrool, in Kirkcudbright, and with a cremation burial at Embo, in Sutherland; this was a secondary deposit at the edge of the chambered cairn already mentioned.

Gold armlets and rings were also produced; a hoard of such pieces from Duff House, in Banff, had been deposited in an inverted cinerary urn with a cremation burial. One of the largest hoards of gold ornaments is that found in 1857 at Law Farm, Morayshire, where about thirty-six twisted ribbon armlets, all except one of gold, were discovered in the course of ploughing.

Two other hoards illustrate the range of Middle to Late Bronze Age material. From Glentrool, in Kirkcudbright, objects dating from about 1100 BC were discovered beneath a large rock; they include a rapier, an axe, razors, chisels and punches, a pin, glass and amber beads. The pin, which has a flat nail-like head and a loop on one side of the shank, is of north German type and, like two examples in Ireland, it indicates trade connections, perhaps with the Elbe valley. At Pyotdykes, Angus, two swords (one of which had a wood and leather scabbard) and a spearhead were found during ploughing; the spearhead is decorated with a gold band round its base. This hoard dates to about 750 BC.

In the Late Bronze Age, between about 900 BC and the middle of the first millennium BC, a series of fine weapons show the practical and prestige aspects of combat. It is likely that the shields of beaten bronze
59 like that from Auchmaleddie, Aberdeenshire, were made primarily for ceremonial occasions rather than the battlefield; it has been proved by

59 Bronze shield, Auchmaleddie, Aberdeenshire

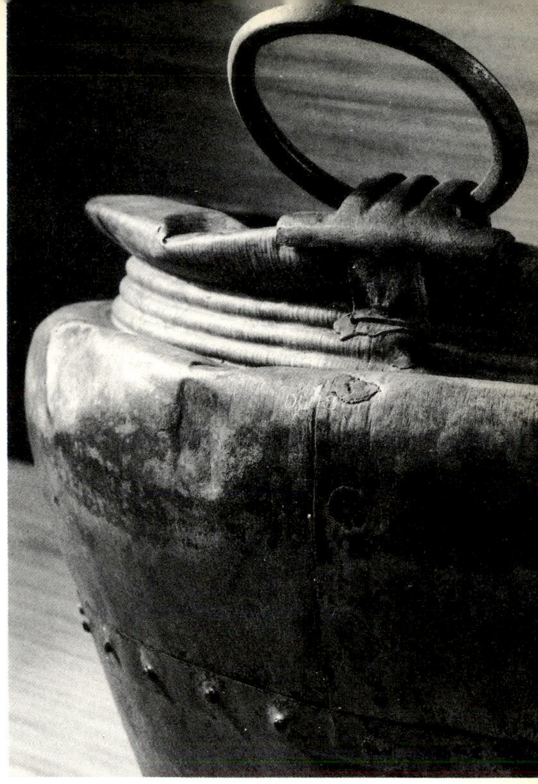

60–1 · Bronze cauldron, Hatton Knowe, Peeblesshire

practical experiment that leather shields are more effective than bronze shields in withstanding blows from a bronze sword. Sheet bronze cauldrons like that from Hatton Knowe, Peeblesshire, are also of eighth-century date, and when coupled with the contemporary flesh-fork from the collection of bronzes from Killeonan, in Argyll, suggest feasting in a Celtic tradition with the forking out of the champion's portion.

The techniques involved in the casting of bronzes changed at this time, and lead was added in varying amounts to the mixture of copper and tin to make a bronze that flowed more freely during the casting process. Hoards illustrating the range of such Bronze Age metalwork have been divided into several broad groups, though not all finds fit neatly into only one category: ritual, merchant's and founder's hoards. A very few deposits appear to be of a ritual or votive nature. About 1780 five or six bronze shields were found in the course of peat-cutting at Luggtonridge, in Ayrshire; they seem to have been set out in a ring, though the original account does not make it clear whether they were upright or flat, and they appear to have been votive in character. Hoards which appear to be the stock in trade of a merchant dealing with a few 'sales lines' can also be identified, as for example, at Kalemouth, Roxburgh, where fourteen axes were found in a cache in the river bank, or the dozen or so rapiers found at Drumcoltran, Kirkcudbright. The objects in such deposits are for the most part complete; the raw materials of a smith, on the other hand, might contain imperfect or damaged pieces that could be melted down for use on a subsequent occasion. The role of the 'itinerant smith' should not be overstressed, as ethnographic parallels taken from recent primitive society show the smith to be based more or less permanently in a village or tribe. Perhaps such caches of metalwork represent local collections ready to be transported at a later stage to the central bronze-smith. The hoard from Peelhill, Lanarkshire, for example contained twenty-eight spearheads, a sword, a socketed axe and a ferrule; many of the spearheads were fragmentary or damaged and the sword had been deliberately broken into three pieces.

62 Bronze sword, Cowgill, Lanarkshire

An important hoard was discovered in Duddingston Loch, in Edinburgh, during dredging for marl in 1778; the objects included swords, spearheads and a fragment of a bucket. The better preserved were presented to King George III and were subsequently lost. The surviving pieces were all bent or broken in antiquity and many appear to have been subjected to heat. Several objects or hoards of later eighth- to seventh-century BC date have been found on Arthur's Seat, above Duddingston Loch, and it is likely that there was a settlement with a bronze-smith on the slopes of the hill at about this time.

62 Swords such as those from the Duddingston Loch hoard, which belong to a type known as Ewart Park, after an example from Northumberland, are widespread throughout eastern Scotland and are also well represented in hoards from the west coast and Western Isles. Clay moulds for the manufacture of Ewart Park swords have been found on Traprain Law, East Lothian, and at Jarlshof, in Shetland. The use of this class of sword continued until about 600 BC as hoards from Tarves, Aberdeenshire, and Grosvenor Crescent, Edinburgh, contain pins of the distinctive 'swan's-neck sunflower' class, which are related to examples from north Germany. Exotic gold-work, on the other hand, shows contact with Irish raw materials and design. A cup-
63 ended ornament and lock-ring found at Whitefarland on Arran are objects for personal adornment, the latter perhaps a hair decoration. One of the most spectacular hoards of gold was made on the farm of Coul, on Islay, in 1780 when thirty-six gold armlets were ploughed up, 'all looped on to one – in a bunch', but all, except perhaps one, are now lost.

In the north-east of Scotland, along the southern shores of the Moray Firth and into Aberdeenshire, there is a series of distinctive bronzes that indicates either close trading contacts or indeed settlement from north-west Germany around 700 BC. They include penannular bracelets with out-turned terminals such as those from the Sculptor's Cave, Covesea, Morayshire, and Balmashanner in Angus.
64 Similar bracelets occur in the hoard from the Braes of Gight, Aberdeenshire, associated with a Class II razor and with an elaborate necklet with eighteen pendant rings – a type with convincing continental parallels. It seems unlikely that settlement by a new element of the population would be indicated mainly by decorative bronzes, and it is more probable that these objects indicate trade contacts with North Germany and Scandinavia.

Rather later contacts with continental markets are indicated by a small number of bronzes of broadly seventh-century BC date; these include the swan's-neck sunflower pins already mentioned and distinctive types of swords and razors, with an example of the latter from Traprain Law. The Adabrock hoard on Lewis includes several examples of such exotic material as well as objects of normal Late

Bronze Age types – socketed axes, a tanged chisel, razors and fragments of a beaten bronze vessel with cross-shaped handle attachments. A hoard from Horsehope, Peeblesshire, has several objects that are parts of cart-furniture or harness-fittings; the pieces do not appear to be full-size, however, and it is possible that they are from a model 'cult-waggon'. Two socketed axes found with the other bronzes may be compared to examples from the merchant's hoard from Kalemouth, Roxburgh, dating to about the late eighth century BC. About the middle of the first millennium BC iron-working was introduced, but, because of the poor survival qualities of the new metal, our knowledge of the types is very slight; there is an iron ring for example with the hoard of bronzes from Balmashanner, in Angus, but as the objects were found during ploughing its context is not perhaps ideal. Adoption of the new technology is likely to have been gradual; from Traprain Law, for example, there is an iron copy of a looped and socketed axe of bronze style, 'a laborious effort to translate a type appropriate to bronze into a foreign and unsuitable material'.

63 Gold hoard, Whitefarland, Arran

Settlements and agriculture

The various styles of pottery and metalwork described along with radiocarbon determinations provide much of the chronological framework for the Bronze Age, but, although burials and cairns doubtless indicate the vicinity of settlements, very few houses or field-systems dating to the second millennium BC have so far been discovered. At

64 Bronze hoard, Braes of Gight, Aberdeenshire

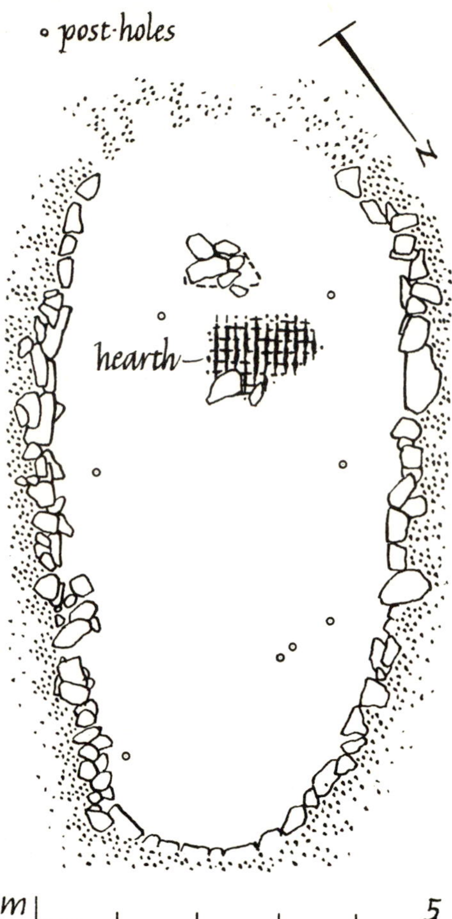

65 House, Northton, Harris

65 Northton, on Harris, there was a stratified sequence of occupation from the Neolithic to comparatively recent times. The earlier levels, which contained Hebridean and Unstan wares as well as bone tools, have a radiocarbon date of 2461 bc±79 (BM-705), but there were no remains of houses. A settlement of the beaker period overlies these levels; set into the blown sand, the most complete structure was oval on plan measuring 5.5m by 4.3m, and consisted of a well-built revetment of water-worn boulders standing to a height of about a metre. In the interior there was a central hearth and a series of stake-holes that the excavator interpreted as the remains of a light hut or tent, for which the stone-work provided some additional protection from the elements. Radiocarbon determinations for the two levels of beaker activity on the site are 1654 bc±70 (BM-706) and 1531 bc±54 (BM-707). Domestic tools included bone points, smoothed bone implements, as well as objects of flint and stone. Four small bone combs were probably used for decorating beaker ware and provide one of the surest indications of the local manufacture of such pottery.

Because of the height of the surrounding sand-dunes at Northton there was no opportunity to examine the adjacent land-surfaces for traces of agriculture; at Rosinish, on Benbecula, on the other hand, the dunes have been eroded by wind, and areas of the ground surface showing traces of plough cultivation have been laid bare. The plough marks were visible as dark lines of humic material standing out from the lighter sand, which the bottom of the ploughshare had scarred. A shallow ditch divided two areas of ploughing and it may be interpreted as a field-boundary. The plough used would have been an ard, a simple type of wooden plough that was probably drawn by a pair of yoked oxen; the stone bar-shares found in contemporary contexts in Shetland and Orkney belonged to such ploughs. Parts of wooden ards survive from Milton Loch, in Kirkcudbrightshire, and Lochmaben, in Dumfriesshire, both with radiocarbon dates within the later first millennium BC. The crops grown at Rosinish were barley and wheat, though the former was clearly predominant.

The fragmentary remains of a structure similar to that found at Northton have recently been excavated at Sorisdale, on Coll, and a link with both Rosinish and Kilellan, on Islay, is the presence here of large shouldered storage jars. At Kilellan and Ardnave, both on Islay, extensive middens with decorated pottery of second millennium BC date as well as animal bones underline the importance of sites on the *machair* (a fixed dune pasture over a calcareous rich shell-sand). Such fertile soils clearly attracted early settlement, but there was an obvious risk of being engulfed in a subsequent sand-blow. This process can provide a detailed sequence of archaeological events and one of the most important of such sites is that currently being excavated at the Udal on North Uist. The small house at Ardnave measures 4m by 3m and, like the Northton example, is oval on plan. The walls have, however, been upstanding, not merely set into the sand. The house was entered between two large upstanding slabs, and there is a short baffle-wall outside the doorway to afford some protection from the wind.

Circular house-plans have also been discovered including those at Kilpatrick and Tormore, on Arran, Cul a'Bhaile, on Jura, and at Muirkirk, in Ayrshire. Circular houses were constructed with large upright timbers forming an inner circle with the roof resting on the uprights and sloping down to the outer stone wall; they were thus much more substantial structures than the impermanent huts or tents envisaged for Northton and Sorisdale.

The stone and timber house at Cul a'Bhaile, on Jura, measures about 7m in diameter and is set within a boulder-built enclosure-wall surrounding an area of about 77m by 64m. This exciting excavation shows that even the outer house wall may have been reconstructed on several occasions and that the internal post arrangement may have been altered and renewed in the course of occupation. At Tormore and Kilpatrick, extensive areas of field banks and clearance cairns were associated with circular houses that were in some cases rebuilt on a number of occasions within the second millennium. An extensive system of plot boundaries has been discovered on the Moss of Achnacree in Argyll; three banks protruding from beneath blanket peat have

been examined by excavation and their extent below the peat has been identified by probing. Smallscale excavation of bank B showed that it was made up of boulders forming the outer faces of a wall some 1.5m wide with an inner core of earth, gravel and smaller stones thrown up from flanking quarry-ditches. The banks indicate fields some 200m
66–7 square in extent. They belong to about 1359 bc±50 (SRR-219), if a single analysis from the old land surface beneath bank B can be taken to provide a general indication of date; the peat had started to build up about 980 bc±80 (N-1468). The formation of an iron pan probably made drainage difficult and the resultant waterlogging hastened the growth of the blanket bog. Pollen analysis has shown that the banks were built on heathland and it is not at all clear whether they represent the boundaries of pastoral enclosures or of tilled fields.

Fieldwork in Perthshire has shown the presence of many hut-circles associated with field-systems and small cairns that are probably of second millennium BC date, but only a programme of excavation coupled with pollen analysis is likely to advance this problem. The homesteads and settlements of Arran and Perthshire were not enclosed by any surrounding defensive wall or stockade but were, like the individual farmsteads of Shetland, at the centre of groups of fields and grazings. Lowland farms are likely to have been on the same sites as more recent buildings, and we are unlikely to find archaeological traces of them except as crop-marks on aerial photographs; it is again to more upland locations that we must look for evidence of settlement. In the course of fieldwork in Peeblesshire, officers of the Royal Commission on the Ancient and Historical Monuments of Scotland realized that groups of circular or oval platforms, measuring between 10m and 20m in diameter situated along the slopes of the upper valley of the River Tweed, were in fact the sites of timber houses, and more recently over twenty similar settlements have been found in the upper Clyde valley. Such 'unenclosed platform settlements' are often grouped in two or three rows on the hillside or strung out along the contour and are most frequently found on south-facing slopes at about 300m OD. The platforms were constructed by excavating a semicircular quarry-scoop into the hillside and piling up the material on the downhill side with careful revetment to make a circular foundation. Excavations at Green Knowe, Peeblesshire, have shown the presence of timber houses, which were in some cases reconstructed on several occasions. Finds recovered included vessels akin to 'flat-rimmed ware', stone rubbers and saddle querns, none of which can provide useful dating evidence. Radiocarbon dates, however, show that the occupation of platform settlements was under way by the last quarter of the second millennium BC. Groups of small cairns at such sites as Green Knowe, Peeblesshire, and Normangill Rig, Lanarkshire, indicate smallscale plot cultivation nearby, but considering their general situation, it is more likely that the economy of such settlements was to a large degree pastoral.

One of the most important contributions that carbon-14 has made to Scottish archaeology has been the provision of a number of chronological pointers to the extensive settlement remains in Shetland, Orkney and the northernmost counties of Scotland. The large building

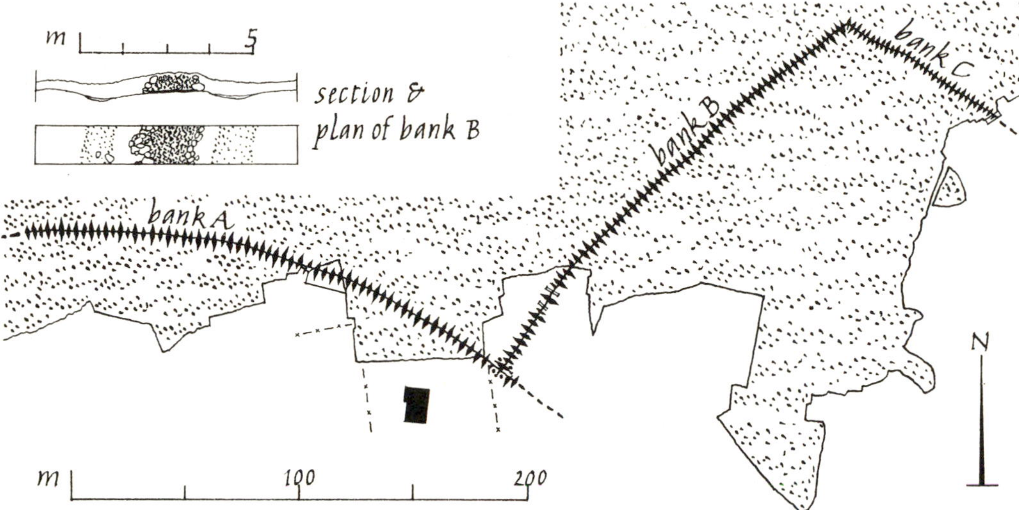

66 Field banks, Moss of Achnacree, Argyll

67 Field bank, Moss of Achnacree, Argyll; cutting through bank B (scale in 50 cm divisions)

at Stanydale, which had a series of central posts as additional roof support, may have been a public meeting place rather than a house. At Ness of Gruting, Charles Calder excavated a stone-based house which seems to have been reconstructed on a number of occasions. Between the house and Seli Voe there is evidence of small agricultural plots in the form of cairns and banks of gathered stones. A deposit of grain under the wall was contemporary with the building of the house; comprising both naked and hulled barley it yielded a radiocarbon date of 1564 bc$\pm$120 (BM-441). The use of upright stones or piers of masonry rather than timber posts is an important structural feature of a number of houses, suggesting perhaps that the small amount of available timber was reserved for roof support.

Excavations by John Hedges on two burnt mounds in Orkney, Liddle and Beaquoy, have shown that these enigmatic piles of fire-shattered stones are the result of a particular cooking technique and that they are associated with houses dating to the later second millennium BC. The cooking method involved the boiling of meat in a stone-lined trough of water by placing heated stones into the trough along with the water. The water could be kept on the boil by adding more stones, and the stones if they shattered would be thrown out on to the ever-increasing mound of fire-reddened debris. Baking and steaming of food could also be achieved with heated stones. Such cooking places were frequently sited near a stream and they may to this day be detected in the north as crescentic mounds of stone, sometimes with the remains of a trough still visible. Excavations at Liddle showed the trough to be at the centre of a building, with a series of compartments radiating from the walls and divided from one another by well-set upright slabs. The finds included ard-shares, hammer-stones and fragments of bucket-shaped vessels with flat rims. Over four hundred burnt mounds are known from the Northern Isles, but it is only in recent years that their purpose and date have become clear.

At Jarlshof, on the southern tip of mainland Shetland, there is evidence of bronze-working within the framework of a settlement. The earliest periods are represented by undefended settlements; the better preserved houses of the first period (houses II and III) have thick stone walls with projecting piers of stone helping to subdivide the internal area. House II was also partly used as a byre for there was a tethering ring made from the vertebra of a whale partly built into the wall and a dished floor allowing liquid manure to be collected in a central sump. House III has a central paved area with recesses on either side and a further chamber at the end. This house was used, some time after its initial construction, by a smith for over two hundred pieces of clay moulds were discovered including matrices for at least eight socketed axes, seven swords, a sunflower pin, and a gouge. This activity is of eighth- to seventh-century BC date. The stone implements from this period include slate 'axes' and 'choppers' as well as small sub-rectangular vessels of steatite (soapstone). The pottery is of hard-fired wares with a variety of rim forms. At one time thought to have affinities with wares in the north-east at such sites as Old Keig, Loanhead of Daviot and Covesea, it can now be seen that such a simple ceramic tradition is of long duration and of little help as a chronological indicator.

A rather smaller cellular settlement, forming the first period of occupation at Clickhimin, near Lerwick, was associated with similar pottery and with fragments of 'Shetland knives'. These are tools for skinning, split flakes of porphyry for example, which have been found in such earlier contexts as Ness of Gruting and Stanydale. Jarlshof, however, provides an unusually rounded picture of the economy of the Late Bronze Age, with the presence of sheep of Soay type and cattle; barley was ground in trough querns. Fishing also played a part with the discovery of cod and ling bones; seal hunting was undertaken and there are a few bones of walrus and whale.

5

Warrior Celts

The centuries between about 900 BC and 500 BC saw novel and far-reaching changes in the prehistoric lifestyle of Scotland, as elsewhere in the British Isles. The Scottish bronze industry expanded, adopting new techniques and producing new types of weapon and tool, and the appearance of exotic imports such as beaten bronze vessels from continental Europe implies the existence of a wealthy and extrovert home market. The fact that so much bronze-work was deliberately buried and not recovered indicates considerable social unrest, and it is against this background that the first defensive forts appear in the sixth or seventh centuries BC. The distribution of locally manufactured bronze swords and spearheads coincides with that of the early forts with which they were contemporary. Settlements and homesteads enclosed by timber palisades also appear at this time. Towards 500 BC, the establishment of an iron industry was under way, and the acceptance of iron as a proper material for tools and weapons must gradually have made an enormous impact upon everyday domestic life. We have to assume that a new language, the P-Celtic Gallo-Brittonic language, was introduced into Scotland around the middle of the first millennium BC, but there is no direct evidence as to how or exactly when this happened: it was certainly well established before the advent of the Romans. The introduction of a new language ought to involve physical immigration of new settlers, in this case Celts, but their number need not be large.

Forts

Apart from the Late Neolithic defensive enclosure at Meldon Bridge, the earliest fortifications in Scotland appeared in the mid-first millennium BC, perhaps even before 600 BC, in the shape of timber-laced forts. In some cases the ramparts were damaged by fire in antiquity, thus providing charcoal for radiocarbon dating, and samples from five forts range from 1186 bc±60 (BM-444) at Cullykhan, Banffshire, to 35 bc±40 (GaK-996) at Craigmarloch Wood in Renfrewshire. The date of 590 bc±70 (GaK-1224) from Finavon, Angus, may, however, be a more reliable indication of the beginnings of timber-lacing in Scotland, a tradition that seems to have continued throughout the first millennium BC. Occupation in the last few centuries BC is indicated at Abernethy by the presence of a bronze La Tène Ic fibula, an iron ring-headed pin and a bronze spiral finger-ring. Timber-lacing was used as a means of stabilizing both stone walls and

68 Fort, Abernethy, Perthshire, showing beam-slots on the outer face of the inner wall

earthen ramparts, and in either case it consisted of horizontal wooden beams laid at intervals within the core material. Traces of timber-lacing survive in several forms: sometimes, most notably at Abernethy in Perthshire, the rotted timbers left empty beam-slots visible in the stone face of the fort wall. In those cases where the fort suffered deliberate or accidental destruction by fire, the former presence of timber-work is often evident even without excavation, because the extreme temperatures that were attained within the wall as the timber burned caused the stone-work to fuse into distorted masses. Occasionally, the remains of burnt timbers survive in earthen ramparts, as at Kaimes Hill in Midlothian, where a stone-faced rampart contained the carbonized remains of beams as well as a small amount of vitrified rubble. There were traces at Finavon of timber buildings ranged against the inner face of the wall, a practice that would add to the fire-risk involved in timber-laced walls.

The technique of timber-lacing may have been far more common than the known evidence suggests, not only because it is difficult to identify in an unburnt state without excavation, but also because there is reason to believe that it was sometimes employed only in the upper part of the fort wall, the part most likely to have collapsed. Timber-laced forts have a wide distribution on mainland Scotland, but they occur most frequently in central and eastern Scotland and in the Moray Firth area. Their overall distribution correlates well with that of socketed bronze axes, contemporary in the seventh century BC with the earliest timber-laced forts and a vital tool for their construction.

The timber-laced rampart at Kaimes Hill was subsequently replaced by three stone-faced ramparts; the construction of the main rampart is dated by radiocarbon analysis to 365 bc±90 (GaK-1971). In turn this fort was enlarged by building three new rubble and turf ramparts, with the additional and unusual defence of a stone *chevaux de frise* beyond the main rampart. This consisted of pointed stones set upright and close together, and it was a most effective means of hindering any attack, whether the enemy was on foot or horseback. Similar *chevaux de frise* are known in Scotland at the forts of Dreva and Cademuir Hill in Peeblesshire, and this type of outer defence is also found in Ireland, Wales, Spain and Portugal in late prehistoric contexts.

One of the disadvantages of timber-lacing was its relatively short life: once rotted or burnt, the timbers could be replaced only by dismantling the fort wall. In those cases where a structural sequence has been identified, stone-walled forts (including those in which no trace of timber-lacing has been found) were replaced by forts with multiple earth and rubble ramparts. A classic structural sequence was excavated at Hownam Rings in Roxburghshire, where a palisaded enclosure was
succeeded in turn by a stone-walled fort and a multivallate fort until 69
finally the site returned to its original non-defensive status as a settlement. Similarly at Woden Law, Roxburghshire, a stone-walled fort was later translated into a multiple work by the addition of two outer ramparts, prompted perhaps by the impending Agricolan invasion of Scotland. The long sequence at Hownam Rings must have spanned some six or seven centuries, but the material culture remained unchanged despite the structural alterations and all that they imply about social conditions. The excavator suggested that 'only the leadership changed', bringing innovations in warfare. This useful evidence would carry greater weight if the site had been extensively excavated, but the areas dug were very small and included very little of the interior.

In some forts, excavation has yielded traces of unenclosed settlement on the hill-top prior to its fortification, and it is likely that many more such settlements existed. Forts were built throughout Scotland,
including the Atlantic seaboard, but more than 90 per cent of the total 70
of some 1,500 are concentrated south of the Forth-Clyde valleys, primarily in south-east Scotland. Palisaded works are also concentrated in the latter area, though the pattern of their distribution is weighted more by the survival of surface traces, for which conditions in the Cheviot hills are ideal. In comparison with English hillforts, Scottish forts are generally small, but there are two distinctly large forts on Traprain Law and Eildon Hill North (Roxburghshire), both of which show a succession of fortifications and, at their largest extent, enclosed about sixteen hectares. Little is known about their internal arrangements, although some three hundred house-sites are visible on

Overleaf

69 Fort, Arbory Hill, Lanarkshire

70 Fort, Dun Mara, Lewis

71 Cross-ridge dyke, Woden Law, Roxburghshire (scale in feet)

the surface of Eildon Hill North, implying dense permanent occupation. The function of hillforts is still the subject of controversy, and in Scotland the problem is intensified by lack of information. There is insufficient dating evidence to allow hillforts to be related specifically to the pattern of contemporary non-defensive settlements, but it seems likely that they were themselves permanently occupied rather than used merely as places of refuge when the need arose. As elsewhere, the prime significance of hillforts lies in their social implications for the emergence of tribal territories, and perhaps for the role of pride and prestige in Celtic society.

Cross-dykes

In many cases, forts in the Cheviot hills of south-east Scotland possess additional protection in the form of outlying cross-dykes. These are short linear earthworks which span ridge-tops and promontories, thereby controlling access and movement along these essential routes. Most consist of a ditch with either a single bank or a bank on each side, and in the latter case one bank is normally larger than the other. Five cross-dykes span the neck of land between the promontory of Woden Law with its hillfort and the main ridge of Cheviot hills in Roxburghshire; this was the route later chosen by Roman engineers for Dere Street, and it was the only means of easy access to Woden Law. The
71 centre three dykes survive as slight univallate works and were perhaps built earlier than the larger flanking dykes, one bivallate and the other consisting of a bank between two ditches. Cross-dykes occur in Yorkshire, Wales and on the chalk downlands of southern England, and it is clear that the idea of such control barriers was a common response to similar geological and social conditions. Proximity to hillforts is

most frequent in southern Scotland and southern England, but the Cheviot dykes do not appear to have played the dual role of barriers and land divisions that has been identified in Wessex.

Palisaded homesteads and settlements

In the Cheviots, cross-dykes appear to be related to palisaded sites as well as to hillforts, emphasizing the early date of some of these earthworks. Although palisaded sites were occupied at broadly the same time as forts, there is evidence to show that they were often the first stage in a structural sequence that led on to forts, either stone-walled or earthen.

Palisaded sites in Scotland ought not to be divorced from those in north-east England, with which they form an homogeneous group. The site at Huckhoe in Northumberland yielded evidence that there was no great delay in time between the construction of the palisaded settlement and that of the stone-walled fort, and the radiocarbon date of 510 bc±40 (GaK-1388) for the palisade is also a useful chronological indicator for untimbered stone forts. Comparable dates have been obtained for the palisaded phases preceding forts at Burnswark, Dumfriesshire (500 bc±100, GaK-2203b) and Craigmarloch Wood, Renfrewshire (590 bc±40, GaK-995).

Palisades were used to protect both settlements and homesteads; the distinction between these two depends upon the number of houses and thereby the size of the social unit: one to three houses need represent no more than a single family living in a homestead, whereas more than three houses are likely to represent more than one family living in a communal settlement. Without excavation, it is often impossible to estimate the number of houses, and the size of the enclosure can be misleading, but in many cases traces of timber-built houses are clearly visible as grooves or rings in the turf. The enclosing palisades consist of closely spaced wooden posts set upright into narrow bedding trenches: the chocking stones that supported each post can be seen in the photograph of Hownam Rings. Most sites possess either a single 72

palisade or a double palisade with the two concentric trenches set

72 Fort, Howman Rings, Roxburgh; palisade (scale in feet)

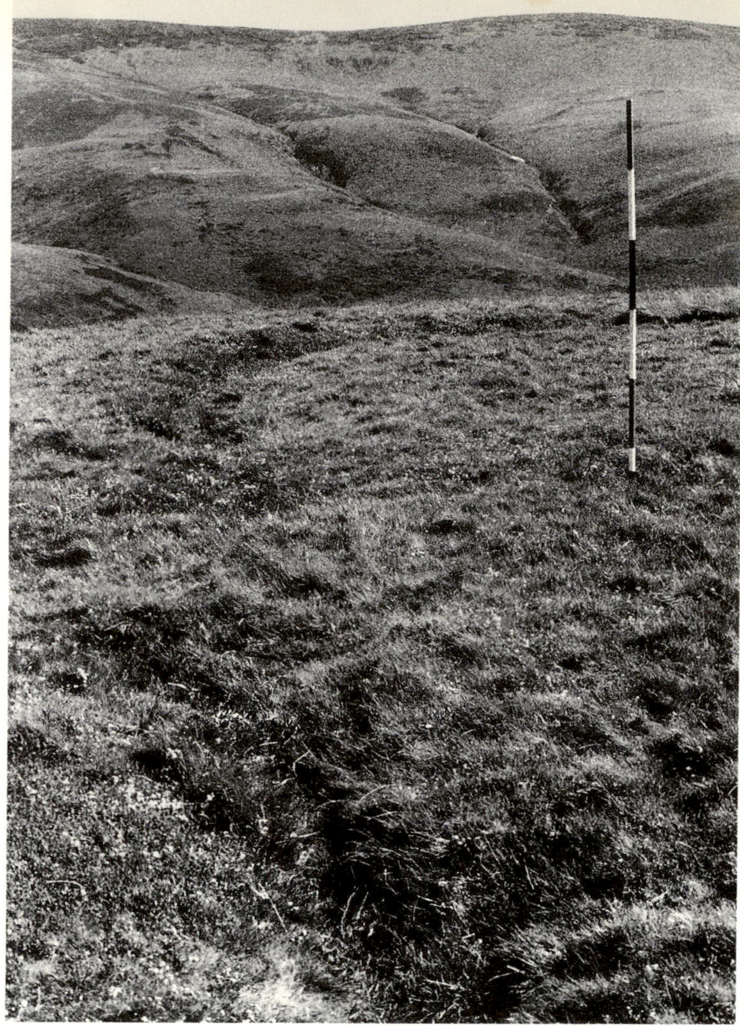

73 Palisaded homestead, Greenbrough, Roxburghshire (scale in feet)

between 1.5m and 3m apart. Occasionally there is an outer palisade perhaps providing space for penning sheep or cattle. The use of double palisades is normally confined to the larger sites. Most palisaded sites have a single entrance, either a simple gap with a large terminal post for
73 the gate on either side, as visible on the surface at Greenbrough Hill in Roxburghshire, or, in the case of some double palisades, the two trenches were linked together on either side to form a short entrance passage. Excavation of the settlement at Hayhope Knowe, Roxburghshire, revealed both types of entrance; an oval enclosure had been formed by a double palisade with an outer single palisade, and there were two opposing entrances.

Broxmouth

In 1956, aerial photography revealed a previously unknown multivallate enclosure on a low hill near Dunbar, East Lothian, and recent excavations by Peter Hill have uncovered a hillfort of considerable complexity. It was preceded by an apparently unenclosed homestead, consisting of a large circular timber house. The hillfort was originally

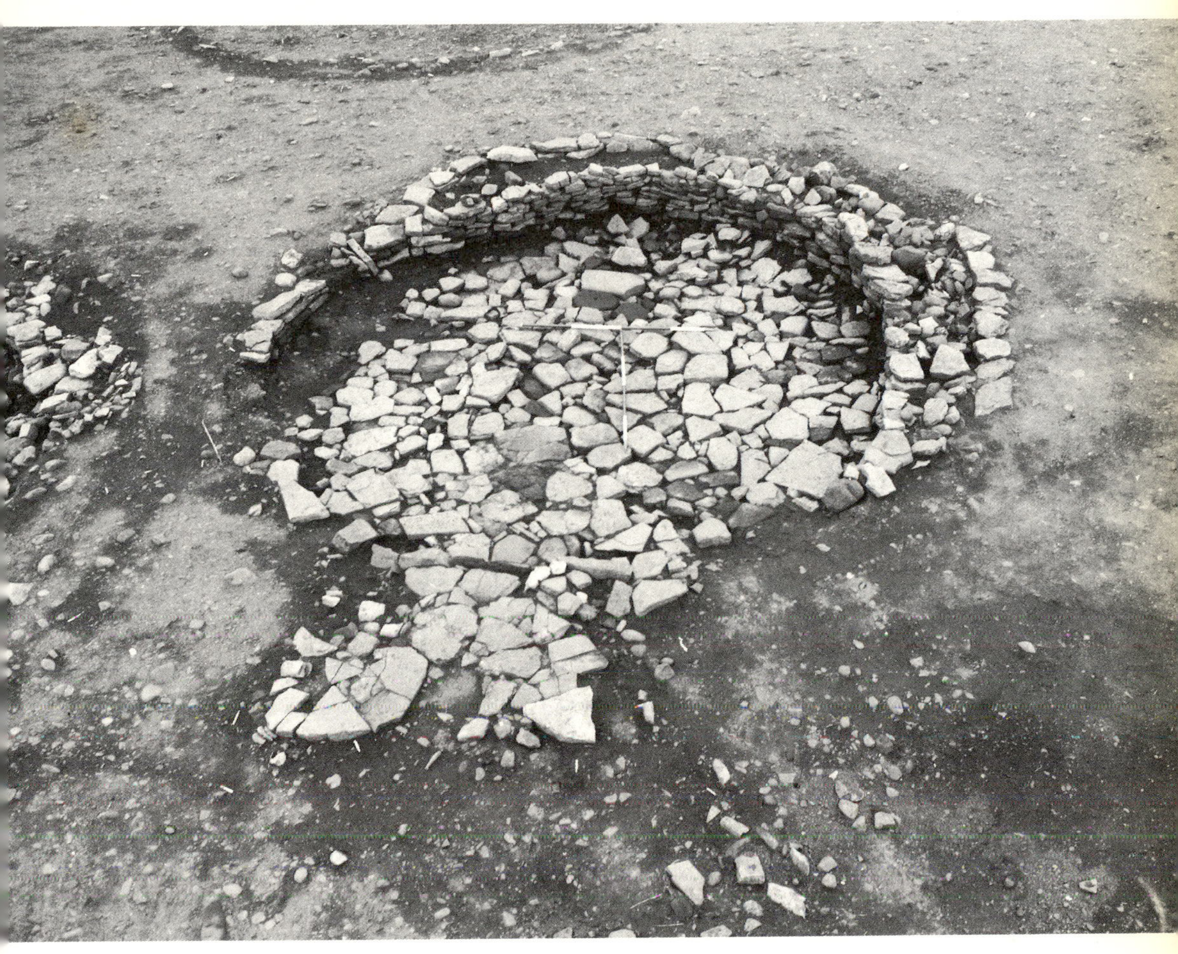

74 Fort, Broxmouth, East Lothian; house 4 in its initial form (scales in 50 cm divisions)

univallate with two opposing entrances, but subsequently its design underwent four major periods and several minor phases of modification, during which the fort became alternately bivallate and univallate and its entrances were rebuilt in different ways. Almost the entire interior of the hillfort was excavated, revealing five houses of ring-groove type up to 11m in diameter, but ploughing must have destroyed others. Three scooped stone-built houses represented post-fort occupation of the site, and it is likely that at least one of these houses was built on top of an earlier ring-groove house. The stone-built houses had clearly been occupied over a considerable period of time, and the photographs of house 4 give an impression of their structural complexity; 74–5 initially the house consisted of a stone wall, with timber posts supporting the roof, and an earthen floor, and subsequently the area of the house was reduced by refacing the wall internally, and the floor was paved. At this stage, the timber posts supporting the roof were presumably founded on pad-stones. House 4 had an external porch both before and after its floor was paved. Deposits of ox skulls at the base of the house wall may be connected with ritual dedications.

75 Fort, Broxmouth, East Lothian; house 4 in its later form

A cemetery of nine inhumation graves lay immediately beyond the outermost ditch of the fort, and another four burials were found within the fort. The form of the graves varied, but most were lined and covered with stone slabs, aligned NNE-SSW, and they contained loosely flexed burials; the majority of the skeletons represent men and women who died in their early twenties. These burials are a useful addition to the sparse data available about funerary practices at this period; one of the Broxmouth burials had been placed in a deep circular pit, a type of grave that has also been found, though containing crouched inhumations, at the nearby palisaded enclosure at Dryburn Bridge.

Burials

It is clear that the burial of the dead was not observed in uniform ways throughout Scotland, although inhumation rather than cremation was the normal rite. Inhumations in cists have been found, for example, at Moredun and Granton, in Edinburgh, both containing two crouched bodies, the former associated with two brooches and a ring-headed pin of iron, and the latter with a spiral finger-ring and a penannular brooch. Both date to the first or second centuries AD. At Airlie, Angus, an inhumation in a cist was accompanied by a Roman glass cup of second- to fourth-century date. Graves for extended or flexed inhumations are also known. At Burnmouth, Berwickshire, a man aged about thirty-five had been buried in a stone-lined grave along with a short iron dagger, two bronze 'spoons' and a number of pig bones; the pig joints may have been intended to provide sustenance during the journey to the next world. A large cist from Lochend, Dunbar, East Lothian, contained the remains of some twenty-one inhumations, accompanied only by two iron penannular brooches and an iron stud of the first or second century AD. Recent excavation of the Sculptor's Cave, Covesea, Morayshire, has uncovered several lower jaws in the later Bronze Age layers at the side of the cave, and it has been suggested that heads may have been kept hanging up in the cave, and that the jaws became detached in the course of time!

Perhaps the most important indication of wide-ranging burial traditions has been the identification of a number of cemeteries of barrows surrounded by square ditches which are now visible only as crop-marks on aerial photographs. Such barrows have central grave-pits and are characteristic of burial practices in Iron Age Yorkshire. Several cemeteries have been found in Angus including that at Invergighty Cottage where four barrows form a block about 12m square. At Boysack Mills a barrow about 5m square had a deep grave-pit at its centre, which contained the remains of an inhumation burial in a wooden coffin.

Homesteads and settlements

Contemporary with hillforts, duns and latterly brochs in the second half of the first millennium were settlements and homesteads enclosed by earthen banks and ditches, mostly non-defensive in character. Among the few excavated examples is Scotstarvit in Fife, where an area about 29m in diameter was enclosed by a low bank and ditch; it contained a single, unusually large and elaborate timber house, 18m in diameter, which had been reconstructed twice. Dating evidence was lacking, but it should probably be seen as the home of a Celtic farmer of some substance and prestige in the late pre-Roman Iron Age.

Earthwork construction continued into the Roman period, in conjunction with both timber and stone houses. In south-east Scotland and northern England, the replacement of timber by stone for houses seems to have taken place during, and perhaps as a result of, the Roman occupation, but this transition is absent from south-west Scotland, where timber houses continued in fashion throughout the period. At one time, there appeared to be virtually no native settlements in this area, because the stone-built sites so common in the eastern uplands were lacking, but a programme of intensive fieldwork in East Dumfriesshire has shown that there are plenty of equivalent sites, built as small embanked enclosures containing circular wooden houses. Excavation of one of these sites at Boonies, an oval enclosure of some 0.07 hectares, revealed a lay-out typical of Romano-British

76 Broch, Mousa, Shetland

settlement in which the houses were confined to the rear of the enclosure, leaving a yard, often slightly sunken, at the front. Traces of thirteen timber buildings were found, representing at least seven successive and often superimposed phases of construction; the site was essentially a homestead with one house, which had been rebuilt at various times, until the final phase of occupation when the number of houses expanded to five. The enclosing bank consisted of earth and rubble derived from an external ditch, and the entrance was a simple gateway, 2.5m wide, between the stone-revetted terminals of the bank. Burnt wood from beneath the bank yielded a radiocarbon date of ad 108±47 (SRR-300), indicating that the enclosure is likely to have been built within the first or second centuries AD, a date supported by the presence within the bank of a bronze penannular brooch that ought not to be earlier than the first century AD.

In the Cheviot hills, the dominant type of settlement in the Roman period is characterized by an oval or circular stone-walled enclosure, containing stone-built houses opening off a sunken yard. Excavation has shown that the stone houses were often preceded by timber houses. It is thought that the hollowed aspect of these yards may be the result

of prolonged trampling by livestock. A homestead at Crock Cleuch in Roxburghshire contained one circular stone-built house on a platform 2m above the sunken floor of the yard, together with traces of possible ancillary sheds or barns. Occupation of Crock Cleuch and of a rectilinear homestead at Hownam Rings seems to have extended into the post-Roman period: an iron knife of fifth- to seventh-century type was found at the latter site, while a bronze annular brooch of Anglian style was recovered from Crock Cleuch. There is a concentration of stone-built homesteads in the area around Yeavering in Northumberland, which may account for the location there of the later royal seat of the Anglian kings.

Brochs

By about 100 BC, a new and unique type of fortification had evolved in Scotland: the broch. Almost five hundred brochs have been recorded, mostly in the far north of mainland Scotland and in the Northern Isles but also in western Scotland and the Hebrides, and they are entirely a Scottish phenomenon. Brochs are essentially dry-stone towers, and

there is a considerable degree of uniformity in their design and construction, despite their wide geographical distribution, that must in part reflect the short chronological span of some two hundred years during which they were built. It has also been suggested that they were erected by itinerant professional engineers. Brochs are circular with a tapering profile that is reminiscent of a modern cooling tower, and they are characterized by the height and massive thickness of their walls, and by their peculiar hollow-wall construction. The broch of
76–7 Mousa in Shetland survives to a height of 13m and must originally have reached a height of 15m or more, and its wall occupies no less than 64 per cent of the overall diameter of 15.2m; Mousa is the best preserved of all surviving brochs, and it may well be the most extreme example both in height and proportions. The characteristic hollow wall of the broch was achieved by building an inner and an outer casement wall bonded together by horizontal stone slabs or lintels, which in effect created a series of superimposed galleries within the wall. A stairway led clockwise up through these galleries, presumably to the wall-top; a single entrance at or just above ground level was the sole aperture in the broch wall, and the wall-top must have provided a vital look-out point. This hollow-wall construction must have been designed to lighten the wall and, together with the thickness of the wall, it allowed the broch to be built to considerable height. The construc-
78 tion of the wall may be seen clearly at Dun Carloway in Lewis and at Dun Telve in Inverness-shire, together with the vertical openings in the interior wall-face which played a dual role in helping to lessen the weight of the structure and in allowing air and light into the staircase.

A protruding ledge or scarcement running round the interior of the broch at a height of between 1.5m and 3.3m is likely to have carried a timber gallery, supported by vertical wooden posts for which a ring of post-holes has been found in several recent excavations. At Dun Telve and Mousa there is a second scarcement at a height of 9m and 4m respectively, which probably supported a roof over the gallery, and it is likely that other brochs were originally built with such upper scarcements. This timber gallery and the intramural cells commonly found at ground level represent living accommodation, and the floor of the broch was furnished with a central hearth and sometimes storage tanks. The question of how brochs were roofed is unlikely ever to be resolved, as there is no direct evidence; an overall roof at wall-top level would be impractical for several reasons, including stress on the walls, vulnerability to winds and scarcity of suitable timber to span the diameter of the broch. Whatever form the roof took, it is likely to have rested on the upper scarcement. The only weak point in the defence of a broch was its entrance, but the length of the entrance passage through the thick broch wall made it a narrow and easily defended tunnel. Checks and bar-hole for a massive wooden door occur at varying distances along the entrance passages, and in a few brochs there were two doors.

77 Broch, Mousa, Shetland; ground-plan and section

78 Broch, Dun Carloway, Lewis

Brochs display considerable uniformity as a class of monument, but in one respect, their ground-plan, it is possible to identify two architectural types: ground-galleried brochs and solid-based brochs. The first type has a gallery or both cells and galleries within its wall at

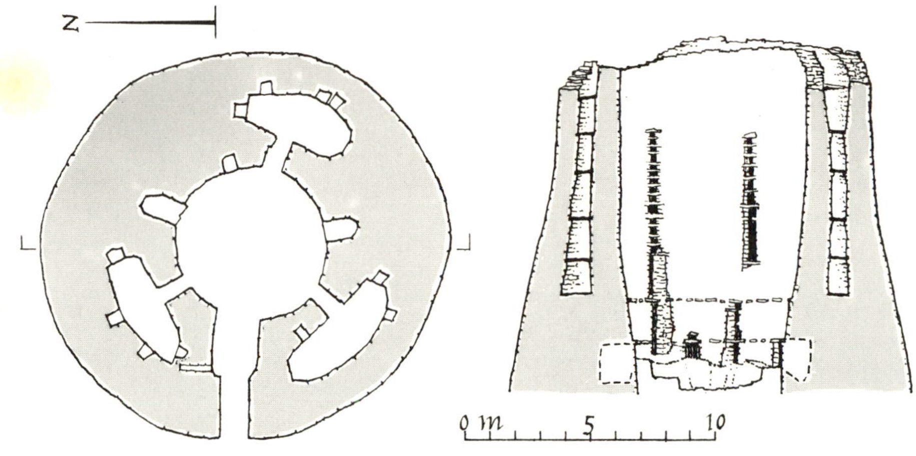
0 m
5
10

79 Semi-broch, Dun Ardtreck, Skye

ground level, while the second has a solid wall at ground level which is broken only by the entrance passage and perhaps two or three cells. This distinction between ground-galleried and solid-based brochs is vital to the problem of their origins, and the geographical distribution of the two types suggest that the broch evolved either in the Hebrides, where most ground-galleried brochs are found, or in north Scotland and the Northern Isles, where the solid-based type predominates.

The geographical distribution of brochs as a whole is heavily concentrated in north Scotland and the Northern Isles, where the available building stone is ideal for dry-stone masonry. John Hamilton has argued that Orkney was a centre of political and maritime power in the later Iron Age and that the broch developed in Orkney as an expression of prestige as well as defence. Orkney lacks any earlier form of fortification that might be seen as ancestral to the brochs, however, and the existence of small forts and duns with galleried walls in the Hebrides led Euan MacKie to follow the alternative hypothesis, first suggested in the 1920s, that brochs originated there. He would see the massive solid-based brochs of the far north, with doors set well down the entrance passage, as the later and more advanced development of a broch-building tradition that evolved in the Hebrides from the earlier galleried duns. More specifically, MacKie has pinpointed the island of Skye as the birthplace of the broch: within their Hebridean distribution, brochs are concentrated on Skye, as is a group of closely related galleried duns that MacKie terms semibrochs. These have high hollow walls similar to the brochs, but instead of being circular they are built as curving lengths of wall fortifying promontories, where the line of
79 defence is completed by natural precipices. The semibroch of Dun

Ardtreck on Skye was excavated by MacKie, and a radiocarbon date of 55 bc±105 (GX-1120) was obtained from charcoal in the artificial platform on which the fortlet was built. This date is barely early enough to make Dun Ardtreck ancestral to the brochs, but it does not invalidate the idea that the building tradition represented by Dun Ardtreck and other galleried fortlets lies behind the development of the brochs. The broch design was quickly adopted elsewhere. The uniformity of the design and its adoption by communities of widely differing cultural tradition makes very convincing MacKie's suggestion that brochs were built by professional engineers, commissioned presumably by local chieftains. Brochs clearly became fashionable, probably as much for the prestige involved as for their defensive qualities.

There is an outlying scatter of brochs around the firths of the Forth and the Tay and in southern Scotland that has always been difficult to explain. Various theories have been put forward involving alliances between broch-using people from west or north and the native tribes of central and southern Scotland during the first and second centuries AD, but the most economical solution lies in acceptance of the idea of professional broch-builders. Brochs may well have been commissioned by leading families seeking protection against the Roman army. Two of the most recently excavated brochs, at Buchlyvie and at Leckie in Stirlingshire, revealed traces of a timber house replaced by the broch; at Buchlyvie, the primary house was a most substantial structure more than 8m in diameter, and the same hearth formed the central feature both of the timber house and of the solid-based broch that replaced it in the late first century AD. The finds from both sites include bronze jewellery and Roman imports, and it is clear that they were the homes of wealthy families. Leckie appears, like the broch at Torwoodlee in Selkirkshire, to have been destroyed in the early second century AD, perhaps as a result of Roman punitive raids.

The Roman army with its war machines was probably the only force capable of successful attack on a broch. That the broch of Mousa was built to last may be gauged from saga references to two occasions in the Viking age when the tower, then some eight or nine hundred years old, was used as a refuge. Brochs were normally sited with an eye to natural strength, and in the Hebrides and western Sutherland additional defences are rare. Elsewhere in northern Scotland and especially in Orkney and Shetland, however, outlying defences are common and often elaborate, taking the form of outer walls or ramparts. The fact that the causeway through the outer defences is often aligned with the entrance into the broch suggests that prestige rather than practical defence may have been a dominant factor. At Gurness in Orkney, the broch was circled by three stone-faced ramparts and ditches, and at Midhowe on Rousay, the rocky promontory on which the broch stands was cut off by a truly massive wall with a ditch on either side. The broch of Burland in Shetland was built on a small promontory surrounded on three sides by precipitous cliffs and defended on the landward side by three ramparts and ditches; in its heyday, the whole fortification must have been a most impressive and formidable sight. Despite the essentially coastal distribution of brochs, the lack of outer

80 Bu Broch, Stromness, Orkney (scales in 50 cm divisions)

defences associated with island brochs may indicate that the threat against which they were built was not sea-borne but emanated from their mainland neighbours. In social terms, the age of the brochs must have been a foretaste of the internecine strife of the Viking Age.

The earlier phases of settlement at Jarlshof in Shetland have already been described, and they were separated from the broch construction levels by a layer of wind-blown sand: the site would appear to have been abandoned for a time before new settlers decided to build a broch there. Less than half the broch survives, the rest having been destroyed by coastal erosion, but originally this was a solid-based broch with two or more cells within the wall at ground level, and it measured about 19m in overall diameter. An unusual external feature is a walled courtyard attached to rather than encircling the broch; no structural features were found within the surviving area of the enclosure. An aisled roundhouse was later inserted into one end of the enclosure, and the wall of the latter is thought to have been robbed of stone to build the roundhouse, which presumably replaced the broch as living accommodation. This in turn was demolished to build two wheel-houses, bringing the history of the settlement into the mid-first millennium AD. Aisled roundhouses and wheelhouses are structurally closely related forms of stone-built house: both are circular and both have radiating piers of masonry that help to support the roof and divide up the perimeter of the house floor area into cubicles. In the aisled roundhouse, the piers are free-standing, creating an aisle round the inner perimeter of the house, whereas the piers in a wheelhouse project from the outer wall like the spokes of a wheel. The Jarlshof excavations were thus useful in providing evidence for the post-broch sequence of settlement, but the hiatus in the stratigraphy of the site immediately preceding the construction of the broch meant that there was no information about the social environment into which the broch had been introduced. For this reason, Hamilton decided next to excavate the broch site at Clickhimin, on the outskirts of Lerwick.

The broch at Clickhimin was built on a small islet in a loch, and, 81
although its situation involved considerable effort in transporting building stone, it possessed natural defensive strength. It is a solid-based broch, almost 20m in diameter, with two intra-mural cells, and it survives to a height of some 5m; there is evidence for a timber gallery 1.8m above the floor and for paving of the broch floor immediately below the gallery. The low height of some of these galleries, especially in Hebridean brochs, may suggest that the area beneath them was used as byre accommodation for livestock. The archaeological importance of Clickhimin centres not on the broch but on the Iron Age forts that preceded it, and here the interpretation of the evidence uncovered by excavation remains controversial. The islet is enclosed within a massive stone wall about 3m thick, and just inside the entrance to this primary fort is a large free-standing stone building known as the blockhouse. This is an arc of masonry 13m long and 4.1m wide, pierced at ground level by an entrance passage-way, and there is evidence not only for a first floor but also for a timber range

81 Broch, Clickhimin, Shetland

against its inner face. Hamilton argued that the blockhouse was originally designed as the entrance to the primary fort, but that, subsequent to the building of the blockhouse, it was decided to make the fort bigger, with the result that the blockhouse became a free-standing chieftain's house inside the completed fort. Similar blockhouses occur in Shetland at the Loch of Huxter in Whalsay, where it forms the entrance (though separately built) into a stone walled fort on an islet, and at Ness of Burgi near Sumburgh, where the blockhouse is free-standing within a promontory fort. These blockhouses are unique to the Shetland Iron Age. Hamilton's interpretation of the function of the blockhouse at Clickhimin has been challenged by MacKie, who would see it as the entrance gateway of a second fort with a partly galleried wall and thus as proof of the arrival of the Hebridean semibroch tradition in Shetland. We believe that the Clickhimin evidence is not strong enough archaeologically to bear either narrative; inevitably such a complex site raises problems that, because of the destruction of early levels by later building activities, cannot be resolved satisfactorily. Sometime in the second century AD, by which time the broch had gone out of use, a wheelhouse was built inside the old tower.

Both Jarlshof and Clickhimin had been explored by earlier excavators, and very few of the brochs excavated in recent times have been undisturbed. One such undisturbed site is Dun Mor Vaul on the Hebridean island of Tiree, where MacKie has found evidence of a broch built in the first century BC and partially demolished probably in the late second or early third century AD. The broch stands on a rocky knoll on the foreshore of the island, and it represents the typical Hebridean ground-galleried broch; its overall diameter is 18.2m and its wall occupies 45 per cent of that diameter. It survives to a height of 2.2m, with a scarcement course about 1.4m above floor level. Outer defences consisted of a wall encircling the summit of the knoll and an outer earthen rampart across the landward access route. Finds include bronze and silver spiral finger-rings, rotary querns, glass beads and bone dice, and a series of eight radiocarbon determinations was obtained from the site as a whole, ranging from 1195 bc±90 (GaK-1096) to ad 490±200 (GaK-1520), which underlines the problems of using radiocarbon dating within an expected short chronological context. Once the broch-tower had been abandoned, the site became a domestic farmstead during the third century AD.

Duns

The term 'dun' is used in Scotland to distinguish a class of small fort enclosing an area up to about 375 sq. m, usually approximately circular or oval, and characterized by a thick dry-stone wall. Duns have a wide distribution in western and southern Scotland, but most are to be found in Argyll; their distribution overlaps with that of brochs in the west, but the two types of structures are essentially complementary in their geographical location. Some were built on level ground, but most occur on rocky knolls, promontories or isolated rock stacks with a degree of natural strength, and additional protection is

82 Dun, Leccamore, Luing, Argyll (scale in 50 cm divisions)

sometimes afforded by outer stone walls restricting access to the dun. The wall of the dun was normally built with a solid rubble core between stone facings; traces of vitrifaction at a few sites indicate the use of timber-lacing, a technique that may as yet be undetected at other duns where the timbers have not been burnt. Timber-lacing was one way of stabilizing the wall; another was to build the outer face with a marked batter. Excavation and careful planning in the course of fieldwork has revealed a third device, a revetment within the core of the wall; this may be seen at several sites including Kildonan Bay and Kildalloig in Kintyre. Occasionally a galleried wall was employed, perhaps to allow the wall to be built to a greater height or, as at Kildonan Bay where a short stretch of wall over very uneven bedrock was galleried, in order to provide maximum stability.

The galleried wall provides a clear link in building tradition with brochs, and there are other structural features common to both classes of fortification, which show that their builders possessed considerable architectural skill. These include entrance passages furnished with checks and bar-holes for the door, intramural cells and stairways leading to the top of the wall. The dun of Leccamore on the island of 82
Luing is roughly oval on plan, measuring about 20m by 13m, enclosed by a wall up to 5m thick and surviving to a height of 3m. It has an entrance at either end; one is checked for a door with bar-holes on both sides, while the other has a corbelled guard-cell opening off one side of the passage, giving access to an intramural stair.

Excavations of a number of duns have suggested that their internal arrangements may have taken the form of timber ranges built against the inner wall-face, but the evidence is scanty and uncertain. At Ardifuar in Mid Argyll, a remarkable galleried dun survives to a height of 3m, and the presence of a scarcement 1.5m above floor level provides convincing evidence for such a timber range. Duns should probably be regarded as fortified homesteads – or even, in the extreme case of the dun at Sunadale in Kintyre, which is only about 6m by 4.5m internally, as individual fortified houses. Although timber-laced duns may be as early as the seventh or sixth centuries BC, it is thought that most solid-walled duns were probably contemporary with brochs in the first two or three centuries AD, and they should be seen as alternative fortifications in an area where, for some reason, brochs were apparently rarely appropriate to the prevalent social conditions. Fieldwork has identified a structural sequence at Dun Skeig in Kintyre in which a stone-walled fort was partially overlain by a vitrified dun, and the wall of the latter was then robbed to provide core material for a second dun.

Several Argyll duns have yielded evidence of reoccupation, after a period of abandonment; Kildalloig appears to have been abandoned finally in the eighth century, while traces of medieval occupation have been found at Dun Fhinn and Kildonan Bay. The ninth-century penannular bronze brooch from Kildonan need indicate no more than chance loss by a visitor. The small galleried dun at Dun Cuier on the Isle of Barra appears to belong both in construction and occupation to the mid-first millennium AD: the pottery is very late Iron Age in form and decoration, the finely decorated bone combs have sixth- and seventh-century parallels, as do in broader terms the bone pins, and the small stone mould has been identified as a mould for glass studs with Irish parallels of seventh- or even eighth-century date.

Duns were clearly a very successful form of fortified homestead, the construction and use of which may have spanned a thousand years, contemporary with other shorter-lived types of settlement such as brochs and wheelhouses. Only crannogs matched the enduring advantages of the dun.

Crannogs

A crannog is a timber house built on an artificial, or partly artificial, island, and it represents a form of defended homestead that was apparently first adopted in the latter half of the first millennium BC and continued to be built into late historical times. These small islands were built close to the shores of lochs, sometimes linked to the shore by causeways, and they consist of layers of timbers and brushwood, consolidated by stones and vertical wooden piles driven down through the layers. Some appear today as small stone islands or grass-grown mounds in reclaimed fields, but many more may exist totally sub-
83 merged in lochs; an underwater survey of Loch Awe in Argyll identified twenty crannogs along the shores of the loch, many of which are below water level and were previously unknown. Most crannog excavations were carried out in the later nineteenth century, following the

interest aroused by the discovery of lake dwellings in Switzerland in the 1850s; the search for comparable buildings in Scotland was facilitated by extensive land reclamation by draining shallow lochs. The first systematic excavation was carried out in 1878 at Lochlee in Ayrshire by Robert Munro, who was to become the leading British authority on crannogs and lake dwellings. Several of these early excavations yielded huge collections of finds, including wooden and leather artefacts preserved by the waterlogged conditions, though these same conditions made excavation difficult. The organic finds from Lochlee included wooden vessels, leather boots, wooden clubs and a small wooden dug-out – the latter essential for access to the mainland – and there was an impressive collection of Roman artefacts of the second century AD. It is likely that these Roman finds date only the latter part of the overall period of occupation, for the crannog was clearly in use over a considerable length of time.

One of two crannogs in Milton Loch in Kirkcudbrightshire was excavated in 1953 by C. M. Piggott; at the time, the only dating evidence was an enamelled bronze fastener of the first or second centuries AD, but subsequently two radiocarbon dates have been obtained from oak samples from the substructure of the crannog, and these indicate that the crannog may have been built as early as the fourth century BC. One of the structural piles gave a date of 490 bc± 100 (K-2027), and one of the horizontal timbers, formerly an ard-head and stilt from a plough, gave a date of 400 bc±100 (K-1394); both these samples were oak and may have been of some age before they were used in the construction of the crannog. The beam of a similar ard or plough was found in a peat bog at Lochmaben, Dumfriesshire, and it has yielded a radiocarbon date of 80 bc±100 (K-1867). The use of such ploughs in Scotland at least as early as the late third millennium BC is indicated, as we have seen, by the stone bar-shares found in Shetland and Orkney which would have been fitted to wooden ards.

The crannog in Milton Loch was connected with the adjacent shore by a causeway about 3m wide, marked by upright timber piles, which were presumably supports for an original corduroy trackway. On the opposite side of the crannog, a hornwork of piles and stones was thought to be the remains of a small harbour, but it was submerged to an extent that made excavation impossible. Traces of boat-docks have been recognized at several of the crannogs in Loch Awe, but none has been excavated. The crannog itself at Milton Loch had been built as a raft on a bed of thick mud: 'the whole island could be made to shake by jumping on it'. Some of the substructure had been washed away, but nevertheless an almost complete plan was obtained. Large logs had been laid side by side to make a platform about 12m in diameter, which had been carefully surfaced with split logs of alder to act as the floor of the house; the platform was surrounded by a band of numerous piles, the innermost of which were interpreted as the uprights of the outer wall of the house, while the outer piles were thought to have supported an external platform, about 1.5m wide, all round the house. A hearth built of large flat stones with a covering of clay occupied an area about 3.6m square at the centre of the house. Little evidence survived to indicate the superstructure of the house, but the arrange-

83 Crannog, Ardanaiseig, Loch Awe, Lorn, Argyll

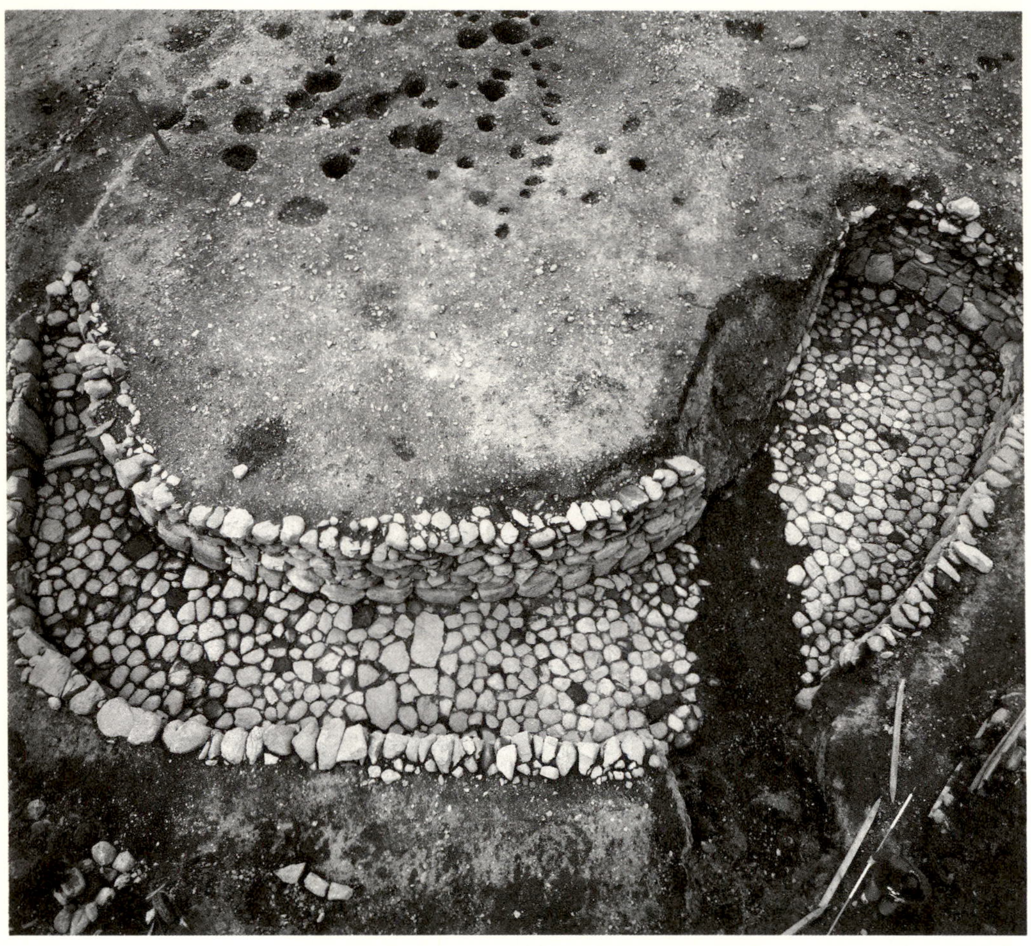

84 Souterrain, Newmill, Bankfoot, Perthshire

ment of internal timber piles and the remains of wattlework suggested that there may have been an inner rectangular room containing the hearth and that the surrounding outer area may have been subdivided by radial partitions. The threshold into the inner room was marked by a large timber with square mortice holes for door-posts. Apart from the wooden ard-head and the bronze ornament already mentioned, there were few artefacts, perhaps because of the weathering of the original floor level: a spindle-whorl and a fragment of a quern were the only stone tools, and two large wooden gorges were interpreted as fowling rather than fishing equipment.

One of the most productive crannogs in terms of finds was Hyndford in Lanarkshire, where an assemblage of metal, glass, pottery and stone artefacts included much Roman material of late first century AD date. It is thought that this material derived from the Roman fort at Castledykes, which is only 3km from Hyndford, though the mechanics of how the artefacts reached the crannog are uncertain. The discovery of a fine torc of bronze beads strung on a thin iron necklet, together with other bronze and glass jewellery, suggests that the occupiers of the crannog were people of substance. Anne Robertson has argued that the exchange of Roman and native goods took place initially in the annexes attached to most Roman forts, which became trading areas. She has stressed the high quality of Roman material found on native sites as evidence against the idea that such material was obtained by looting abandoned forts. J. G. Scott has recently taken this line of argument further, suggesting that the contact between Roman and native was deliberately encouraged by the Romans, and that the contact was manifested not just in goods but in carpentry and construction techniques.

Souterrains

Souterrains, or earth-houses, form a numerous but little studied class of monument in Scotland. They are stone-built underground structures and as such have survived well until recent times, but their discovery is usually accidental and many have been destroyed virtually unrecorded. About two hundred souterrains have been found, concentrated in groups in Angus and Perthshire, in Aberdeenshire, in Sutherland and Ross and Cromarty, in Skye and the Outer Hebrides and in the Northern Isles, and outliers are rare beyond these groups. Dating evidence is meagre, but they appear everywhere to be a phenomenon of the first three centuries AD; until recently dating relied upon stratigraphy, usually secondary to a broch, or finds of second-century Roman artefacts, and predictably the first radiocarbon dates for a souterrain from Newmill near Perth have balanced the date 84
range by indicating that the souterrain was already in use early in the first century. A date of 55 bc±90 (GU-1022) was obtained from charcoal immediately beneath the entrance ramp, and the destruction of the souterrain was dated to ad 195±55 (GU-1019). It is clear that the building of souterrains should not be regarded as a cultural indicator but simply as a common response to the need for storage facilities for food and other products. Within their wide geographical distribution in Scotland, souterrains exhibit considerable variation in design and building technique.

In Orkney and Shetland, souterrains were designed essentially as subterranean chambers approached from the surface by sloping passages; apart from the entrances, which could be camouflaged, these structures were invisible at ground level. The passages were roofed with horizontal stone slabs, and the chambers were covered either in the same way with lintels as at Grain on mainland Orkney or by corbelled domes as at nearby Rennibister, but in either case the weight of the roof and the earth above it rested partly on the walls and partly on free-standing stone pillars. In contrast, the souterrains of eastern Scotland are sometimes only partially subterranean and must have had timber roofs above ground level; in plan they consist essentially of a passage, which gradually widens along its length. They are normally built on well-drained slopes, the passage following the natural contours, and on average they are more than twice the size of their northern counterparts: the passage is often about 15m in length and in rare cases may be up to 58m in length. Some of these souterrains were not only visible at ground level, with their roofs if not their walls protruding well above the surface, but they appear to have been almost focal points for the small domestic settlements to which they were attached. Traces of surface structures were found at several sites; at Ardestie and Carlungie I in Angus there were stone-built houses, approximately circular or oval with diameters of 3m to 4.5m, with paved floors, while at Newmill in Perthshire there were large circular houses built of timber, the largest and latest of which was about 17.6m in diameter and included the entrance to the souterrain within it. The Newmill souterrain was an imposing structure some 20m long with a paved floor, and it widened to 4m across at its far end, thus providing vast storage space. With a long, ridged timber roof, this souterrain and its attached huge timber house must have dominated the Newmill settlement, and they underline the lack of knowledge about social organization at this period: were the house and souterrain in communal use or do they represent the establishment of a chieftain? The latter is perhaps more likely in a developed Celtic society and, with the Roman army in the vicinity during the lifetime of the souterrain, the provisions stored there may not all have been destined for home consumption. Prior to the Newmill excavation, there was a tendency to assume an heirloom character for the exotic Roman artefacts found on eight of the north-east Scottish earth-house sites, but the Newmill radiocarbon dates strengthen the possibility that some souterrains were in use in the first century AD and therefore that more direct contact with the Roman army may be represented by these finds. For the most part the finds consist of sherds of second-century pottery of Roman manufacture and fragments of glass, but an imported bronze brooch of late second- or third-century date was found at Carlungie II. Souterrain excavations rarely yield artefacts even of native origin, presumably because they were kept clean and free of occupation debris, and there is an obvious need for more excavation of domestic structures associated with souterrains.

Wheelhouses

A very distinctive type of stone-built house became fashionable in the Late Iron Age in the Outer Hebrides and, to a lesser degree, in the Northern Isles. This was the wheelhouse, so described because it resembles a wheel in plan: circular, with a central hearth and the periphery of the interior subdivided by radial piers of stone-work. In some cases, there is a gap between the piers and the house-wall, and this type is sometimes known as an aisled roundhouse, though the aisle is rarely wide enough to be negotiable. The primary function of the piers must be connected with roof support, though the bays that they created were no doubt useful for storage and perhaps sleeping accommodation. The bays appear to have been roofed over in some cases by overlapping stone slabs, and, in the aisled type of house, the piers were bonded into the outer wall by lintels at the same level. There were two methods of building the outer wall, either a thick free-standing structure or an inner face built as a revetment against the sand into which the floor of the house had been sunk.

Two wheelhouses have been excavated in the Drimore area of South Uist, both buried by blown sand and well preserved. A Cheardach Mhor was a true wheelhouse, although the piers were not bonded in with the main wall; the latter had only an inner stone face revetted against the sand. The inner area of the house, within the ends of the piers, was about 6.5m in diameter, and additional roof support was provided by five irregularly spaced post-holes, two of which were whale vertebrae set in clay and wedged with stones. Both here, and at the neighbouring site of A Cheardach Bheag, there were bizarre deposits of animal material: thirty-two ox teeth had been buried beside one of the piers, while the hearth at A Cheardach Bheag lay partially enclosed by an arc of about twenty deer jawbones, set close together with the teeth downwards. The jawbones may have been decorative rather than part of some ritual, as nothing comparable has been found elsewhere. The entrance into the wheelhouse was narrow, just over 0.6m in width, and there was no trace of door arrangements. The nearby wheelhouse at A Cheardach Bheag was also sunk into the sand with a revetment wall and an internal diameter of about 9m, but this was of the aisled type with a narrow gap between the piers and the main wall. It was linked to a smaller aisled wheelhouse, only 5.3m in diameter, but this was thought to have been a later addition. A free-standing aisled wheelhouse was excavated at Tigh Talamhanta, Allasdale on the Isle of Barra; here the structures were unencumbered by sand, and surface traces allowed the identification of a complete farmstead, of which the wheelhouse was the main dwelling house.

Few wheelhouses have been identified in northern Scotland, where there is considerable variety in design among post-broch settlements. Late modifications to the interiors of brochs often include radial partitions, and sometimes, as at Clickhimin, a wheelhouse was built inside the partially dismantled wall of the broch.

At Jarlshof, an aisled wheelhouse was succeeded by at least two wheelhouses within the area of the old broch yard, and the overall structural sequence implies that there was a simple evolution from the stone roundhouse of the pre-broch Iron Age first to an aisled version and finally to the wheelhouse proper. A similar sequence may exist in Orkney, but there is as yet little information about the pre-broch Iron Age. Excavation of the chambered tomb at Quanterness revealed a later house at the tomb entrance; this is a simple stone-built roundhouse, about 7m in diameter, with a wall about 0.8m thick, which was occupied over a long period. The associated pottery compares well with that from the pre-broch roundhouses at Jarlshof, and radiocarbon dates for the primary occupation at Quanterness indicate a period around 700 BC.

Whatever their origins, wheelhouses reinforce strongly the impression already given by brochs of close contacts between the Hebrides and the Northern Isles during the later Iron Age, and these contacts were to continue into and to receive fresh stimulus during the Viking Age. Wheelhouses are rarely closely datable but their position in the overall sequence of building traditions is clear: they belong to the post-broch era of the third to fifth centuries AD, though individual sites may well overlap either end of that chronological range.

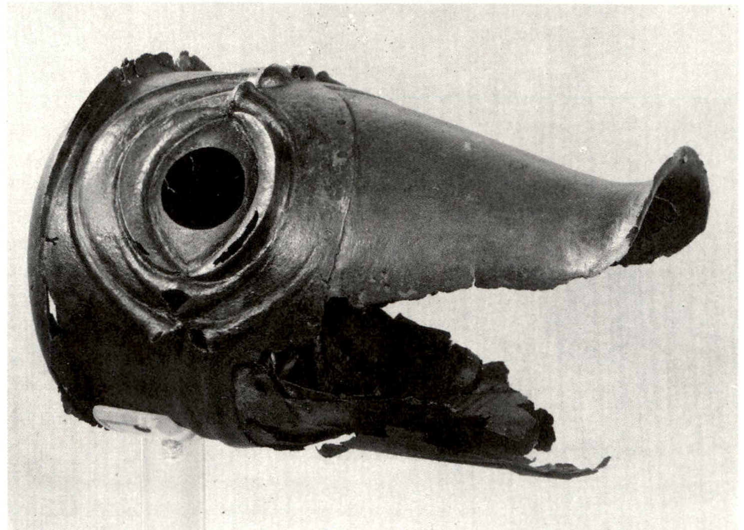

85 Trumpet mouth in the shape of a boar's head, Deskford, Banffshire

86 Sword scabbard, Mortonhall, Edinburgh

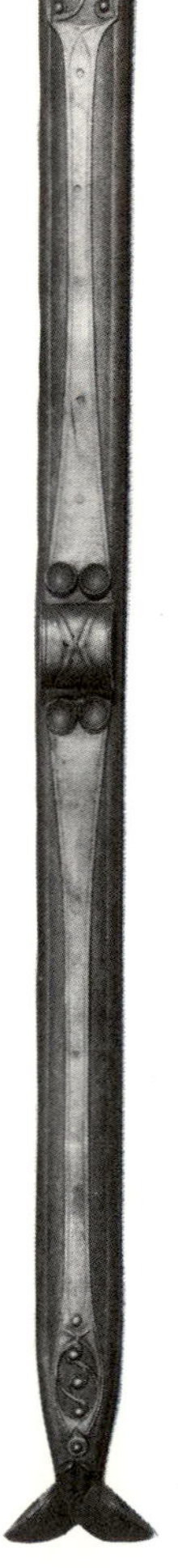

Social structure and art

The fortified sites described in this chapter imply a turbulent society and a way of life in which inter-tribal or family squabbles resulted in raiding and armed skirmishes. From the archaeological evidence alone we can infer little more about the nature of society in Scotland than this, and it is not clear how far classical descriptions of the social structure in Gaul in the first century BC should be used as a model for other Celtic areas. There the upper tier was an aristocratic class from which the ruler (a king in some Celtic societies) and noble families were drawn; the ruling élite also included the religious men, prophets and bards (druids, *vates* and *bardi*). The next group comprised farmers, who held property and whose wealth might be counted in the number of cattle they owned, as well as craftsmen, including the blacksmith. Below them were the unfree and the slaves. Irish sources show a similar hierarchical social structure, and in broad terms this is likely to have been the case for Scotland.

Apart from impressive fortifications, the best evidence for a rich warrior aristocracy comes from a series of metal objects, which evoke
85 the noisy tumult of the Celtic warrior bands. A bronze trumpet mouth in the shape of a boar's head from Deskford, Banffshire, belongs to the later first century AD; originally it had a hinged wooden tongue and it would have had a long trumpet-tube like those depicted on the cauldron from Gundestrup in Jutland. Noise played an important part in Celtic battle tactics as a preliminary attempt to intimidate the enemy. Several richly decorated sword-scabbards have also been
86 found in Scotland including that from Mortonhall, Edinburgh, which is made of sheet bronze of two different colours in order to emphasize the pattern. The long slashing swords of the Celtic warriors have not frequently survived, nor have other iron weapons like spearheads or
95 shield fittings. The depiction of defeated warriors on the Roman

87 Torc terminal and gold coins, Cairnmuir, Peeblesshire

88 Decorated bronze strip, detail, Balmaclellan, Kircudbrightshire

89 Bronze armlet, Culbin Sands, Morayshire

distance-slab from Bridgeness, West Lothian, incorporates two rectangular shields, with round bosses to protect the hand-grip, and an elaborately hilted sword. The naked barbarians illustrate the traditional Celtic disdain for defensive armour, though Agricola does not mention ritual nakedness among native troops at *Mons Graupius* (see p. 123).

Both Agricola in the first century AD and Cassius Dio in the third describe the use of war-chariots by the tribes of eastern Scotland, though they had gone out of fashion on the continent by the second century BC. Light two-wheeled chariots drawn by two small horses harnessed on either side of a pole are illustrated on Celtic coins and are represented by discoveries in burials on the continent and in Yorkshire. Some bronze horse-harness and trappings belong to types also found in the south, and this indicates contact through trade with tribes beyond the Cheviots.

An elaborate bronze pony-cap was found, together with two bronze terminals from drinking-horns, at Torrs, Kirkcudbrightshire; a date in the second century BC has been put forward for the fashioning of the pony-cap and for the horn-terminals, with a place of manufacture in east-central England, but neither suggestion is more than tentative. The motifs of the repertoire of Celtic craftsmen included lyres, palmettes, scrolls and tendrils derived from classical art to which were added an exciting irrationality of layout or a three-dimensional reality that is distinctly Celtic. The interlace of the later Christian art of the Celtic west derives from Germanic sources.

In 1806 a shepherd-boy found part of a torc-terminal, three other torcs of gold alloy, and 'upwards of forty' coins of gold alloy at Cairnmuir, Peeblesshire; sadly only the torc-terminal and two of the coins still survive, but the torc is a fine example of Celtic craftsmanship of 87

Norfolk/Lincolnshire schools, dating to the early first century BC with parallels from Snettisham and Sedgeford, in Norfolk. The terminal is of cast gold alloy with additional decoration achieved by punching. The coins belong to a Gallo-Belgic class (XB) dating to the first half of the first century BC.

An example of engraved decoration may be illustrated from the hoard of metalwork, including an elaborate bronze mirror, found wrapped in cloth at Balmaclellan, Kirkcudbright, in 1861; the orna-
88 ment on a crescentic strip of bronze, of which a detail is illustrated, has been carried out with a pair of compasses to provide the outline which was then filled in with engraved basket-work. This piece probably dates to the second half of the first century AD.

Among the most distinctive examples of Celtic craftsmanship of north-east Scotland are elaborate armlets, including spiral armlets
89 with snake heads at the terminals, like that from Culbin Sands, Morayshire, dating to the later first century AD. A snake bracelet and armlet have been found in the course of the excavations of the broch of Hurly Hawkin, and of the souterrain of West Grange of Conon, both in Angus. Spiral armlets such as these lie behind a series of cast armlets also found in the north-east, which belong to the late first century and the second century AD. The two armlets from Castle Newe, Strathdon, Aberdeenshire, found at the entrance to a souterrain, are decorated with high relief scrolls and trumpet patterns as well as with discs of inlaid enamel.

Kenneth Jackson has used Irish tales to evoke Celtic society of earlier times; although the tales were not written down until the later first millennium AD, they record aspects of life of many centuries earlier, and because of the activities of almost professional story-tellers they were probably passed on from generation to generation with little change. The drinking-horn terminals, tankard hold-fasts and cauldrons of the archaeological record provide the tangible evidence of life round the chieftain's board. Mirrors, neck ornaments, rings, bronze and bone pins, and dice help to illustrate not only wide ranging trade contacts but also provide an insight into leisure and dress. We should not, however, allow the ostentatious side of Celtic society to overshadow the architectural skills both in stone and in timber and the undoubted success in farming or stock-rearing (and indeed raiding), which formed the economic basis for that society in Scotland.

6
Roman Scotland

Gnaeus Julius Agricola

In AD 80 the Roman governor of Britain, Gnaeus Julius Agricola, acting on the orders of the Flavian emperor Titus, advanced through the Scottish Lowlands, reconnoitring as far north as the Tay. He seems to have subdued the Lowland tribes without a battle and secured his conquests by the construction of a network of forts connected by roads. Southern Scotland was incorporated within the Roman empire, and for the first time can be said to have entered 'history'. The Roman historian Tacitus was Agricola's son-in-law and his biography of Agricola contains an account of the campaigns. The occupation of southern Scotland is generally assumed to have been influenced by the disposition of the various Lowland tribes; the paucity of Roman forts in the territory of the Votadini, for example, is taken to indicate that there was no hostility from this quarter. The Selgovae, occupying the upper valley of the Tweed, may have been considered to be the main threat. The Roman army may have been divided into two main columns advancing on the east along the line that was later to be known as Dere Street and later still the A68, from Corbridge to the Forth, and in the west through Annandale and the upper Clyde valley. The roads linked the main lines of forts and fortlets, which served to control the local tribes. To the north, garrisons were established on the Forth-Clyde isthmus. Tacitus tells us that 'if the courage of the army and the glory of the name of Rome had permitted, the limit of Roman influence would have been found within Britain itself', and it may well have been that the creation of a permanent frontier on this line, was considered rather than taking the whole of the island into the Empire.

In the two years following the advance into southern Scotland, Agricola's concern was to consolidate the Roman hold over the conquered territory and in the south-west he constructed forts at Dal- 90
swinton and Glenlochar and a fortlet at Gatehouse of Fleet. A series of forts at the exits of the mountain passes of southern Perthshire (Fendoch, Dalginross, Bochastle, Malling, by the Lake of Menteith, and Drumquhassle) have been interpreted in two ways; the more traditional approach is to see them as part of Agricola's preparations for his intended march into Strathmore and beyond, because by blocking the mouths of each glen he could protect his supply route to the

90 Roman forts, Dalswinton, Dumfriesshire

north. The building of a new legionary fortress at Inchtuthil on the River Tay near Dunkeld may be considered the hub of Agricola's projected occupation of northern Scotland. A second interpretation of the evidence is that Agricola would not have had time to build these forts at this stage in the campaign, but rather that they belong to the period of the following governor, whose name is not known. In AD 83 Agricola was ordered to advance north of the Tay, and Tacitus recounts how Agricola employed his fleet to harass the enemy. The advance did not go unchallenged; it was not until the following year, however, that the major pitched battle was fought.

Mons Graupius

In AD 84 Agricola sent his fleet ahead to intimidate the enemy, and he marched north through Strathmore and the Mearns into Aberdeenshire, and at a place known to Tacitus as *Mons Graupius* 'the strength of all the tribes', numbering some 30,000 men, was lined up for battle. One of the leaders of the native forces, Calgacus, 'the swordsman', is the first inhabitant of Scotland whose name is known to us, at least in its Roman form. Tacitus' account of the battle begins with a speech by Calgacus, a moving and cadenced oration in which an attempt is made to present the barbarian point of view, and Agricola is given a suitably rallying reply. One of the particular interests of the battle is that it was a clash not only of armies but also of styles of warfare and weaponry. The long slashing sword of the Celts was quite unsuitable for the close combat of Roman tactics, and the native infantry was put to flight; the Roman cavalry had a vital role to play not only in defeating the chariots of the Celts but also in routing the final advance. The picture Tacitus evokes of stray chariots, horses panic-stricken without a driver, rushing upon the Romans on the flank and in front, sums up the native collapse.

Tacitus did not attempt to describe *Mons Graupius* as a war-correspondent would, though he must certainly have heard first-hand accounts of the battle; the absence of a detailed description of the topography of the site has meant that its location has been a matter of speculation since antiquarian studies began in Scotland. As knowledge of the system of marching camps has increased, however, a site within the north-east has been favoured; O. G. S. Crawford, for example, suggested a position near Raedykes, inland from Stonehaven. There are similarities between Tacitus' description of the topography of the battle and the Raedykes area, but it is hardly far enough north to be reached only at the end of a summer's campaigning, as Tacitus infers.
Marching camps, laid out by the Roman army on campaign, are the 91
earthwork perimeters of tented compounds; the ditches, now silted, from which the bank material was thrown up, appear as crop marks on aerial photographs, but some are also visible on the ground. The discovery of such camps from the air, however, accompanied by selective excavations at Ardoch for example, has suggested that camps of similar acreage belong to single campaigns and indicate the Roman advances into Scotland of several distinct periods. Taking the latest first, camps of 63 acres and 130 acres may be thought to indicate the campaigns of Septimius Severus in the early third century, while

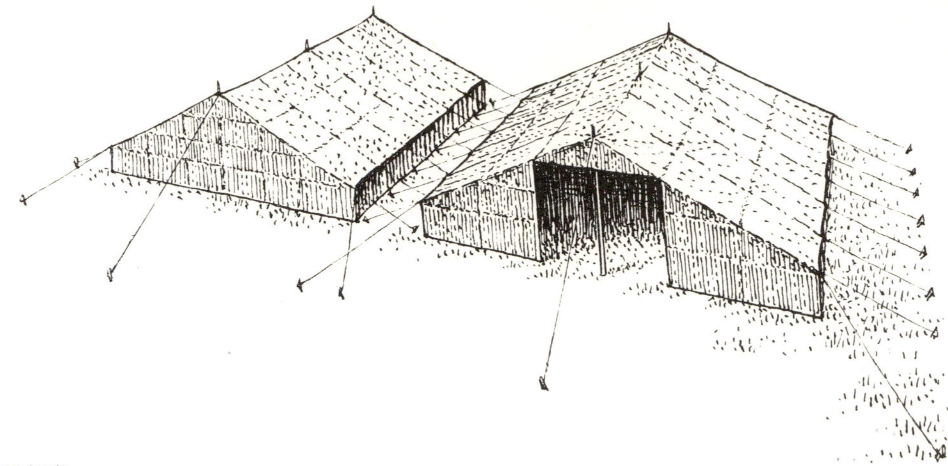

91 Roman tents

camps of about 30 acres, 109 acres and others with distinctive out-
92 turned entrances of Stracathro type (as at Malling, in Perthshire) have been linked to Agricolan campaigns. The discovery of such camps in Moray led Sir Ian Richmond to suggest that *Mons Graupius* was probably fought in this area. In 1975 J. K. St Joseph discovered an unusually large marching camp at Durno, in central Aberdeenshire; the area of the camp, some 144 acres, may be seen as the concentration of troops prepared for that important battle with the northern tribes. The camp at Durno, moreover, is close to one of the most conspicuous mountains in Scotland, Bennachie, a site that could well have acted as the rallying point for the Caledonii. St Joseph has persuasively set the scene round Bennachie for the battle described by Tacitus, and there seems a strong possibility that that mountain is in fact *Mons Graupius*.

After his victory Agricola ordered his fleet to sail round the island, and wintered his troops in the south. Agricola's governorship came to an end at this point, and it was left to others to complete his programme of fort- and road-construction. This, however, had in part to be abandoned because Roman losses on the Danube frontier led to the withdrawal of troops from Britain, and the more northern forts, in Strathearn and Strathmore, were dismantled. The legionary fortress of Inchtuthil was abandoned around AD 86 before building was finished.

The date of the withdrawal of troops and of the dismantling of the defences at Inchtuthil and Stracathro is unusually well documented as unworn *asses* of Domitian, struck in AD 86, have been discovered there; such coins would have become worn quickly once they had been released for circulation, and it seems probable that they came from the mint not long before the demolition of the forts. That the dismantling of the system of fortifications was part of an orderly withdrawal has been demonstrated by excavations at Inchtuthil and at Fendoch.

It has recently been suggested that a series of watch-towers that runs from Ardoch to Strageath and thence eastwards along the Gask Ridge, perhaps as far as Bertha, may date to the period immediately following the withdrawal from Inchtuthil. These timber watch-towers, surrounded by a bank and a ditch, were intervisible and seem to have been designed to provide surveillance along the frontier. However, this system seems to have had a short life, being abandoned together with most of the other forts north of the Cheviots in about AD 90.

Newstead, Broomholm, Dalswinton, Oakwood, Milton and Glenlochar in southern Scotland seem to have been held at least until the end of the first century. Newstead itself was refortified on a grand scale, befitting its new role as a frontier post, with a massive rampart and ditch. The barrack-blocks, probably for legionaries, were provided with stone foundations. Some impression of the trappings of fortress life will be gained when we look at the finds from Newstead in greater detail. These forts, and all others north of the Tyne-Solway isthmus, appear to have been abandoned about AD 105, possibly when more troops were withdrawn from Britain for service on the continent. It was on the Tyne-Solway line in the 120s that Hadrian's Wall was constructed.

92 Roman fort and temporary camps, Malling, Lake of Menteith, Perthshire

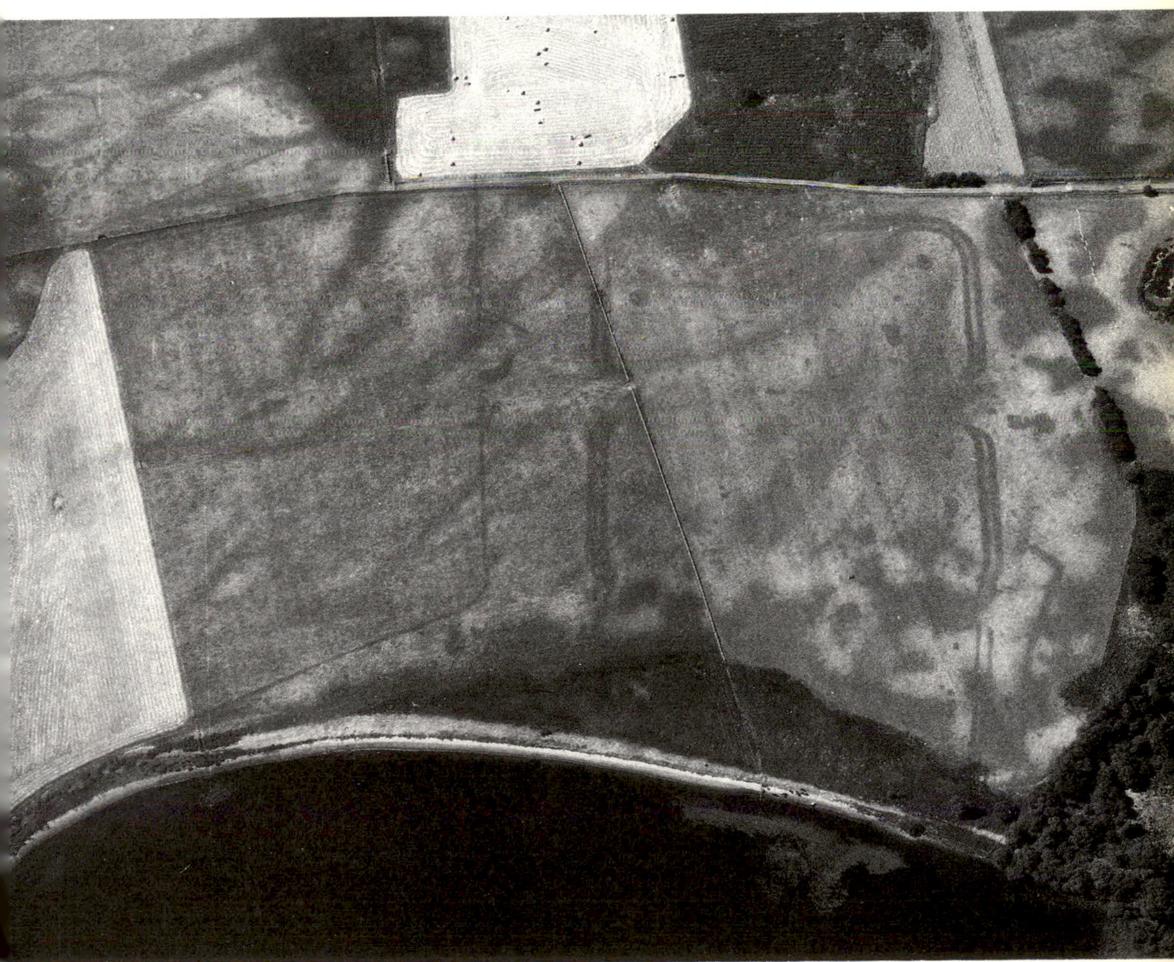

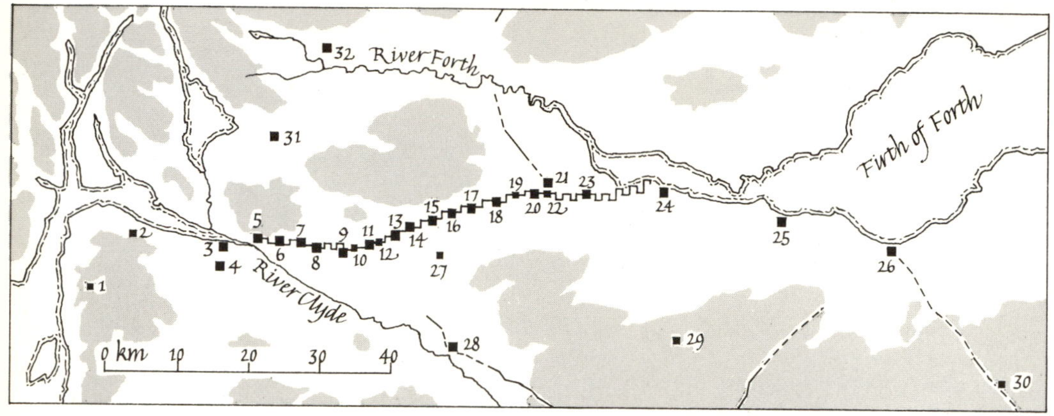

93 Antonine Wall showing forts and fortlets

1 Outerwards
2 Lurg Moor
3 Barochan
4 Old Bishopton
5 Old Kilpatrick
6 Duntocher
7 Castle Hill
8 Bearsden
9 Balmuildy
10 Wilderness Plantation
11 Cadder
12 Glasgow Bridge
13 Kirkintilloch
14 Auchendavy
15 Bar Hill
16 Croy Hill
17 Westerwood
18 Castlecary
19 Seabegs
20 Rough Castle
21 Camelon
22 Watling Lodge
23 Mumrills
24 Carriden
25 Cramond
26 Inveresk
27 Mollins
28 Bothwellhaugh
29 Castle Greg
30 Oxton
31 Drumquhassle
32 Malling

The Antonine Wall

In AD 138–9 Roman forces again advanced into southern Scotland; the governor of Britain, Q. Lollius Urbicus, had orders from the emperor, Antoninus Pius, to reconquer the Lowland tribes and to establish a new frontier further north. Coins and an inscription provide the evidence for the date of the successful campaigns in AD 142; they also indicate the date of initial work on the permanent frontier, known to us as the Antonine Wall. The disposition of the Lowland forts broadly follows the same lines as in the earlier period.

93 The Wall ran from Bridgeness on the Firth of Forth for forty Roman miles to Old Kilpatrick on the north bank of the Clyde; the line chosen runs along the southern edge of the series of river valleys that make up the isthmus; the Rivers Forth and Clyde themselves form no part of the frontier. Several components made up this new frontier: a turf-built rampart, at least 3m high, set on a stone founda-
94 tion about 4.3m wide, and, in front of the rampart, a broad ditch with a counterscarp bank on its outer margin. To the south of the Wall, and running parallel to it at a distance of some 45m, was the main line of communication – the Military Way. The building of the Wall was

94 Antonine Wall, Watling Lodge, Stirlingshire

undertaken by detachments of the Second, Sixth and Twelfth Legions, who commemorated the completion of their allotted stretches by setting up 'distance slabs', stones carved with a panel recording the length constructed and the legion, and often with suitable decorative motifs. On several distance slabs defeated and disconsolate barbarians 95 are shown. To the native Caledonians, the architectural and engineering feat of the construction of the Wall, presumably surmounted by a timber parapet and walkway, with the complex military organization of forts and fortlets along its length, must have been an awesome reminder of the alien authority in southern and eastern Scotland.

Passage along the Military Way was undoubtedly an important aspect of Roman control as well as an essential supply route for victualling the forts. Some supplies at least would have come by sea from the ports on the Forth and Clyde. The discovery of coriander, opium poppy and figs, none of which is native to Britain, at Bearsden serves to demonstrate the wide trading contacts of the Wall-forts, and pottery from Britain and Gaul, and wine from southern Spain can be demonstrated archaeologically or inferred from other evidence. Corn would also be brought in from areas to the south or from the continent.

95 Distance slab, Bridgeness, West Lothian; detail showing defeated barbarians (*far left*)

96 Signalling platform, Bonnyside East, Stirlingshire (*left*)

Bridges were provided over rivers and streams. In order to improve passage across the River Kelvin, a bridge with masonry piers and with a timber superstructure was built a little distance to the north-west of the fort at Balmuildy. Communication by beacon fires was also important; six signalling posts abutting the rear of the Wall have been 96 discovered. They are found in pairs; one pair lies to the west of Croy Hill and the other two pairs on either side of Rough Castle. The excavation of one example revealed a stone base, some 5m square, with a capping of turf. Signalling to the north and south of the Wall, rather than along it, has been inferred. The communication system also continued beyond each end of the Wall; to the east, a road must have linked Cramond and Inveresk to the Wall line; on the west, one fort and at least two fortlets were sited on the south side of the River Clyde. The road linking these sites continues beyond Outerwards towards the Firth of Clyde near Largs and Fairlie, and it has been suggested that there may have been a harbour of Roman date on the coast, possibly at Irvine.

The sixteen known forts, which accommodated the frontier garrisons, were spaced along the Wall at average distances of some 3.2km; the siting of a fort, however, was determined as much by considerations of topography as by mathematics. Strategic reasons seem to have affected the troop distributions, with the weight of the garrison lying to the western half of the Wall, where there were no forward positions, such as are found in the east at Ardoch, Strageath and Bertha. These outpost forts were designed not only to provide advance positions on the east of the country, from which most trouble was presumably expected, but also to provide cover for Fife, rather in the manner of the watch-towers of the Flavian period. Computation of the total garrison strength on the Wall at the beginning of this period has led to the conclusion that it was only slightly less than that of Hadrian's Wall, which was in fact twice as long.

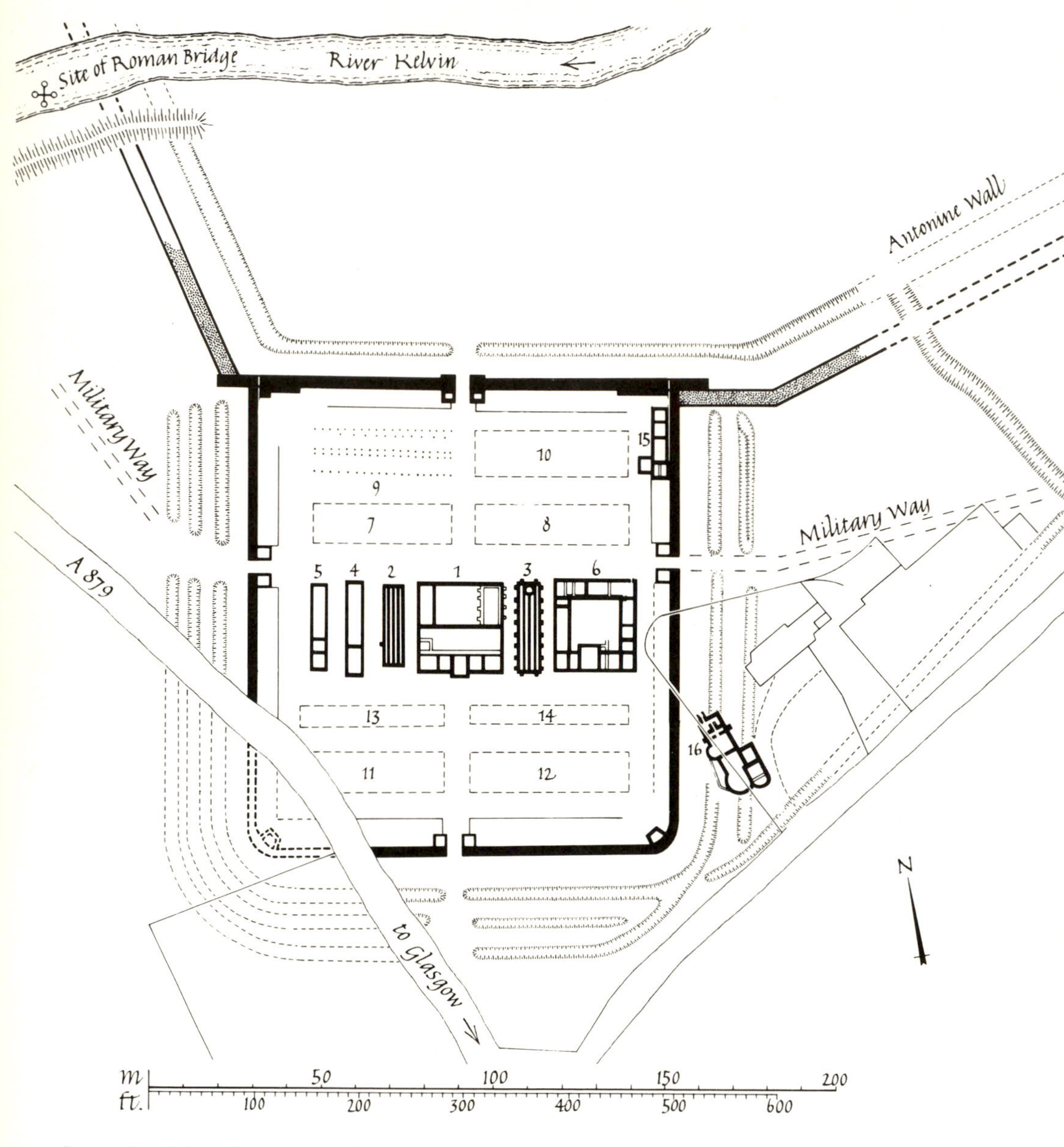

97 Roman fort, Balmuildy, Lanarkshire

1 Headquarters building
2–3 Granaries
4–5 Workshops
6 Commandant's residence
7–12 Barracks
13–14 Workshops
15–16 Bath-houses

98 Roman fort, Rough Castle, Stirlingshire

The reoccupation of the Lowlands was planned in some detail, and the garrisoning of the isthmus took place even before the construction of the Wall. Two groups of Wall-forts have been identified, the earlier group preceding the construction of the Wall and a later group added to the rear of the rampart. Of the earlier group Balmuildy has projecting wings of stone against which the Wall was to abut, and it may even be that the original intention was to build a stone frontier. The Wall itself was built from east to west, but it is clear that forts such as Balmuildy were planned, if not finished, before the construction of the adjacent stretches of Wall. This form of bonding with the Wall, which has been compared to the junctions of the mile-castles on Hadrian's Wall, would be less successful where the linear boundary was of turf. The forts of the second group, for example Rough Castle and Cadder, were added to the rear of the Wall. As well as such differences of relationship with the Wall, the forts are of varied size and therefore garrison. Balmuildy and Cadder may have housed quingenary cohorts, but the larger size of Mumrills, together with an inscription to a cavalry regiment of Tungrians, combine to demonstrate the presence

97 98 99

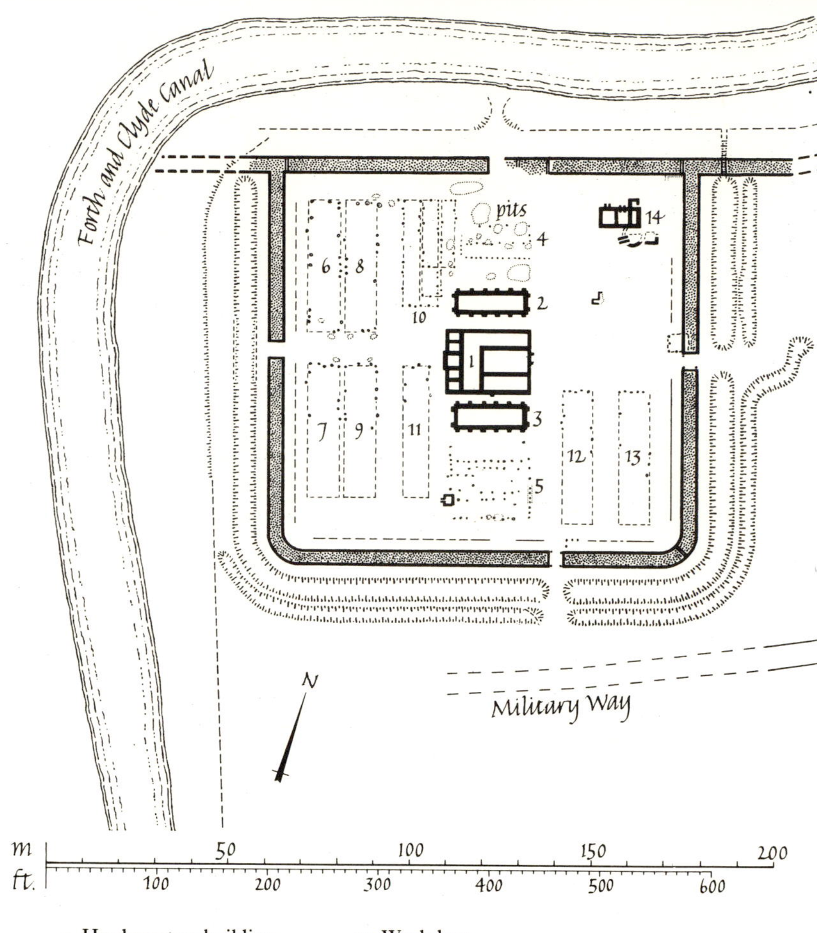

99 Roman fort, Cadder, Lanarkshire

1 Headquarters building
2–3 Granaries
4–5 Timber buildings
6–9 Barracks
10 Workshop
11 Storehouse
12–13 Barracks
14 Bath-house

there of a cavalry garrison. A tombstone from Mumrills is evidence for local recruitment into the Roman army, for it is erected to Nectovelius, a Brigantian serving in the Second Cohort of Thracians.

The impressive archaeological evidence for the Antonine period of occupation in Scotland does not mean that the historical facts are altogether clear. A possible revolt among the Brigantes in northern England is one reason given for the reorganization that seems to have taken place in the 150s, but there is sadly very little historical or numismatic information for this period. There is evidence of destruction of at least two forts, Birrens and Newstead, the former just before AD 158, but many of the other forts appear to have been abandoned peacefully. After the death of Antoninus Pius in AD 161, the northern Wall was given up in favour of the Hadrianic frontier, and the forts in southern Scotland were finally abandoned. Though the Antonine Wall may no longer have had the status of a frontier at this time, the occupation of a number of the forts, Castlecary for example, may have continued after the main withdrawal. It has been suggested that there are similar reasons for the Antonine advance and retreat: the former was not to gain territory, but perhaps to allow the emperor to gain military prestige; the withdrawal might thus imply that this policy could be abandoned and that the troops might more usefully be deployed elsewhere. The use of outpost forts sets the scene for Roman involvement in Scotland from the death of Antoninus Pius to the middle of the fourth century; such forts served as the bases for auxiliary infantry and cavalry units which could provide effective supervision of the frontier area by patrolling and scouting.

The Severan campaigns

In the early years of the third century AD the Scottish tribes proved sufficiently troublesome for a major expedition against them to be mounted. Herodian recorded that the governor of Britain wrote to the emperor in the following terms: 'the barbarians had risen and were over-running the country, carrying off booty and causing great destruction, and that for the effective defence either more troops or the presence of the emperor was necessary'. Accordingly in AD 208 the emperor, Septimius Severus and his sons Caracalla and Geta, came to Britain with additional men to be deployed against the Maeatae and the Caledonii in eastern Scotland and the Highlands. The tribes apparently made overtures of peace, but, as a resounding military victory was at least one reason for the imperial family's presence in the north, negotiation was not contemplated. In order to provision the troops during the campaign, and indeed the subsequent reoccupation of Scotland, additional granaries were constructed at South Shields on the Tyne; Cramond on the Forth was refortified. A completely new legionary base at Carpow on the Tay was constructed, presumably as the linch-pin of the new occupation. The Severan advance of AD 208, however, is indicated not only by such substantial structures as the legionary bases, but also by temporary camps of sixty-three acre size. Keithock, near Stracathro in Angus, is the furthest north of this group, but the Roman army is not thought to have penetrated the heartland of the Caledonii on this occasion. The tribes, however, were forced to come to terms, and the historian Dio stated that they lost 'not a small part of their territory'. Severus may have considered that Carpow on the south shore of the Tay was the most suitable forward station for the legionary troops, a base that also had the advantage of good maritime communications. The agreement with the tribes was not long lasting, however, for the Maeatae and later the Caledonii joined in revolt. The emperor was too ill to lead the army in a renewed attack, but Caracalla marched as far north as Stonehaven, if the interpretation of the pattern of camps of 130-acre size is to be believed. In AD 211, on the death of his father, Caracalla quickly concluded an agreement with the Maeatae and Caledonii, and along with other members of the imperial family, he returned to Rome. Building at Carpow was not, however, stopped until some time after AD 212, when the fort was demolished and abandoned.

100 Roman fort, Ardoch, Perthshire

Throughout the next century comparative peace was maintained by troops stationed in only four forts, High Rochester, Risingham, Bewcastle and Netherby. These forts held *cohortes milliariae equitatae* – mixed cavalry and infantry units – ideally suited to patrol work. These were the largest units in the Roman army below the legions. The soldiers in these units, and the scouts attached to them, appear to have patrolled an area from Hadrian's Wall as far north perhaps as the Tay.

Forts and practice siege works

After this outline of the Roman occupation of Scotland, we may now examine other sites and finds that help us to build up a picture of Roman military life on the northern frontier. For, although the main periods of Roman rule were short, the surviving field monuments are 100
among the most impressive remains of the Roman army anywhere in the Empire. The Wall and the system of forts, signal-stations and road communications must have struck both the Roman soldiers and native warriors as a considerable achievement; the almost complete lack of mention of the frontier in the historical record is a reflection of how far from the centre of power and interest it was.

Newstead

The most important of the excavations sponsored by the Society of Antiquaries of Scotland was that undertaken at Newstead, near Melrose, by James Curle between 1905 and 1910, the longest almost continuous excavation in Scotland of its day. Its success is to be gauged not only by the quality of the finds and by Curle's discussion of them in a European context, but also by the standard of recording in general. Curle notes that his residence within a mile of the site enabled him 'to make frequent, often daily, visits to follow the progress of the digging'.

The site is on the south bank of the River Tweed, overlooked by the majestic Eildon Hills to the south-west, a position which Curle says 'commended itself to more than one generation of Roman military engineers'. Indeed Ian Richmond has shown that four periods of occupation can be distinguished: first an Agricolan fort of most unusual outline, with dog-legged sides and with the gateways at the re-entrants. This fort was dismantled about AD 86. In the second period the fort became the major outpost in the north for the last decade of the first century AD and was protected by a massive rampart and ditch of more conventional outline. A bath house and an adjacent building interpreted as a guest house for official travellers were discovered outside the fort on the west. It may be that this period ended in disaster as the internal buildings have been destroyed by fire, and the rubbish pits, from which so much exciting material has been discovered, contain weapons and querns that would not have been dis- 101–4
posed of had the withdrawal been more orderly; the possibility that some of this material is of ritual deposition has also to be considered. In the subsequent Antonine period there are two phases of occupation during which the fort was protected by a stone-faced rampart and a series of smaller ditches, first two and finally three. The rubbish pits

101 Brass cavalry parade-helmet, Newstead, Roxburghshire

102 Bronze cavalry parade-helmet, face-mask, Newstead, Roxburghshire

contained many objects that demonstrated the magnificence of frontier life; amongst the discoveries were several cavalry helmets, including a brass example richly decorated with a naked winged figure standing upright in a chariot to which are harnessed a pair of leopards, and an elegant bronze parade-helmet; sword- and shield-fittings; spear- and arrow-heads; bronze wine-flagons; and many examples of high-class table-ware. The practical tools of the carpenter and the smith are reminders of the essential day-to-day maintenance that such a camp and the weapons of its occupants would require. Curle's excavations

also recovered samples of botanical and animal remains – the latter including the bones of horse and large quantities of oxen and sheep.

Several views of the destruction of the fort and of the deposition of material within the pits have been put forward. The burning may have been part of the demolition of the fort by Roman soldiers themselves, in order to render useless anything that the natives might have sought to salvage; the use of Roman dressed stones in the souterrain at Crichton, Midlothian, and in the fort at Rubers Law, Roxburgh, shows that the pillaging of building materials did indeed take place.

103 Spearheads, arrowheads and bolts, Newstead, Roxburghshire

104 Swords, Newstead, Roxburghshire

The pits thus contain material dumped before evacuation of the fort by a force that wished to travel with as little surplus equipment as possible. There is also the possibility that the pits are the result of a tidying-up operation by a Roman force subsequent to withdrawal. Ritual depositions, either by the troops of the garrison during the period of occupation or by the barbarians following the putative sacking, have been suggested. There are over one hundred 'pits', some originally dug as wells, and their fillings need not all be of similar origin. The ritual nature of the fillings of a number of pits has been argued by Anne Ross and Richard Feachem, while William Manning's solution that surplus and damaged equipment was buried 'because it could not easily be transported', perhaps sacrificed with some degree of ritual, couples two of the possible interpretations.

Training areas

Two native forts formed the focus for Roman military training, namely
105 Woden Law, in Roxburghshire, and Burnswark, in Dumfriesshire. Woden Law is situated at the point where Dere Street leaves the Cheviots and comes down to Kale Water, a tributary of the River Tweed; to the north-west along Dere Street are the marching camps of Pennymuir, the small fort of Cappuck, and Newstead. The position of the native fort on this route has led to the suggestion that the Cheviot section at least may be a line of communication of greater antiquity than the Roman period. The earthworks enclosing the native fort on the south and east sides are best explained as the result of field-training in the construction of siege works and in the use of siege engines. The temporary camps at Pennymuir are seen as providing the tented accommodation for the detachments on exercise. At Burnswark too a spectacular native fort seems to have been used as the centre for a training school in the use of slings, bows and ballista. The use of two such prominent sites for exercises with siege engines would have had a depressing effect on native morale.

Religious life

A wide variety of gods, as recorded by the altars and statuettes set up to them, was worshipped in Roman Scotland; they include gods of the Roman pantheon – Jupiter, Mars, Mercury, Apollo and Fortuna – as well as more local deities or personifications – Brigantia, Britannia and Maponus, for example. A god from the eastern Empire, Jupiter Dolichenus, from Doliche in Syria, was worshipped at Croy Hill, while gods from the Germanic world are recorded from Birrens and Cramond. A relief carving of Brigantia, the personification of the tribe, was found at Birrens in 1831, in the ruins of a building outside the fort. Cocidius, a native deity associated with Silvanus and Mars, was also worshipped in Scotland, and his shrine may have been at Bewcastle, in Cumberland. Birrens may have been near the cult centre of the god Maponus, the native equivalent of Apollo; a sandstone slab from the fort has an incised dedication to the god and a figure that has been interpreted both as a dog and as a serpent, the former perhaps being the more likely.

105 Hillfort and practice siege works, Woden Law, Roxburghshire

Very few burials have been found, but cremations in pottery urns have been discovered near Cramond, at Croy Hill and Newstead. An unusual cremation burial from High Torrs, Luce Sands, Wigtownshire, was associated with fragments of two vessels of samian ware of late second- or early third-century date, an iron finger-ring with an intaglio, and fragments of what may be a cooking-pan. A cist-burial, containing the double interments of two warriors who may have been Roman auxiliaries, accompanied by their weapons, was found in the course of gravel-working near Camelon in 1975.

The demolition in 1743, of what must have been a Roman temple near Camelon, Arthur's O'on (or Oven), was the archaeological scandal of its day and is still a chilling reminder of the vulnerability of ancient monuments to 'gothic' destruction. Perhaps built as a trophy to commemorate a victory, the circular beehive-shaped building stood to a height of over 6m; fortunately it had been well recorded in 1726,

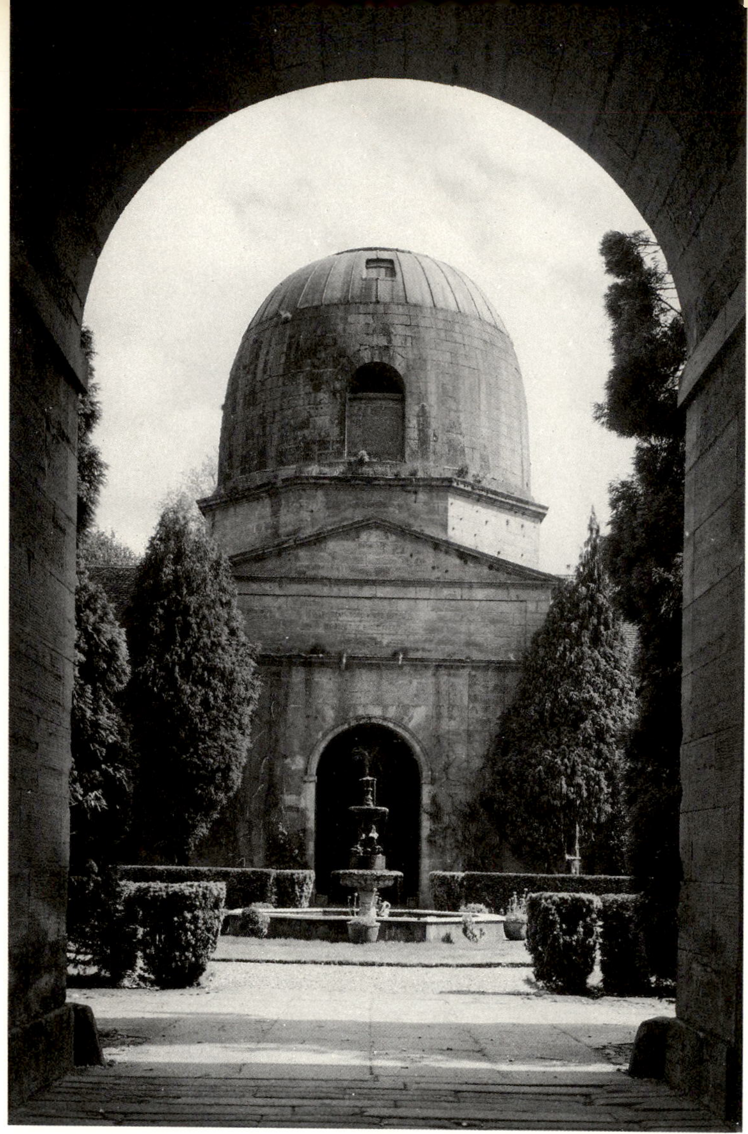

106 Arthur's O'on; replica on the stable block of Penicuik House, Midlothian

and in the 1760s a fullscale replica of the O'on was constructed, as a
106 dovecot surmounting the stable block at Penicuik House, by Sir John Clerk of Penicuik, one of the most eminent of Scotland's early antiquaries.

Roman Scotland is a military study, and there is little evidence of civilian life beyond the forts. From other frontiers, however, it may be suggested that there would have been civil settlements outside many forts, and excavation has demonstrated the presence of an extensive settlement to the east of the fort at Inveresk on the Firth of Forth. Here were found both timber and stone buildings, and one area was rebuilt on at least two occasions within a period of almost twenty-five years. An officially recognized civil settlement existed at Carriden near the east end of the Antonine Wall.

There were two different reasons for the Roman army's presence in north Britain. Sometimes, as in the advance of Antoninus Pius, such a

show of military success could be useful in political terms in Rome itself; sometimes, as with Severus, political reasons were coupled with the need to protect the southern part of the province from the unruly barbarians in the north. It is thus difficult to assess the importance or impact of these episodes on the early history of Scotland. On another frontier, Andreas Alfoldi has described the way that 'high-handed actions of the Roman imperialists and the arbitrary behaviour of the 107
restless rapacious barbarians, threatening to destroy the very foundations of civilized life, confronted one another'. He continued that '"pax Romana" was only a justification of a world empire by conquest'. Scotland was never Romanized; trade, however, brought the scattered native communities into a wider framework than we have been able to trace archaeologically in earlier periods, and it is even possible that some part of the agricultural production of the Lowlands may have been geared to providing a surplus for the Roman authorities. A terracotta model of a bale of hides or fleeces from Dun Fiadhairt, Skye, is probably a votive offering by a Roman merchant, trading, among other things, in hides. The Roman army must have relied on local production of dairy products and fresh meat, but such contacts were at best comparatively superficial.

John Mann has suggested that the tribal amalgamations to the north of the Tay, culminating in the rise of the Picts in the fourth century, can be ascribed to Roman pressure in the south. Indeed he goes so far as to say that 'the Pictish Kingdom was a product of the Roman presence in Britain'. If this is so, it is a significant, and rather unexpected, contribution to the future history of what is now Scotland.

107 Roman sculpture, Croy Hill, Dunbartonshire, showing three soldiers with legionary tunics and cloaks, long shields (scuta), helmets and spears or swords

7

Britons, Angles and Scots

Britons

The tribes of the part of north Britain that fell between the Walls appear to have enjoyed a special relationship with the Roman authorities to the south; the Votadini on the coastal plain of the Lothians and Berwickshire, the Selgovae in the Upper Tweed valley, the Novantae in the south-west and the Damnonii in the Clyde Valley were thus quite distinct from their more belligerent northern neighbours beyond the Forth-Clyde line. There are also differences in the languages spoken by the two groups; the former speaking a P-Celtic dialect, and the latter using a tongue in which an earlier strand of Celtic may be detected; the northern tribes also spoke a non-Celtic, and in fact a non-Indo-European language, Pictish.

The Picts are first introduced in AD 297, when the writer Eumenius, in a historical allusion, describes the Picti and the Hiberni as the enemies of the Britons. Ammianus Marcellinus, a fourth-century historian, tells how, in about AD 360, the Scots (from Ireland) and Picts broke treaties, raided the frontier region and terrified the inhabitants, who were already exhausted by a series of previous defeats. In a concerted attack the Picts, Scots and Attacotti, with the help of Saxon pirates, ravaged parts of the Roman province in AD 364. Alarmed by a further 'conspiracy of barbarians', in AD 367 the emperor Valentinian despatched Theodosius, an able general, who restored Roman authority as far north as Hadrian's Wall in the following year. In AD 382 Magnus Maximus campaigned against the Picts and the Scots. But further raids are recorded from AD 394, and the famous soldier, Stilicho, is reputed to have dealt with them, though not necessarily in person, finally subduing the northern invaders about AD 396; in 401 or 402, however, he withdrew his forces to the continent to meet the threat of the invading Goths. Henceforth the British tribes beyond Hadrian's Wall had to evolve their own defences and increasingly their own political identities.

One of the most remarkable discoveries of Scottish archaeology illustrates the turbulent frontier life; it was made on Traprain Law in May 1919 when, in the course of the excavation of the hillfort, one of the workmen brought up a silver bowl on the end of his pick. Further examination revealed the top of a pit, measuring about 0.6m in diameter, the excavation of which uncovered over one hundred pieces
108–10 of Roman silver plate – the richest hoard ever found in Scotland. The silver included parts of ten flagons, fifty bowls, nine spoons as well as a

wine-strainer, handles, fittings and mountings. Four coins are important dating evidence; struck for Valens (AD 364–78), Valentinian II (AD 375–92) and Honorius (AD 395–423), they indicate that the hoard was deposited during or after the reign of Honorius. The silver had been cut up and folded into small packets with the bowls and flagons flattened and contorted. There were eight small folded pieces of silver plate made ready as if for melting down. In two of the other packets of silver were small amounts of base metal. Such treatment indicates that the silver was not in use by a chieftain on Traprain Law before it was hidden, but rather that it was regarded as bullion. It is not altogether clear, however, whether or not it is the loot of a pirate band based on the hillfort and raided from a wealthy Roman establishment in southern England or the continent, or whether it represents a transaction with Roman authorities to the south, either as a diplomatic bribe or possibly as a payment for the service of the warrior bands in the army of the frontier. The interpretation of the hoard as pirate loot finds less favour with archaeologists today than do the other two solutions, but the several possibilities serve to underline the complexity of the political situation in the early fifth century.

Several of the items of silver bear motifs that are of Christian inspiration, and though there is no suggestion of their ecclesiastical use at Traprain, they demonstrate the potentially Christian character of much of the Late Roman world. One of the flagons has repoussé decoration illustrating four Biblical scenes – the Fall, the Betrayal, the Adoration of the Magi and Moses striking water from the rock. The bowls of two of the spoons are inscribed with the Chi-Rho monogram; the perforations on the base of a strainer are laid out to form the same Christian symbol and round the upper part of its bowl the perforations form the letters of the name of Jesus Christ in Roman capitals.

The Votadini emerge in the early historical period as the kingdom of the Gododdin, with strongholds presumably at Stirling, Edinburgh and on Traprain Law. The capital of the kingdom of Strathclyde was

108–10 Silver objects, Traprain Law, East Lothian; flagon with Old Testament scenes, goblet and spoons

on Castle Rock, Dumbarton; the centres of power in Dumfries and Galloway are less clear. No structural remains of this period survive on Traprain Law or on the Castle Rock, Edinburgh, and even the location of *Urbs Giudi*, another important centre, is uncertain, although Stirling and Cramond have both been put forward. Traprain Law, from a consideration of the surviving defences and the objects recovered from the excavations, seems to have been abandoned by the middle of the fifth century AD – perhaps with the transference of power to a centre further west.

On Dalmahoy Hill, near Edinburgh, there are the substantial remains of a stone-walled fort on the summit of the hill with a series of defended terraces on the lower slopes. Although Dalmahoy has not been excavated, comparison with a number of smaller sites, notably Dundurn, Perthshire, Rubers Law, Roxburghshire, and Dunadd, Argyll, led Robert Stevenson to suggest that it was of Dark Age date and excavation has since confirmed such a date for Dundurn. The discovery of dressed stones of Roman origin in the core-material of the wall of Rubers Law also indicates a date about the fourth or fifth century AD for this fortification; a Roman signal-station on the summit of the hill may well have been used as a quarry for the later fort. There is no doubt about the status of Castle Rock, Dumbarton, for it is mentioned by the Venerable Bede who, describing the Firth of Clyde, identifies a centre of the Britons strongly defended up to his day, which was called Alt Clut. 'Clyde Rock' can be none other than Castle Rock, Dumbarton, and excavation by Leslie Alcock has confirmed the existence of a timber and rubble rampart constructed after AD 600 and destroyed in all probability in a Viking raid in AD 870. The finds included sherds of imported pottery, glass vessels and tanged iron knives. The Mote of Mark, Kirkcudbright, is another key site to our understanding of this period; excavations, undertaken in 1913 and 1963, have shown there to be several phases of occupation; the most important was of sixth-century date and included the construction of a timber-laced defensive wall surrounding the summit of the rocky hill. The extensive finds produced evidence of metalworking in bronze and iron, and the discovery of imported pottery indicates the trading contacts that west Scotland enjoyed at that time.

Pottery imported from continental workshops has been found both on sites of secular and, to a lesser extent, ecclesiastical, importance in northern and western Britain, including Dumbarton Rock, and Dunadd and Dunollie in Argyll. Several categories of imported ware, not all of which have so far been found in Scotland, have been identified, Class A being fine red table-ware, some with Christian symbols stamped on them, and Class B comprising wine or oil containers with distinctive ribbing or comb decoration, found in south-west England and south Wales, but also discovered on Dumbarton Rock. Class A was first recognized at the important monastic site of Tintagel in Cornwall; the wine or oil imported in the Class B amphorae may have been for use in the service of the mass, but sherds of this type have also been found in secular centres such as Garranes, Co. Cork and Degannwy, Caernarvonshire. While the dates and origin of these classes of vessel are still a matter for discussion, Class A may be considered to be of East Mediterranean and North Africa origin and to be of late fifth- to sixth-century date, and Class B to be of East Mediterranean and Black Sea origin and broadly of later fifth- to early seventh-century date. One fragment of red-slipped ware related to Class A and probably of North African origin, which has been found on Iona, is thought to date to the second half of the sixth century. Class C, found in Cornwall, is now thought to be medieval; Class D are small mixing vessels also in a grey ware, with a distinct spout for pouring, and have been discovered at Dunadd, Argyll, and Mote of Mark in Kirkcudbright. Although the origin and date of this style is not altogether clear, workshops in south and west France active in about the fifth and sixth centuries seem to be the most acceptable geographical and chronological suggestions. The most important category of material is known to archaeologists as Class E or E ware; drinking vessels, bowls and pitchers in the distinct wheel-made wares of this class have been found at several key sites of this period, including Mote of Mark in the south-west, Buston Crannog and Dumbarton Rock in Strathclyde, Dunadd, Dunollie and Kildalloig Dun in the territory of the Scots and Craig Phadrig and Clatchard Craig in Pictland. Such pottery implies that these sites were enjoying direct or indirect trade with western Gaul in fifth to early eighth centuries AD. Charles Thomas has rightly pointed out that French wines are more likely to have been traded in the cask rather than in pottery vessels, and it is possible that the pottery trade is an adjunct to some more important but intangible commerce such as this.

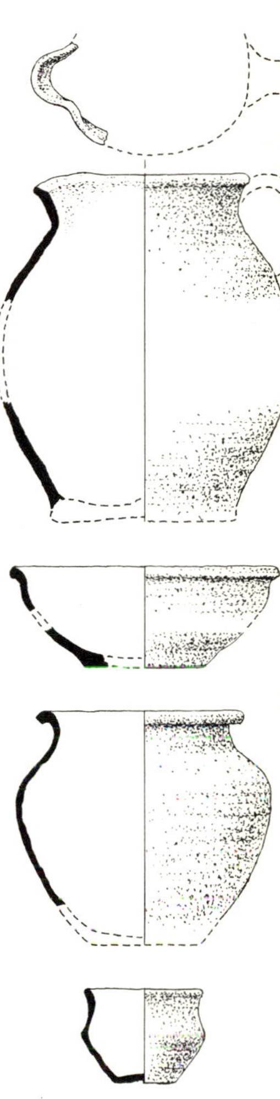

111 Imported pottery of Class E

The use of timber in construction is an important element on a number of sites, including hillforts, crannogs and palisaded works, the latter visible as crop-marks on aerial photographs. At Doon Hill, Dunbar, East Lothian, two timber halls were excavated by Brian Hope Taylor between 1964 and 1966; the earlier is a British hall dating to the second half of the sixth century, and the later, because of its similarity to the halls of Yeavering, Northumberland, belonged to the conquering Angles of the seventh century. The halls of both periods are enclosed within a timber palisade. The earlier hall is an important indication of the building traditions in timber of the Britons and demonstrates their considerable skills in carpentry. Measuring about 23m in length, it was built with the side-walls supported by substantial timber uprights, but the end-walls were made of squared timbers set in foundation trenches; there was a large compartment in the middle of the hall with smaller flanking rooms at either end. Some impression of the rich fittings in such halls may be gleaned from the epic poem, *The Gododdin* by Aneirin, which describes an unsuccessful British attack on the pagan Angles of Northumbria, who by the later sixth century were menacing their southern borders.

Sophisticated use of timber is also present in the construction or reconstruction of crannogs, particularly in south-west Scotland at Buston, Lochlee and Lochspouts in Ayrshire; the sequence of building or the stratification of the finds from these nineteenth-century excavations are not, however, always clear. The carefully constructed timber substructure at Buston was the foundation for a large circular house with a central hearth. Crannogs are often discovered in water-

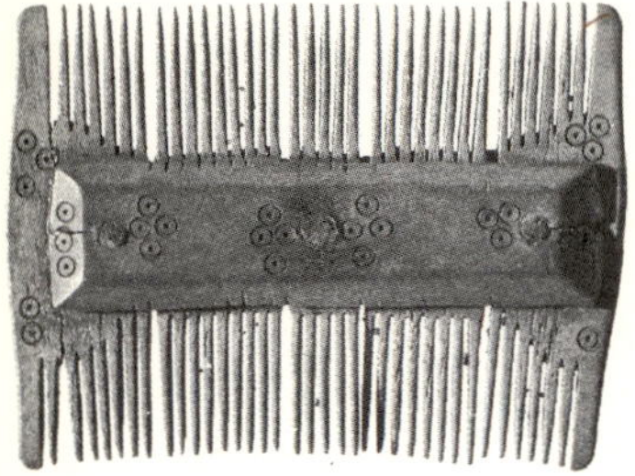

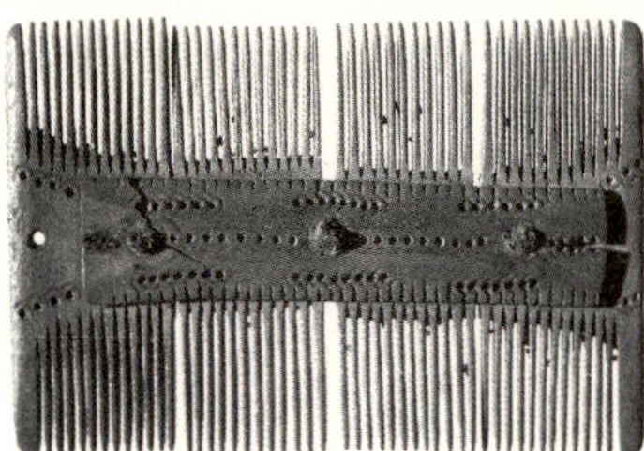

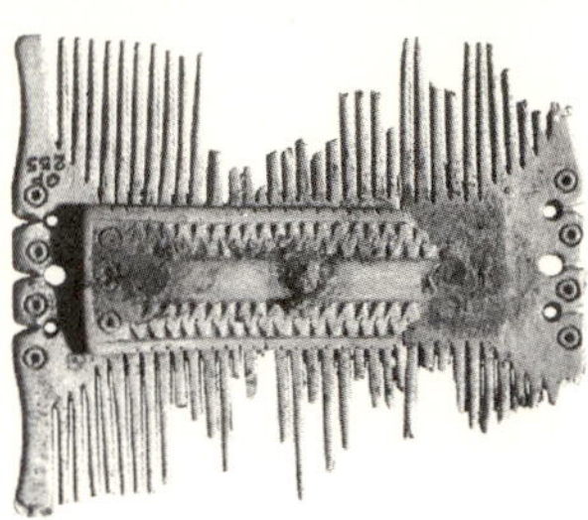

112 Bone combs: left and middle, Buston Crannog, Ayrshire; right, Dunadd, Argyll

113 Iron spearhead, knives and point; antler crossbow-nut, Buston Crannog, Ayrshire

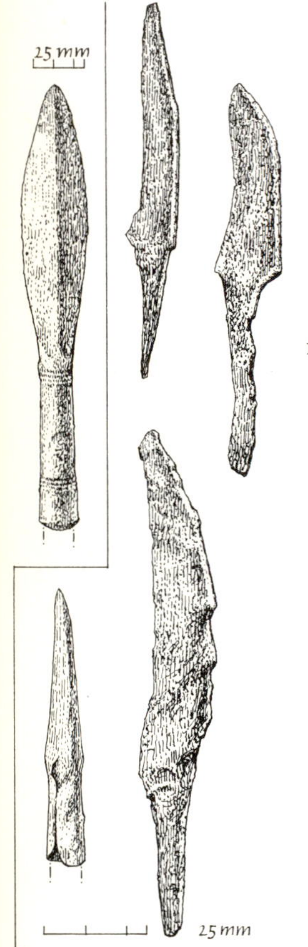

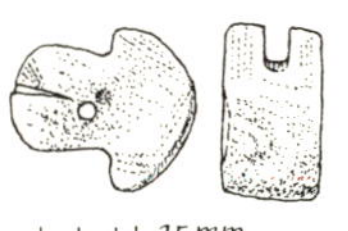

logged situations, and at Buston, for example, such conditions have preserved an unusually full range of artefacts including bone combs, pins, the nut of a cross-bow, iron knives, spearheads and arrowheads, as well as beads of jet and glass. The date of the occupation (or at least of one of the periods of occupation) is provided by imported pottery of Class E ware and by a forgery of an Anglo-Saxon coin of approximately the eighth century. Class E ware has also been reported from the crannog of Loch Glashan, Argyll, a structure probably constructed by the Dalriadic Scots; the extensive assemblage of wooden finds recovered (including bowls, troughs and paddles) strikingly illustrates the potential for preservation that such sites offer.

The British kingdoms appear to have been converted to Christianity from the fifth century, and the archaeological evidence thus provides information not only about defensive and settlement sites, such as Dumbarton, but also about ecclesiastical monuments and cemeteries. Galloway seems to have been converted by the mid-fifth century, and memorial stones dating to the late fifth or early sixth centuries from Yarrowkirk, Selkirkshire and the Catstane, near Edinburgh, attest the
114 presence of Christian communities in the eastern kingdoms. In Galloway the important centres of Whithorn and Kirkmadrine have memorial stones bearing inscriptions in Latin, dating from the late fifth to the seventh centuries.

The first saint whose influence in Scotland has been recorded by later historians is Ninian, a bishop with a see based at Whithorn, in Wigtownshire, probably active in the later fourth and early fifth centuries AD. It has recently been suggested that Ninian was not so much an evangelizing saint as pastor to an existing Christian flock in Galloway; although he may have undertaken missionary work in this area, wide-ranging travel within northern Scotland is not thought likely. The position of a bishop within the hierarchy of the church means that it is unthinkable that Ninian would have been sent to Whithorn, had an appropriate ecclesiastical framework not already been in existence. The early church in north Britain thus had an episcopal organization in a late Roman tradition, rather than one based on monasteries. Bede recorded that Ninian built a church of stone in a manner to which the Britons were not accustomed, but doubt has been cast on the precise meaning of his words. The stone foundation of a small chapel visible to the east of the present Priory at Whithorn is probably of seventh-century date or even later.

A sequence of ecclesiastical remains on the small tidal island of Ardwall, off the Kirkcudbright coast uncovered by Charles Thomas between 1964–5 begins with a series of extended inhumations which

114 Early Christian inscribed stone, Manor Water, Peeblesshire

may be as early as the late fifth century in origin. In the second period a small timber oratory or chapel was built on the site and further burials were added to the cemetery. The timber building was replaced, perhaps in the early eighth century, by a stone chapel associated with
further burials. A range of memorial stones and crosses was found on 115
this important site, including one probably dating to the mid-eighth century set up to a person called Cudgar; this name is of Germanic rather than Celtic origin and Thomas has linked its presence to the penetration of the Angles into the south-west.

Our knowledge of Kentigern (or Mungo), the patron saint of Strathclyde, who appears to have been active in the later sixth century and died in 612, comes from a *Life* written in the mid-twelfth century; the centre of his ministry is not known, but one possibility is that Kentigern was based at Govan where there is a concentration of monumental stone sculpture, admittedly of rather later date than the saint's activities. A more traditional site is Glasgow itself.

The spread of Christianity can be shown by the introduction of a new burial tradition – extended inhumation, unaccompanied by grave-goods, in a long cist or grave, usually oriented east and west with the head at the west end. In the absence of grave-goods it is difficult to suggest a date for such cemeteries, as long-cist burials occur both in earlier and in later contexts. However, cemeteries where the cists are

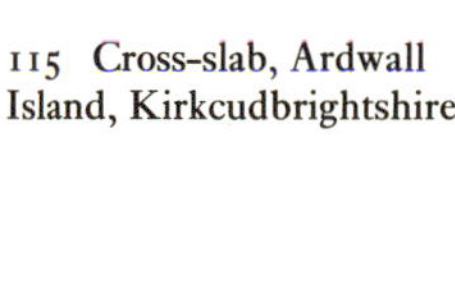

115 Cross-slab, Ardwall Island, Kirkcudbrightshire

116 Catstane, Midlothian, view by James Drummond, 1849

aligned east and west may be assumed to be of Early Christian date, and to represent the burial grounds of the small agricultural communities of the surrounding district. Some cemeteries are laid out in such regular lines that markers indicating the position of each grave must have existed, perhaps an upright stone with a simple incised
116–17 cross. The Catstane, near Edinburgh, standing to one side of a carefully laid out series of long cists, is of later fifth-century or early sixth-century date and bears a memorial inscription in Latin. The large number of long-cist cemeteries in the Lothians implies a considerable Christian presence there.

The Anglian advance into the south-east lowlands of Scotland from Northumbria led to the collapse of the British authority in the Lothians and eastern Borders; in AD 638 Edinburgh fell, and in AD 642 Stirling. North of the Forth, however, the Picts, after an initial defeat, held their ground, and King Bridei defeated a Northumbrian army at Nechtanesmere, near Dunnichen in Angus, in AD 685. The later history of the kingdom of Strathclyde is beyond the scope of this volume; it continued to play an important rôle in the politics of Scotland until the early eleventh century, when, with the end of its royal dynasty, the kingdom fell to the Scottish king Malcolm II and was granted to his grandson and heir, Duncan.

Angles

The invasion of the Angles, Saxons and Jutes is one of those 'turning-points' of English history known to every schoolboy; from a Scottish point of view the position is more complex. The advance of the Northumbrian Angles into the south-east Lowlands in the second quarter of the seventh century may not have been followed by intensive settlement, although doubtless the ruling British families fled, if they were able, to areas still held by British kings. But the evidence of history and of place-names shows how important was the Anglian presence in the south-east; archaeologically there is less to offer. At Doon Hill, Dunbar, East Lothian, a second timber hall overlying that already described, is almost identical in size and construction to seventh-century structures at Yeavering in Northumberland, and there is no doubt of its Anglian origin.

Both in the south-east and in the south-west, where the Angles gained control of the British kingdom of Rheged (an area round modern Carlisle) by marriage into the royal house, the most striking evidence of Anglian, or more properly Northumbrian, presence is in monumental sculpture. In the south-east the most notable pieces include cross-shafts from Aberlady, East Lothian, and Abercorn, West Lothian, and a slab from a shrine, now at Jedburgh Abbey. The symmetrical vine-scroll ornament with birds and animals intertwined on the Jedburgh fragment suggests a date in the late eighth or early ninth century. In the south-west, in Dumfriesshire, the sculptured cross at Ruthwell and the fragments of crosses at Hoddom help to

117 Catstane, Midlothian; part of the long-cist cemetery (scale in 50 cm divisions)

118–19 Ruthwell Cross, Dumfriesshire, details of scroll ornament and Mary washing Christ's feet

underline the international influences present in Northumbrian art. The Ruthwell Cross is probably one of the most important monuments of Dark Age Europe; it bears carving of a high order, including the
118–19 glorified Christ, Christ with Mary Magdalene washing his feet, and elaborate vine-scroll ornament with intertwined birds. In the margins there is a long runic inscription, forming parts of the *Dream of the Rood*, one of the most beautiful Anglo-Saxon religious poems, in which the story of the Crucifixion is told by the Cross. The Ruthwell Cross may be dated to the mid-eighth century. Rosemary Cramp has summarized the elements present in this magnificent Cross, 'where the explanatory Latin inscriptions with the figural panels combine in a great theological meditation on the recognition of the divinity and power of Christ, and the runic poem framing the animated scrolls emphasizes, with the birds and beasts in the vine, the relation of creation to God, and man's position in the hierarchy of creation. No other Cross illustrates so perfectly the intellectual background of Northumbrian Christianity.'

The archaeological evidence of the major Christian centres, however, remains slight. Bede recorded, for example, a monastery (and a bishop's seat) at Abercorn, to the west of Edinburgh, a monastery at

Old Melrose on the Tweed, but, in the absence of largescale excavations at such sites, their interpretation on the ground is uncertain. St Cuthbert entered monastic life at Melrose in the mid-seventh century, before moving with his abbot, in AD 664, to Lindisfarne, in Northumberland. Whithorn was the seat of a Northumbrian bishop, and Coldingham, in Berwickshire, was another important monastic site, but no structural remains that may be attributed to this period survive. While he was a monk at Melrose, Cuthbert is known to have visited Coldingham, which was a double-house of monks and nuns.

Although the archaeological evidence for the Angles, or Northumbrians, in Scotland is limited, the importance of Northumbrian elements in the art styles both of the Scots and the Picts is very considerable; the Northumbrian form of Christian practice was of more directly Roman origin than that of the Celtic church, and it was the Northumbrian form that was eventually adopted throughout northern Britain. The area between the Forth and the Tweed remained in Northumbrian hands until Lothian was ceded to Kenneth II of Scotland by Edgar in 973, and the River Tweed was finally established as the frontier in 1018 following Malcolm II's victory at Carham on the south bank of the river not far from Coldstream.

Scots

The Anglian advance into the south-east Lowlands of Scotland depended on the strength of their armies in the field; whereas naval ascendancy was the key to the occupation of much of Argyll by families from the territory of Dalriada (properly Dàl Riata) from north Antrim in Northern Ireland. By about AD 500 settlement in Argyll was well enough established for the transfer of the capital of Dalriada from Ireland to Scotland – again emphasizing their maritime supremacy. It was as raiders that such Scotti made their presence felt in the late Roman world, and the word Scotti was probably synonymous with pirates. There is no historical evidence of conflict in their occupation of Argyll, and it might be assumed that the scattered Iron Age communities represented by the small stone-walled defences lacked either the political cohesion or the sea-power to withstand the onslaught. On the other hand they may already have felt a close affinity with their near neighbours from Antrim.

As is also true of the Anglian incomers in the south-east, the archaeological evidence for the Scots is exceedingly scanty, but we are fortunate in that two historical accounts provide complementary view points on the early history and social organization of Dalriada. The *Senchus Fer nAlban* is a record of the genealogies of the royal house of Dalriada; the *Life of Columba*, by Adomnan, is more concerned with intimate and miraculous details of the religious leader's life than with the political milieu. Adomnan offers, however, insights into life at the court of the Pictish King Bridei, which was situated somewhere near Inverness, and also provides some of the detail that can help to explain the archaeological remains of the Celtic Church on Iona and other centres in Dalriada. The *Senchus Fer nAlban* gives a picture of the political organization of Scottish Dalriada in about the seventh century with three main families in control of various areas of Argyll – the kindred of Oengus Mor had the richest island closest to Antrim, Islay; Kintyre, along with Jura and the inner Firth of Clyde, was held by the kindred of Gabrán; Northern Argyll and its islands (including Colonsay) and mainland Lorn were under the sway of the kindred of Loairn. Four strongholds are associated for historical reasons with Dalriada – Dunaverty, possibly Tarbert, Dunadd and Dunollie, but only at the last two has archaeological material of mid-first millennium date been found; many of the duns of the Atlantic seaboard must have been occupied by the intrusive leaders. The successful political take-over by the Irish carpet-baggers was to set a pattern on Scottish history that continued until the '45 – a pattern of kinship and military (or more appropriately naval) obligation.

The political history of the Scots is not our concern here, though it is clear that their more adventurous leaders undertook expeditions, not always successfully, to the east and south-east of Argyll into the territories of the Picts and Britons. The Picts may also on occasion have had some political overlordship over the Scots. It is worth noting one difference, however, in the social structures of the two peoples; the Scots favoured succession within a kinship group, whereas the Picts had a tradition of matrilinear succession. In the latter system, a man was succeeded by his younger brother or by his sister's son. It may be that originally the intention of both systems was to avoid the succession of minors. In 843 the kingship of both peoples became vested in the same man, Kenneth son of Alpin. Kenneth had been king of Dalriada for some two years, and it is not impossible that he had to eliminate other claimants to the Pictish throne before he was able to assume power. He established his court at Scone and founded a royal dynasty that forms the basis of the British monarchy today.

An important result of the Dalriadic settlement was the introduction of that strand of the Celtic language spoken in Ireland (Goedelic) into Scotland; this forms the basis for the Gaelic language spoken in the west of Scotland to this day, its expansion outside Dalriada belonging to a period beyond the limits of this volume. The second linguistic innovation was the use of the ogam script – a method of transcribing the Roman alphabet into a series of strokes through a central line. One inscription, dating to the seventh century or later, which may still be transliterated, is incised on the angle of a standing stone on the island of Gigha, off Kintyre. The Picts also adopted this form of writing but no Pictish ogam is completely understandable.

The archaeological evidence for the Scots in Argyll mirrors the two main spheres of their influence, the one military, the other religious. Excavation at Dunadd and Dunollie, two of their main centres, has provided datable material belonging to this period. The Scots appear to have had no characteristic material culture of their own, and thus these objects of broadly sixth- to ninth-century date found at Dunadd and Dunollie form part of a wider archaeological framework already discussed. Many of the small stone-walled forts of the Iron Age may have been refurbished by the Scottish invaders, though this can only be determined by excavation; in a dun at Kildalloig, near Campbeltown in Kintyre, for example, sherds of Class E ware and a glass dumb-

bell bead comparable to beads from the crannog at Lagore, Co. Meath, have been found. At Dunollie, where the remains are partly masked by the fifteenth-century castle, Leslie Alcock has discovered iron knives, bone combs and pins, and imported pottery all belonging to the seventh to eighth century AD.

120 Dunadd, Argyll

Dunadd, situated in what is now Mid Argyll, has been famous since it was identified as one of the seats of the Dalriadic Scots; standing aloof above the flat valley-floor of the River Add, strategically between Loch Fyne and the Sound of Jura, the rock stack must surely have been an important fortress from Iron Age times. The excavations of the fort, undertaken in the early years of this century and again in 1929, were not of a high standard, and many problems of interpretation remain, including it must be admitted the absence of a well-dated Iron Age occupation-horizon, apart from an iron axe or adze, and a number of sherds of Roman pottery, which might also, of course, belong to a later period. It seems likely that most of the surviving 120

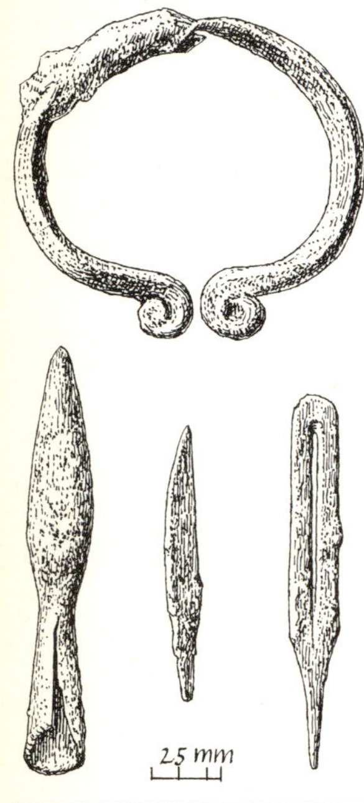

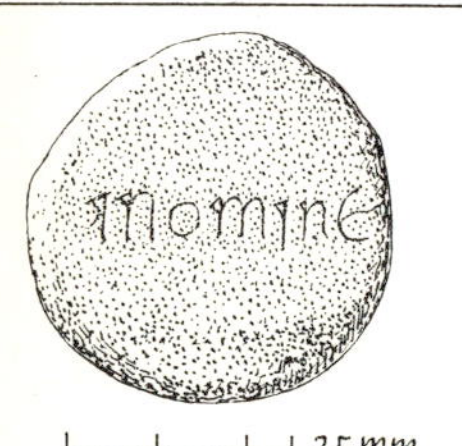

121 Iron ring, spearhead, knife, slotted object and inscribed stone disc, Dunadd, Argyll

defences were built by the Scots; a stone wall encloses the north-west peak, which was further protected by walls at a lower level. A massive dry-stone wall takes in the rather lower flat top of the hill; this was entered along a natural defile in the rock, which must have been provided with stout timber doors. In the main enclosure the excavators found traces of internal walling, and terraces and platforms, still visible today, may have been the foundations for timber halls. On a saddle just below the summit are rock-cut features that are said to have played a part in the inauguration of the Dalriadan kings, though we know that, in 574, Aedán was ordained by St Columba on Iona. The act of inauguration of kings is an accepted facet of Celtic tradition, and the rock-cut 'footprint' and basin at Dunadd may possibly have been used in such rituals. An incised boar and an ogam inscription complete the list of early markings on the rock face; the boar is a symbol current in Pictland, but the carving is not quite in this style and, if it did represent defiant Pictish grafitti, it would, as Alcock has pointed out, surely have been obliterated. The ogam is unintelligible–a characteristic certainly of Pictish inscriptions. The finds recovered from the excavations included sherds of Class D and Class E wares, handled crucibles, iron knives, spearheads and other objects, bone combs and a range of stone implements, including rotary querns and whetstones.

It is possible that St Columba visited Dunadd from Iona, for Adomnan's *Life* records that he went to the *caput regionis* (the most important place in the district), perhaps Dunadd, where he met a ship from Gaul. The account of this visit is a good example of his narrative style: just after the threshing of the grain Columba had calmed a distressed follower by explaining the reason for his unhappiness. 'In this hour sulphurous flame has been poured down from heaven upon a city of the Roman dominion within the borders of Italy; close upon three thousand men, not counting the women and children, have perished, and before the present year is ended, the Gallic sailors arriving from the province of Gaul, will tell you the same.' It was with the same follower that Columba went to the *caput regionis* where the master and sailors of a ship recently arrived did indeed tell them the same story. It is within such a mercantile context that the discovery of the Gaulish pottery on Dunadd becomes understandable; the presence of a Christian community with a knowledge of writing at Dunadd is indicated by the discovery of a small stone disc inscribed with the words 'in nomine' – in the name (of the Lord).

The arrival of Columba and his twelve followers in Iona in AD 563 had a political origin, for the saint felt that he should leave Ireland following his part in the battle of Cùl Dremne. But he chose a remote island, rather than a situation closer to any political centre in Dalriada, for the foundation of what must have been a contemplative religious community. A personal spiritual pilgrimage is more likely to have been among Columba's reasons for leaving Ireland than any sense of missionary zeal among the Picts and Scots, though he had certainly already founded one monastery in Ireland in Derry (and was to found another at Durrow). In their introduction to the *Life of Columba*, A. O. and M. O. Anderson emphasize that Columba's was not a 'penitential pilgrimage among an alien people. It was a monastic life

122 Abbey and *vallum*, Iona, Argyll

in a place remote from centres of human population, and in the company of some friends and kinsmen chosen for their ideals of a spiritual life.' He was making a journey that would not have been undertaken suddenly nor without detailed preparation. John Bannerman has stressed, however, the support that Columba provided for Aedán, king of Dalriada in the last quarter of the sixth century, from the ordination of the king on Iona, to his role as advisor to Aedán at the Convention of Druim Cett. A close connection between the monastery of Iona and the rulers of Dalriada was thus established.

What would the Columban monastery on Iona have looked like and are there any traces still visible today? It is ironic that most visitors miss the main surviving feature of the Celtic monastery on Iona, the surrounding bank and ditch or *vallum*; the remains of this earthwork were first identified on Iona by O. G. S. Crawford in 1933, and can be traced partly on the ground and partly as a crop-mark on aerial photographs. The substantial nature of the rampart and ditch, which was in 122 part dug into the solid rock, shows that the *vallum* dates from a time when the monastery was already well established for in terms of work-effort the digging of this boundary might be compared to the construction of a large henge monument or hillfort. In early Celtic monasteries such an enclosure, which may be rounded as at Nendrum, Co. Down, or rectilinear as at Iona, is not a defensive feature, but rather defines the holy area, and is thus an important legal demarcation. Within the *vallum* the focus must have been a timber church, of which there are now no traces. The wood and wattle cells of the individual clerics, the communal buildings, such as the refectory, *scriptorium*, and the guest house, would be laid out within the enclosure; agricultural buildings, barns and perhaps a corn-drying kiln would be outside the holy area. Many of the stories told by Adomnan about Columba illustrate the importance of the farming routine by the monastic community. The present-day visitor viewing the Benedictine Abbey may find it difficult to envisage the scattered timber buildings of late sixth-century Iona, but, standing above the eastern plain of the island, he may think of

123 Monastery complex, Brough of Deerness, Orkney

124 Beehive cells, Eileach an Naoimh, Garvellachs, Argyll

Columba in Adomnan's moving account, as he, close to his death, 'climbed a small hill overlooking the monastery and stood on its summit for a while. And as he stood he raised both hands, and blessed his monastery . . . After these words, he descended from that little hill, returned to the monastery, and sat in the hut, writing a psalter.'

It is perhaps now easier to evoke the joy of natural things that was so important to the contemplative life of a Celtic monastery on the western coasts of Iona than on parts of the east, but even more isolated and windswept islands and headlands were favoured as retreats for individual monks. In the northern islands of Scotland a large number of hermitages have been identified containing the huts of a group of clerics; one of the most striking of such sites is on the Brough of Deerness in Orkney, where the settlement is on a now detached rock- 123
stack high above the pounding sea. Smaller and more precipitous rocks may have been favoured for solitary contemplation. The best surviving example of a stone-built cell, perhaps belonging to a cleric of the Celtic Church, is on the remote island of Eileach an Naoimh, 124
one of the Garvellach group to the north of Jura; but like so many apparently simple stone structures, its date and context are not known.

Iona shared in the cultural milieu that created the Book of Kells; it is indeed possible that the book was written in the Iona *scriptorium* around AD 800, at a time when the monastery was already experiencing raids from the Vikings, though other centres have also been suggested. Monumental crosses of similar date, St John's Cross and St Martin's Cross, are striking examples of the skills in planning and execution of the monastic craftsmen. The sculpture of St John's Cross finds close parallels in the ornamentation of the Book of Kells; Pictish sculpture, too, may have provided a source of inspiration for the decoration of this book.

In the middle of the ninth century the portable treasures of the monastery, including the relics of Columba himself, were divided between other Columban houses, probably as a result of pressure from the Viking raiders; and the Book of Kells was probably carried to Kells in Ireland during this period. The crosses, however, still stand as testimony to the artistic vitality of Iona. The objects dispersed to safer monastic houses may have included the Monymusk Reliquary, known as the Brecbennoch of St Columba, which was later housed for a time in the Abbey of Arbroath and was carried at the Battle of Bannockburn; the reliquary, one of the greatest treasures of the Scottish nation, is a small wooden box (about 100mm long and 90mm high) with a hinged gabled lid and bronze and silver casing, further decorated with mounts in-filled with interlaced ornament and enamel. One of the bronze terminals of the leather strap, by which it would have been hung round the bearer's neck still survives, and is elaborately decorated in enamel. A date for the fashioning of the reliquary following the translation of the saint, sometime around AD 700, is more probable than the period of his burial on Iona in 597, but the historical sources are silent about what the reliquary actually contained. Another of the objects which may have been transferred from Iona at this time is the psalter known as the Cathach of St Columba, which in historical times became the battle talisman of the O'Donnell family. The psalter is thought to have been copied by Columba himself, and one tradition associated with it is that it was a disagreement over the copying that led to the battle of Cùl Dremne and thus to Columba's decision to leave Ireland.

The political distinctions that have been made between Britons, Angles and Scots have not, as we have seen, been mirrored in their cultural assemblages, and the interlocking influences of Northumbrian and Celtic Christianity and Pictish idiosyncracy form one of the most intractable archaeological and art-historical problems of the next chapter. The distinctions are implied by peopling those geographical areas known from historical sources to have been occupied by the different groups, with Britons or Scots as appropriate; this is clearly an uncertain archaeological method as their limits are not well defined, and some types of site (for example 'nuclear' forts and crannogs) have distributions which cut across such political 'boundaries'. Material culture can, however, help to indicate broad contemporaneity between sites in different regions – imported pottery of D and E ware is a good example – thus emphasizing the importance of trade.

8
The Pictish Kingdom

At first sight, the Picts are easy to identify in the archaeological record; the wealth and individuality of their stone sculpture makes them the best known historical people of early Scotland. New symbol stones, or fragments of them, are still found almost every year, and two small museums are devoted to Pictish monuments at Meigle and St Vigeans. Yet the Picts also remain the least understood historical people, and their abundant sculpture masks the difficulties that archaeologists experience in the positive identification of the rest of Pictish material culture. It is a sad fact that some of the myths created about the Picts through ignorance by classical and medieval authors are still perpetuated even today: the favourite is probably the notion put about by the anonymous twelfth-century *Historia Norvegiae* that the Picts were the size of pygmies and lived underground. Pictish archaeology became a growth area in the 1970s, however, and new information gained primarily by excavation is helping to place the Picts in their true context.

The identification of material attributable to the historical Picts depends upon their chronological and geographical distribution as defined from written sources, place-name studies and sculptured stones. The name *Picti*, 'Painted Ones', first appears in Eumenius' Panegyric of AD 297, and on this basis the Pictish period is taken to begin around AD 300. In broad political terms, the Picti appear to be an amalgam of the two tribes, the Caledonii and the Maeatae, described by Cassius Dio as being in control of the lands to the north of the Antonine Wall in the early third century. The Verona List of AD 313 mentions the Picts and the Caledonians separately, but this is the last historical reference to the latter, and their political transformation into Picts may be assumed to have been complete early in the fourth century. Indeed a reference in 310 to 'Caledones and other Picts' implies that the Caledonians were already regarded as a kind of Pict. The Pictish kingdom came to a formal end in AD 843, when it was united with Dalriada under the Scottish king, Kenneth MacAlpin, and Pictish traditions seem to have been obliterated, with the possible exception of some areas of church and civil government. By the end of the ninth century, even the name of the Picts had vanished from contemporary records: only Kenneth's brother Donald and his sons Constantine and Aed are described as *rex Pictorum*.

The geographical distribution of the Picts was wide, although the heartlands of the kingdom were in eastern Scotland; in effect, Pictish territory included all the lands to the north of the Forth and Clyde rivers, with the exception after about AD 500 of the area in the south-west that had been taken over by the Scots. Place-name studies reinforce the evidence of written records about the area of the Pictish kingdom, most notably in the distribution and interpretation of place-names incorporating the Pictish element *pit*. With few outliers, about three hundred such names are confined to eastern Scotland, north of the Forth and south of Easter Ross. The element *pit* with which all these names begin is derived from the Pictish word *pett*, the closest counterpart of which is the Gaulish word *petia*, meaning 'a share, a piece'; the same meaning is assumed for *pett*, 'a share of land' or 'a piece of land'. Most of these *pit*-names have Gaelic second elements, as in Pitcarmick or 'Cormac's share' and Pitcog, meaning 'share of the fifth part' from Gaelic *coig*, 'five'. This indicates a bilingual background to the names, and they are thought to date from the ninth and tenth centuries, when Gaelic-speaking Scots were settling down amongst the Picts after the union of 843.

Despite their late date, *pit*-names are vivid evidence of the populous areas of Pictland, and the coincident distribution of the monuments known as Pictish symbol stones demonstrates the validity of this evidence even in the heyday of the Pictish kingdom. *Pit*-names are not found, however, in the far north of Pictland, which fell to the Norsemen rather than to the Scots, but here the presence of symbol stones and other elements of Pictish culture, together with the historical evidence, identify the northern mainland and the Northern Isles as Pictish. Symbol stones are by far the most numerous and distinctive class of artefact that can be attributed to the Picts.

Pictish art

The artistic heritage of the Picts in sculptured stones and in metalwork is one of the most enduring contributions to Scottish culture of any early peoples; but the legacy is made all the more puzzling as we do not today understand the meaning that the monumental stones were
125 intended to convey, and the symbols carved on such stones throughout Pictland can now be appreciated only as semi-abstract or decorative art. The stones have fascinated archaeologists and art historians for over a century; they are also some of the most exciting field monuments to visit as they contain rich figural detail and elaborate patterns. Several stones have weathered severely in recent decades and wisely more and more are being resited under cover or in small local collections. The stones provide not only insights into what the Picts looked like and aspects of their day-to-day life, but also illustrate the different strands of influence and tradition that made up Pictish culture.

About 250 stones with symbols survive, doubtless only a small proportion of the original number, and the catalogue and discussion of them published in 1903 by J. R. Allen and Joseph Anderson is still used by scholars as a basis for the classification of the stones. Allen distinguished three main classes of Early Christian monuments in

Scotland: Class I are erratic boulders or roughly prepared slabs, which bear groups of incised or pecked symbols; Class II are more carefully finished slabs, on which a cross as well as symbols have been carved; Class III is a more disparate group of rather later date on which the cross alone has been executed.

Some of the symbols are clear depictions of every-day objects – the mirror and comb symbol for example; others are abstract designs and
are given purely descriptive names – a crescent and V-rod, double disc 126
and Z-rod for example. Animals, real and fantastic, fish and 'serpent' 127
representations also abound. The distribution of Class I stones includes north-east Scotland, Easter Ross and east Sutherland, with a scatter in Fife, Orkney, Shetland and the Western Isles. The symbols on the stones are disposed in such a way that there is no doubt that they are making a statement, which may have been obvious to all Pictish passers-by, rather in the way that advertisements without words are so often clear to us. Charles Thomas has made a thought-provoking attempt to suggest what some of these statements might be. Stones with a single animal symbol (and virtually no other type of symbol appears alone) might indicate the boundaries of the territory of a group

125 Symbol stone, Newton, Aberdeenshire; dumb-bell, serpent and Z-rod symbols

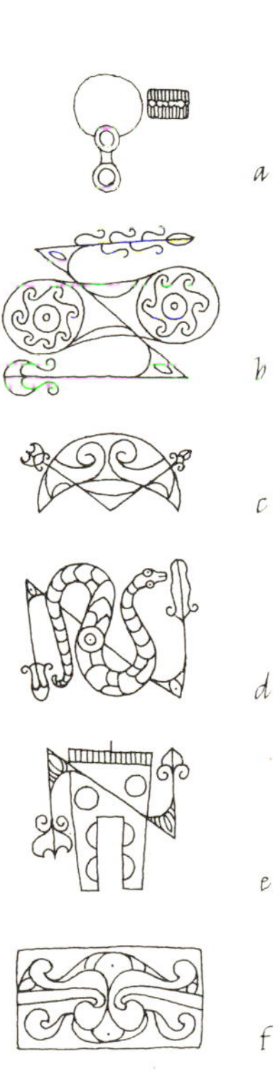

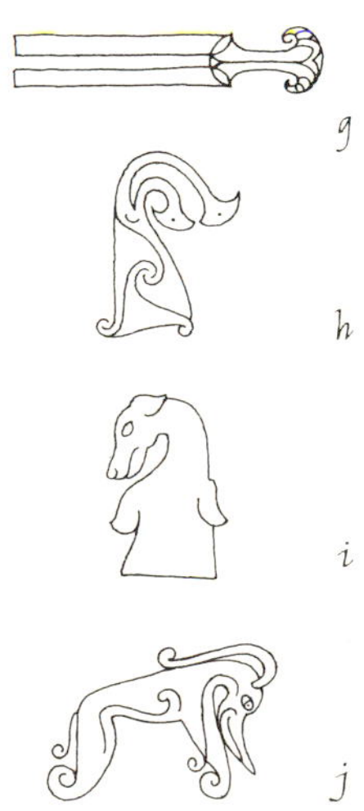

126 Pictish symbols: a, mirror and comb; b, double-disc and Z-rod; c, crescent and V-rod; d, serpent and Z-rod; e, notched-rectangle and Z-rod; f, rectangle; g, tuning-fork; h, flower; i, 'dog's-head'; j, 'Pictish beast' or 'swimming elephant'

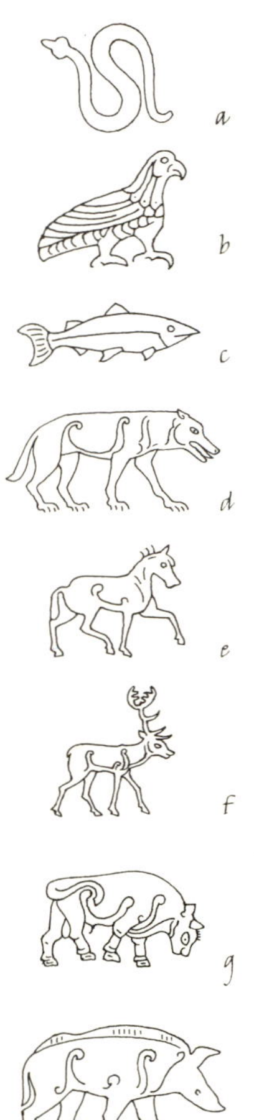

127 Naturalistic symbols: a, serpent; b, eagle; c, fish; d, wolf; e, horse; f, stag; g, bull; h, boar

128 Pictish symbol stone, Dunrobin, Sutherland; fish, tuning-fork and mirror and comb symbols

of people. The slabs with bull symbols from Burghead, Morayshire, might perhaps have been carved there for future use as territorial markers. Stones with between two and four symbols Thomas sees as memorial stones bearing an indication of the person commemorated and perhaps the relationship of the person who caused the stone to be put up. In an anthropological assessment of the symbol stones, Anthony Jackson has put forward the suggestion that they commemorate political and marriage alliances between separate family groups. Isabel Henderson has speculated that the symbolism on both Class I and Class II stones indicates territorial influence and ownership, with the cross of Class II merely an affirmation of the Christian faith by an ecclesiastical institution or a devout landowner. While such interpretations have not been unchallenged, and it is fair to say that we shall never actually know what the stones mean, they indicate the sort of message that the symbols may have been intended to convey. Thomas saw the origin of some of the symbolism in motifs of later Celtic art and in the abstraction of more familiar objects of the Celtic warrior. Isabel

Henderson has suggested that the place of origin for symbol stones of Class I should be sought on the shores of the Moray and Dornoch Firths. The composition and workmanship of the stones in this area are in general of a higher order than those further south. The flagstones which were employed in the north were also more suited to carving than, for example, the intractable Aberdeenshire granite. In an important typological study of the decoration of the crescent and V-rod symbol, Robert Stevenson has shown that it is in Sutherland and in Orkney that the earliest examples may be found, while devolved symbols occur in the north-east of Scotland. The skill of the Sutherland artists can be seen on such stones as that from Dunrobin, with a 128
fish, a 'tuning-fork' symbol and mirror and comb symbol. Examples from other areas include the Newton Stone, Aberdeenshire, and the stone from Dunnichen, Angus. The widespread distribution of broadly similar symbols from the Western Isles, Orkney and Shetland down the east coast to Fife, without any clear precursors in any area, indicates the political cohesion of the Pictish kingdom at this time embracing, as it must have done, groups of peoples, who, in earlier periods, can be shown to have been archaeologically distinct.

The lively animal and bird figures find close parallels in decorated ecclesiastical manuscripts, such as the Book of Durrow, dating broadly to the second half of the seventh century, and a date within the seventh century is usually put forward for Class I stones as well. One of the symbols, the formalized animal known as the 'swimming elephant' or 'Pictish beast', may also be related to such entendrilled animals as those on the Monymusk Reliquary mentioned in the last chapter. As so often in discussing the art of this period, the direction of such influences or contacts remains a matter of opinion; Henderson sees the art of the manuscripts as providing one of the sources for Pictish inspiration, but she also suggests that the style of the eagle, the symbol of St John, in a manuscript now in Cambridge (Corpus Christi College MS 197) has been derived from a Pictish model. In contrast, Julian Brown envisages the manuscript art as providing the inspiration for the naturalism of the Pictish carvings, but he would favour the production of the Book of Kells in a *scriptorium* in eastern Scotland under Northumbrian influence, rather than on Iona or in Northumbria itself. The stones of Class I are the archaeological evidence of an artistically aware Christian milieu in Pictland; it is probably fair to say that, symbols apart, most art historians would see the Picts as absorbing and adapting motifs from other sources. Parallels with manuscript art also raise the possibility that the stones too might have been elaborately picked out with colour, but no evidence for pigment now survives. Symbols on small silver objects from Norrie's Law, Fife, have, however, been highlighted by the use of red enamel.

129 Pictish cross-slab, Meigle no. 5, Perthshire; 'swimming elephant' and mirror symbols

Although symbol stones may be envisaged as memorial stones commemorating a deceased person, very few have been found in association with a grave, and none can be shown to stand at the head of an interment. The stone from Dunrobin illustrated above was discovered in 1854 as one of three cover-slabs of a cist containing the inhumation burials of two adult men accompanied by a corroded iron object. If the stone were carved at the time of the burial it is clear from its position that it was never meant to be seen; if its use as a cover-slab is secondary, the association with the burials is purely fortuitous. In 1942 a delicately incised stone, decorated with crescent and V-rod, 'beast', mirror and comb symbols, was found lying across an irregularly constructed cist at Golspie, in Sutherland, but again this may not have been its original position. More recently, at Garbeg, Inverness-shire, Dunrobin, Sutherland, and Wattenen, Caithness, symbol stones have been found on cairns, but firm association between the stones and burials cannot unfortunately be demonstrated.

Pictish symbols have also been discovered at the mouth of a cave at Covesea, Morayshire, and on the walls of caves at East Wemyss in Fife, but their lay-out is random and we cannot guess what message they were intended to convey. At Covesea, crude crescent and V-rods, 'mirror-case', and fish symbols have been incised on to the sandstone walls of the cave; at East Wemyss the symbols are confused by later graffitti, but fish and double disc motifs are amongst those that can still be made out. The talismanic significance of the symbols is suggested by their appearance on a number of portable objects including a silver pin and silver plaques from Norrie's Law, Fife, and the terminal of the silver chain from Whitecleuch, Lanarkshire. Such pieces are, however, of little help in pinning down the date of the symbol-bearing objects themselves any more firmly. Sadly, too, where symbol-bearing objects have been found in the course of excavations, their context has not been precisely recorded. From the Broch of Burrian, North Ronaldsay, Orkney, comes a small ox-bone with a crescent and V-rod incised on one face and a 'circular disc with notched rectangle' symbol on the other; this is probably a playing man. Such finds are presumably from a secondary phase of occupation of the broch. From Jarlshof, in Shetland, a small circular piece of sandstone with a double-disc and Z-rod symbol, perhaps also part of a game, is a reminder that Shetland, like Orkney, was part of the Pictish kingdom until the arrival of the Vikings.

The cross-slabs of Class II demonstrate the skills of the Pictish sculptors in composition; the distribution of the stones falls in two main areas, a northern concentration in Easter Ross and the adjacent Moray coast, and a southern spread in Angus and Perthshire. The red
130 sandstone slabs of Angus, at Aberlemno and Glamis for example, provided the carvers with an ideal medium for relief expression not only of the crosses, but also of a series of elaborate scenes taken from both Christian and secular sources. The crosses invariably dominate one side of the stone; elaborate interlace emphasizes the shape of the cross with bold relief decoration. The art of the insular manuscripts finds parallels in many of the interlace-, knot- and fret-patterns of the stones and a date within the eighth century is usually accepted for the flowering of Class II. The symbols, often in relief, tend to lose the distinctive linear quality of earlier examples, such as the Dunrobin stone mentioned above, and to become fields for magnificent pattern-
131–2 ing in their own right. The back of the stone at the roadside at Aberlemno illustrates several of these aspects of Class II; prominent crescent and V-rod and double disc and Z-rod symbols have been carved above a hunting scene in which there are four horsemen, three

130 Pictish cross-slab, Glamis, Angus

131–2 Pictish cross-slab, Aberlemno churchyard, Angus; front with cross, 'gripping beasts' and hippocamps, and back with military scenes, cauldron, and notched rectangle and Z-rod symbols

men on foot (two of whom have hunting horns), three stags and three hounds. A more formal hunting scene, but one which is usually considered to be earlier in date, is found on the stone from Hilton of Cadboll, Ross and Cromarty; the bounding dogs of the Cadboll stone provide a sense of excitement in the chase not apparent in the hunters themselves. The Cadboll stone has two side-panels of vine-scroll of Anglian derivation, one of the few stones with Pictish symbols to be so decorated, but the liana-like vine has lost the more intimate character of the Anglian original. Animals, for example at St Vigeans and Moncrieffe House, play an important role in the decoration of Class II stones. The battle scene on the back of the stone in Aberlemno churchyard, an early Class II stone carved in low relief, is a particularly exciting and vigorous overall composition.

The complex range of Christian iconography shows the originality of Pictish sculptors in presenting their own interpretation of a Biblical scene and their use of manuscript patterns. The little scene of Samson killing a Philistine with the jawbone of an ass on the stone from Inchbrayock, Angus, is a distinctively Pictish creation. Representa-

133 Pictish slab, Invergowrie, Angus; horseman with drinking horn

tions of King David as a hunter, warrior or harpist on a number of stones have been discussed by Cecil Curle and Isabel Henderson, and the parallels with manuscript art and other portable objects, such as the Franks Casket, fully explored.

Some of the most assured pieces of Pictish sculpture make use of unusually high relief; the tomb-shrine at St Andrews, Fife, and the stone at the roadside at Aberlemno and the cross-slab from Nigg, Ross and Cromarty, are examples of what Robert Stevenson has described as Early Boss Style, dating to the late eighth or early ninth centuries. The St Andrews tomb-shrine stands apart by its very nature from the rest of Pictish art; originally it comprised four corner-posts, two side- and two end-panels, and a roof. Now only three corner-posts, one side- and one end-panel, and the fragment of another end-panel survive. The high quality of the carving, illustrating scenes from the life of David, makes this one of the most important pieces of art in Pictland. Almost three-quarters of one panel is taken up with a hunting scene of considerable vitality and detail; David the huntsman, 134
attacked by a ferocious rampant lion, defends himself with his sword.

134 St Andrews tomb-shrine, Fife; detail showing David the hunter and David and the lion

135 Pictish cross-slab, Nigg, Ross and Cromarty; detail of front showing Boss style

The other quarter shows David, a classical figure with flowing robes, his hands on the jaws of a lion rending them apart and with a fleecy sheep at his shoulder to confirm the identification. Henderson has suggested specific parallels in Mercian art of the later eighth century for the sarcophagus, and for the Hilton of Cadboll and Nigg stones. Portable ivories or silver dishes of oriental manufacture and textiles have also been put forward as possible sources of inspiration.

135 The stone at Nigg is carved with a central cross, flanked by elaborate panels in high relief and surmounted by a scene of St Paul and St Anthony in the desert. On the back there is a central panel, containing several representations of David, as well as side-panels of interlace and key-pattern. The bosses, which form such an important part of the decoration on the front of the stone, are covered with spiral ornament, key-pattern and interlace work. The use of snakes in the decoration is a feature found both at Nigg and at St Andrews. One of the domed objects from the St Ninian's Isle hoard in Shetland is covered with very similar spiral ornament to two of the bosses on the Nigg stone; several of the animals found on stones at Aberlemno and Meigle, for example, may also be compared to the decoration on the silver bowls from this hoard.

The political strength of the Pictish kingdom was by the eighth century probably situated in eastern Scotland with centres in Perthshire and Angus, where the results of artistic patronage may readily be seen. The continuation of the strong artistic tradition in Easter Ross and southern Sutherland is demonstrated by several magnificent stones, and this area was clearly receptive to influences from far afield. There may have been several major ecclesiastical centres in the north, including perhaps Tarbat, near Portmahomack, in Easter Ross, where

parts of ten cross-slabs have been found, and Kineddar, near Elgin. One fragment from Tarbat is decorated with spiral ornament described by Allen as perhaps the closest of any British stone to the best Irish manuscript decoration; another has scroll-work very similar to that from Hilton of Cadboll.

Stones in the Late Boss Style, dating from the mid- and later ninth century, after the take-over of Pictland by the Scots, include that from Shandwick, Ross and Cromarty, where Stevenson describes the style as having 'run to seed', and St Madoes and Fowlis Wester in Perthshire; the over-elaboration of the symbols, characteristic of this style, is illustrated at Rosemarkie, Ross and Cromarty.

Pictish society

The name *Picti*, 'Painted Ones', implies that the Picts practised body painting or tattooing, and several classical sources refer to such a habit, but the evidence is thought to be unreliable. We cannot know, in the absence of their own written records, whether the Picts called themselves *Picti* or whether they had their own name. Neither Adomnan nor Bede mention personal tattooing, but it is not impossible that some tradition of painted designs, personal or otherwise, lay behind the emergence of Pictish art; the symbols carved on stones may well have been picked out in colour, just as those incised on the silver plaques from Norrie's Law are emphasized by red enamel.

The only surviving written source attributable to the Picts is their king-list, which exists in the form of several Latin manuscripts, which are based on an original list probably compiled in the ninth century in a Pictish monastery. Two notes on the foundation of a church at Abernethy in Perthshire appear in the lists, and it is possible that the original list was compiled there, based on older manuscripts. The list names the kings of the Picts, together with the lengths of their reigns; the first king whose name appears independently in other sources is Brude, son of Maelchon, also spelt Bridei. Apart from this simple list of kings, we know of the Picts only from sources outside Pictland, such as the Irish annals or the writings of Adomnan and Bede. Adomnan mentions two occasions on which Columba needed an interpreter in his dealings with the Picts, and it may be that such difficulties in communication led to some of the myths about them. They appear to have spoken two languages, one a form of Celtic (P-Celtic) and the other a non-Indo-European language in which the unintelligible Pictish ogam inscriptions were written. This unknown language is thought to be that spoken in prehistoric Scotland before the arrival of the Celts, which then survived alongside the Celtic tongue.

It is clear from Adomnan that in the sixth century Pictish society included a class of magicians or pagan priests, but we know nothing about pagan Pictish religion: an amalgam of common Celtic beliefs and pre-Celtic ideas must be envisaged. Kenneth Jackson has demonstrated that the titles of two officials of later medieval Scotland originated in Pictish times: the *mormaer*, who acted as the king's deputy within his own territorial area and collected the royal revenue, and whose high rank was hereditary, and the *toiseach*, who was general of the royal army in the field. There must also have been a Pictish 'admiral of the fleet', for their navy appears to have been of considerable size: even allowing for exaggeration, the reference in the Irish annals to five hundred Pictish ships lost after a great battle implies that the navy was an important weapon to the Picts. The Irish annals record an attack on the Orkneys by Bridei in 682, for which an efficient navy would have been necessary. Adomnan mentions the presence of a *regulus* or regional king from the Orkneys at the court of Bridei at the time of Columba's visit; this Orcadian leader may well have been a *mormaer*, for even in the sixth century it would seem that Pictland was ruled overall by a single king. The Irish annals refer to a 'king of Atholl', another regional leader or *mormaer*, who would be answerable to the king of the Picts. The standardized appearance of Pictish symbols imply not only an organized society but also that the same authority was dominant over the whole of the kingdom. Columba's royal host, Bridei, son of Maelchon, lived in a fortress near the River Ness according to Adomnan, and a base in the Inverness area would be a good central location in a kingdom that stretched from the Forth to the Northern Isles. The forts at Burghead in Morayshire and Craig Phadrig in Inverness-shire have both been cited as candidates for Bridei's royal seat, but excavation at the latter site has shown its ramparts to have been in poor shape in Bridei's time, quite unsuited to a royal fortress. Burghead is chronologically acceptable, but its location hardly fits Adomnan's description of a fortress near the River Ness. The Pictish capital is unlikely to have remained in the north after Bridei, for the seventh and eighth centuries saw constant pressures and conflicts between the Picts and their neighbours to the south and west, and a political centre in southern Pictland was vital. Its precise whereabouts is unknown. The capital was presumably transferred once more to the north during the thirty years or so of the Northumbrian occupation of southern Pictland; the Northumbrians were expelled after the battle of Nechtanesmere in AD 685, and the Pictish king, Bridei, son of Bile, re-established his capital in the south.

The Church in Pictland

Although Columba's mission among the Picts appears not to have been wholly successful, his followers achieved the gradual conversion of the Picts during the rest of the sixth century and into the seventh, building churches and monasteries. Adomnan is silent on the subject of whether Columba baptised King Bridei, but Bede states that Bridei was converted – and that he granted Iona to Columba. It is difficult to identify Columban foundations in Pictland, though tradition would have the monastery at Deer in Aberdeenshire as an early foundation; the early churches were probably built in wood, and traces of them beneath later stone buildings are likely to be slight. Little is known about the organization of the Pictish church, apart from the fact that it was Celtic rather than Roman. The synod of Whitby in AD 663 took place during the Northumbrian occupation of southern Pictland, and there the Pictish church can have had no choice but to accept the reforms imposed upon the Celtic church at Whitby. A bishopric was set up at

Abercorn in West Lothian, but the Pictish victory at Nechtanesmere in 685 turned the bishop and his monks into refugees, and the Pictish church returned to its former ways. The final reformation of the church in Pictland took place around AD 710, when the Pictish king Nechtan, son of Derilei, resolved that his church should fall into line with the teaching of Rome.

Fine metalwork

The obscurity that surrounds Pictish language, the meaning of the symbols and aspects of Pictish society exists primarily in contrast with better-known historical peoples, and it tends itself to blur our appreciation of the extent to which the Picts were in contact with and indeed participating in developments beyond their kingdom. The interaction between Pictish and other art styles has already been described; in metalwork and jewellery, too, common fashions may be seen. A clay mound found during excavation of the fort at Craig Phadrig indicates local manufacture of open-work escutcheons designed to hold the suspension loops on bronze hanging-bowls; comparable escutcheons have been found in Wiltshire and Leicestershire, and the use of hanging-bowls was common throughout Britain and Ireland in the seventh century. The presence of imported Class E ware at Craig Phadrig and Clatchard Craig has already been mentioned as part of a widespread trade pattern. There are links in technique and style between silver hand-pins from Pictish hoards from Gaulcross in Banffshire and Norrie's Law in Fife and the bronze hanging-bowl from Sutton Hoo, and there are several types of brooch and pin current in the mid-first millennium AD that are common to most parts of the British Isles. The hoard from Norrie's Law has a special Pictish
136 flavour as well: the pair of oval silver plaques already mentioned, which are incised with Pictish symbols. This hoard was found almost two hundred years ago and consisted then of more than thirteen kg of

136 Silver plaques, Norrie's Law, Fife

137 Terminal ring from silver chain, Whitecleuch, Lanarkshire

138 Silver chain, Hoardweel, Preston, Berwickshire

silver, but most of it was melted down and only 750g has survived. This includes pins, bracelets and brooches, and the hoard is thought to have been buried in the seventh century. Its size reinforces the impression already given by the great Traprain Law hoard that there was a lot of silver current in post-Roman Scotland, and wealthy Picts may have sported considerable personal finery. Some items of jewellery may be identified as peculiar to the Picts. Heavy silver chains weighing up to 2,877g were made by linking pairs of rings and fastened by broad penannular rings; two of these terminals bear Pictish symbols, and it 137
is likely that the chains were worn as badges of office, perhaps by high-ranking officials such as the *mormaers*. Ten chains have survived, seven 138
of them outside Pictland, south of the Forth, where their presence may perhaps be connected with outlying *pit*-names and the possibility of refugee *mormaers* and their families leaving Pictland after the take-over by the Scots in 843.

139 Silver hoard, St Ninian's Isle, Shetland; bowl, sword chape, spoon and cones

The most famous of all Pictish silverwork hoards is that found in 1958 on St Ninian's Isle, on the west coast of Shetland. It was dis- 139
covered during the excavation of a medieval church site, and it had apparently been buried originally beneath the floor of an earlier church. The hoard consisted of twenty-eight silver objects and the jawbone of a porpoise, all enclosed in a larchwood box of which only a few fragments survived; David Wilson has estimated the date of its burial around AD 800. There are seven shallow bowls, which were probably used at table as drinking-bowls, and a hanging-bowl, a form of vessel that has survived most frequently in bronze rather than silver. Hanging-bowls were fashionable in the seventh century, and a domestic use, perhaps as finger-bowls, has been suggested. Aside from table-ware, the hoard contains sword-fittings, including two very

140–1 beautiful chapes, one of which is inscribed in Latin: on one side, INNOMINEDS 'in the name of God the highest', and on the other, RESADFILISPUSSCIO '[This is the property] of Resad son of Spusscio'. Three unique cones have been interpreted as elaborate buttons or dress-fastenings. All the objects in the hoard are ornamented, some very highly, and Wilson has demonstrated the presence of stylistic elements related to the artistic traditions of Ireland, Pictland, Northumbria, Mercia and southern England. Above all, the hoard is important for Wilson's identification of a specifically Pictish type of penannular brooch. Diagnostic Pictish artefacts are few, and the isolation of this type of brooch will be very useful. There are eleven brooches in the hoard, varying in size from 66mm to 108mm in diameter and all highly decorated. The St Ninian's Isle type of brooch is characterized primarily by its penannular shape and by a number of stylistic features including the presence of a panel with curved ends on the hoop of the brooch. Two other hoards of silver-work in Scotland contain this type of brooch: Rogart in Sutherland and Croy in Inverness-shire, and similar brooches have been found elsewhere in Pictland. A few found their way outside Pictland, most notably to Norway where they occur, presumably the result of looting or trading, in early ninth-century graves.

There is still controversy over the origin of some of the St Ninian's Isle pieces, and over the nature of the hoard, whether ecclesiastical or secular, though most archaeologists favour a secular interpretation. The church was the next best place to a bank, and it is thought likely that the hoard was deposited for safety against the threat of a Viking raid. The presence in the hoard of the porpoise jawbone remains an intriguing puzzle.

142 A delightful bronze pin found at Golspie, Sutherland, has a man's face decorating one side of its head, a rarity in Pictish art where the human face is normally portrayed in profile. There are traces of gilding on the decoration, and the pin is thought to have been cast; style and manufacturing technique leave no doubt that this is a Pictish pin, and the interlace beneath the face link it with one of the St Ninian's Isle brooches. The Golspie area appears to have been a focus of settlement in north Pictland, for it includes fifteen symbol stones, a number of burials and the Rogart silver hoard.

Burials

A large number of post-Roman burials has been recorded in Scotland, most comprising an inhumation lying in a long slab-built cist, but in the absence of grave-goods such burials are impossible to date precisely. Some may well contain Picts, particularly isolated examples dug into mounds covering the ruins of brochs, though some of the presumptively Christian cemeteries may belong to converted Pictland. The possible association of a few symbol stones has already been discussed, and some of these must indicate Pictish graves, even though the symbol stones cannot be proved to have been headstones. The presence in the cemetery of a symbol stone on the Brough of Birsay, Orkney, suggests that the early graves may be Pictish and connected

140–1 Silver hoard, St Ninian's Isle, Shetland; silver chape showing inscriptions on both sides

142 Bronze pin with man's face, Golspie, Sutherland

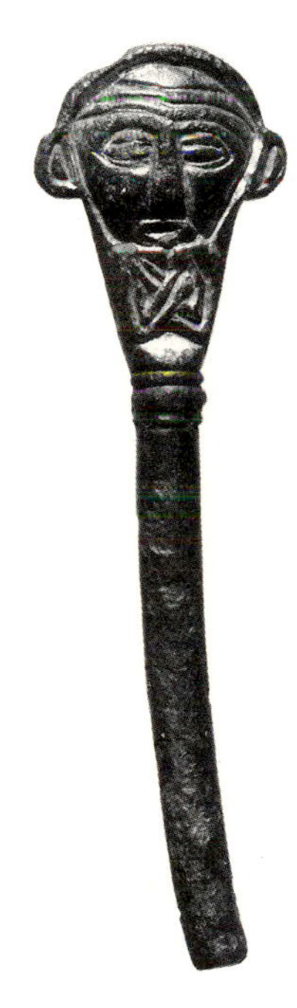

perhaps with evidence from the site of Pictish metalworking, but the stone was found in three scattered fragments and not associated directly with any grave.

There was a distinctively Pictish tradition of grave-construction, which allows the identification of the burials of at least part of the population; with the possible exception of a site at Lundin Links in Fife, these burials belong to northern Pictland. They are characterized by kerbed cairns that enclose burials in long cists. The classic site is at Ackergill in Caithness, where there were two long cists and eight cairns set in a line; seven of the cairns were rectangular or square and the eighth was circular. The cairns consisted of an enclosure formed by a kerb of upright slabs or of horizontal dry-stone walling, with the exception of one square cairn which had no kerb. Most of the rectilinear enclosures had a tall upright stone at each corner, but one had two upright stones set in the centre of one side of the enclosure rather than at the corners. The enclosures were filled with stones and in some cases topped with a layer of small white quartzite pebbles, which must have given them a pleasing appearance. The graves, of which there were sometimes more than one in each cairn, were dug into the sand beneath the cairns. It is not yet known whether there is a chronological difference between circular and rectilinear cairns, but there is some evidence to suggest that the circular form is the earlier. At Ackergill, the circular cairn contained a female skeleton wearing a bronze chain as a necklace, and this is likely to be a pagan burial. It is the only burial known to be associated with grave-goods. The Norsemen in Scotland appear to have adopted the idea of grave-enclosures from the Picts, and the fact that it was the rectangular form that they built suggests that this was the form in use among the Picts in the ninth century.

Comparable circular cairns with horizontal walled kerbs have been found at Keiss Links and Wattenen in Caithness. A rectangular cairn at Sandwick, Unst, in Shetland, had a kerb of upright slabs, with taller stones at the corners and in the middle of each side, but it is not certain whether this is a Pictish or Viking Age burial, though the use of a quartzite capping may favour the earlier date. There are also several examples of circular or rectilinear cairns which, like one of the Ackergill cairns, lack a formal kerb. A rectangular cairn at Dairy Park, Dunrobin, Sutherland, had a rough boulder kerb.

Forts and settlements

In recent years a number of Pictish forts have been identified, and it is likely that this is an area of Pictish studies which will continue to expand. The great timber-laced fort at Burghead on the coast of Morayshire must have been of considerable military and naval importance to the Picts, and radiocarbon dates suggest that it was built in the fifth or sixth centuries and maintained in good condition throughout the Pictish period. Its association with the bull symbol seems entirely appropriate for a military centre. Another coastal promontory fort is Green Castle, Portknockie, Banffshire, where a timber-laced fort wall has been dated by radiocarbon analysis to the mid-first millennium AD, and there is evidence of occupation at a similar period at Clatchard Craig in Fife. Minor domestic occupation of the iron age forts at Craig Phadrig in Inverness-shire and Cullykhan in Banffshire has been identified at this period. Entries in the Irish annals make it clear that Dunnottar on the coast of Kincardineshire and Dundurn in Perthshire were both sites of Pictish forts, and excavation at the latter site has yielded artefacts and radiocarbon dates that are consistent with the annal entry of AD 683 in which the fort was besieged. The timber-laced wall at Dundurn showed the same technique of using iron nails to secure the timbers that is known from Burghead – and from nowhere else in Britain. Leslie Alcock has stressed the high quality of the artefacts found at Dundurn, which included a decorated leather shoe, fragments of a glass beaker and a Class E cooking pot, evidence for jewellery manufacture, and a superb glass boss which may have been intended as ornament for a chalice, crucifix or reliquary.

Most of our knowledge about the domestic settlements of the Picts comes from northern Pictland and in particular from excavations at the Udal, North Uist, and at Buckquoy in Orkney. The secondary settlements that grew up around abandoned brochs in northern Scotland are of great potential interest for this period, and modern excavation of such settlements will add considerably to studies of Pictish domestic life. The identification of settlements in southern Pictland is more difficult; houses are more likely to have been built of timber in this area, and their location will rely heavily on chance discoveries. It is evident that some of the settlements associated with souterrains in Angus and Perthshire in the first two centuries AD continued in occupation after the souterrains had gone out of use, and such occupation may have extended into the early Pictish period.

Excavations at Buckquoy by Anna Ritchie uncovered the remains of a multi-period Pictish farmstead beneath a ninth-century Norse farmstead, with a brief period of abandonment between the two. The site lies on the north-west coast of mainland Orkney, close to the early Christian settlement on the Brough of Birsay which includes evidence of Pictish metalworking; one of the moulds is for a small penannular brooch of the St Ninian's Isle type. No trace of contemporary domestic buildings has been found on the site, but they may lie beneath the later Viking Age settlement. Three successive Pictish houses were identified at Buckquoy, dating to the seventh and early eighth centuries. The
143 earlier two belong to a type known as the cellular house, in which a

143 Pictish farmstead, Buckquoy, Orkney; cellular houses overlain by circular chamber of later house (scale in 50 cm divisions)

central chamber containing the hearth is surrounded by rounded or rectilinear cells; the primary house was incomplete, but comparison with a similar house in the post-broch settlement at Gurness suggests that there were probably five cells, in this case rectilinear, surrounding the slab-lined rectangular hearth. The succeeding house was smaller, about one-third the size of the first house, and there were only three cells; internally it measured about 2.75m by 3.6m, with a small, carefully built rectilinear hearth. The walls of both houses were probably constructed with inner and outer faces of stone and an earthen or turf core, but only the basal courses survived. Their external appearance would have been roughly oval, probably with a turf roof supported by a timber framework.

This cellular type of house was then replaced by a larger and architecturally more advanced house, known as the figure-of-eight house 144–5 because it consists of two basic elements, a large oval chamber and a smaller circular chamber. At Buckquoy, the circular chamber was partially subterranean, 3.4m in diameter, and the base of its wall comprised upright slabs acting as a revetment course with horizontal walling above. Paving in this chamber suggested that its function might have been storage. Collapsed slabs filling the chamber indicated that it had probably had a corbelled roof. The main chamber contained

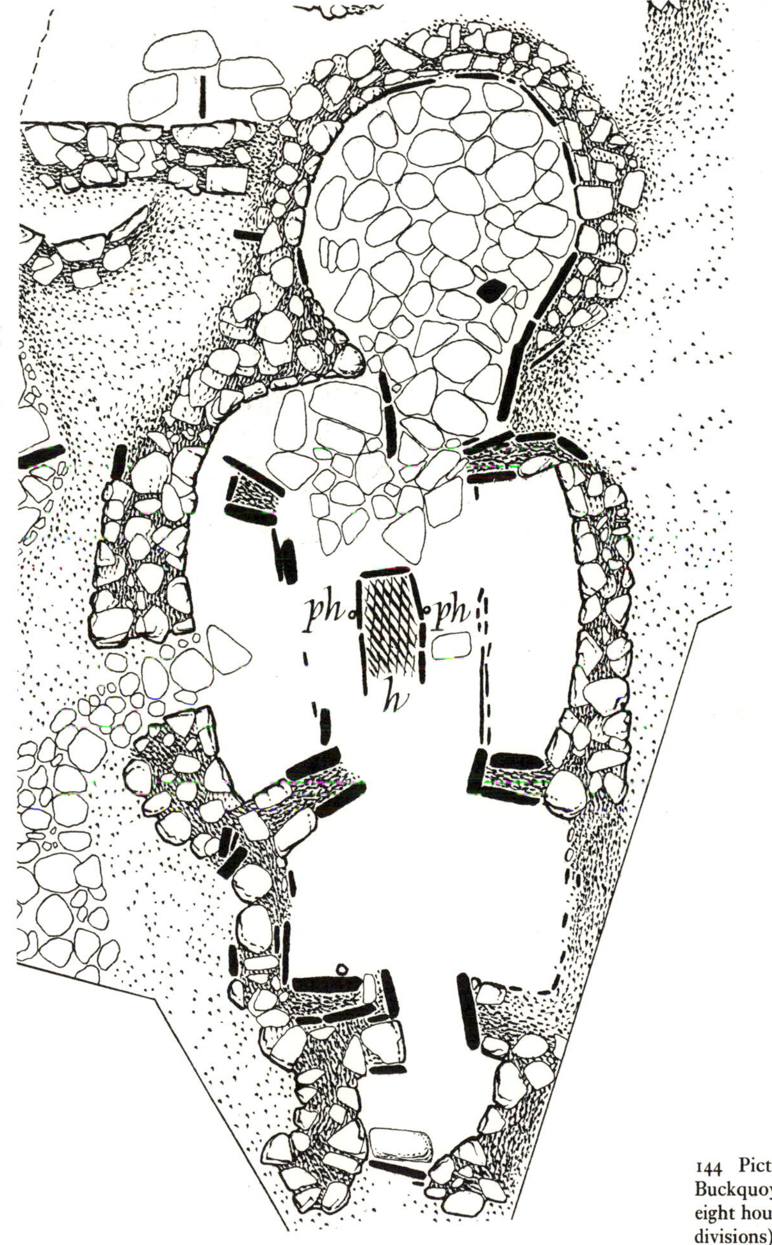

144 Pictish farmstead, Buckquoy, Orkney; figure-of-eight house (scale in 50 cm divisions)

145 Pictish farmstead, Buckquoy, Orkney; plan of figure-of-eight house

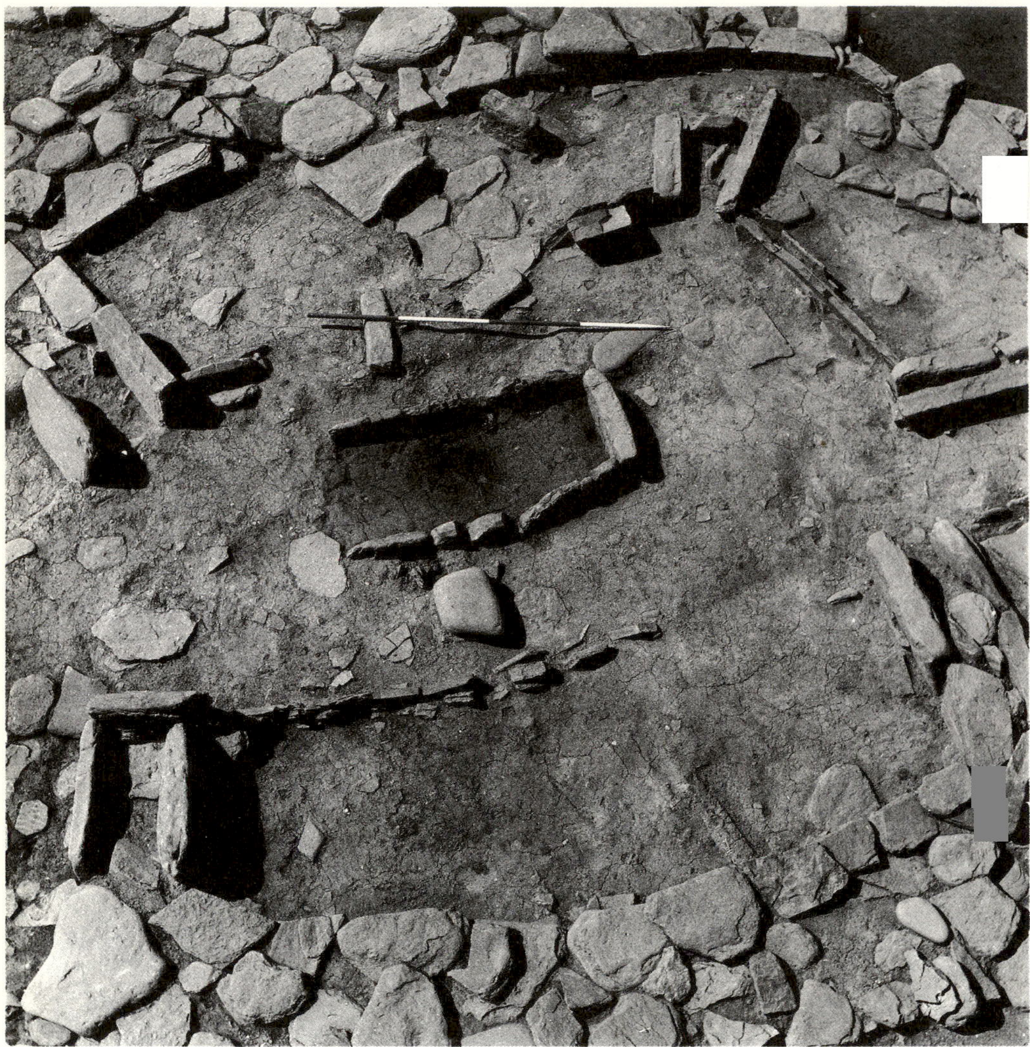

146 Pictish farmstead, Buckquoy, Orkney; main hall of figure-of-eight house, showing hearth and kerbing (scale in 50 cm divisions)

a central rectilinear hearth, paved and kerbed with stone slabs, and low kerbing on either side is likely to have delimited seating and sleeping areas and may even have supported wooden benches. A small rectangular room opened off this main hall, opposite the circular chamber, and a very small entrance vestibule lay beyond, so that the four rooms were arranged in linear fashion. A second entrance opened directly into the main hall. The rooms were separated and the roof partially supported by protruding piers of dry-stone masonry; these piers echo the building traditions seen in wheelhouses. Overall the house measured about 15.8m long internally, and its maximum width in the main hall was about 6m.

Artefacts from these Pictish phases included bone pins, a double-sided composite bone comb, a bone spoon, a little plain coarse pottery, iron knife-blades and stone spindle-whorls. Two artefacts with

147–8 Pictish farmstead, Buckquoy, Orkney; ogam-inscribed spindle-whorl and painted pebble

specifically Pictish connotations were found associated with the figure-of-eight house. One of the spindle-whorls was found to bear an ogam inscription incised round its central perforation; the inscription is unintelligible but the form of the letters suggests a date in the early eighth century. A white quartzite pebble had been painted overall with small circles; eighteen other such painted pebbles have been found, all from sites in the Northern Isles or Caithness and most in contexts datable to the Pictish period. They are thought to have been charm-stones used in treating sick people and cattle, a tradition for which there is considerable evidence from early medieval to recent times. All three Pictish houses at Buckquoy appear to have been abandoned peaceably and their interiors largely swept clean; the late Pictish house is likely to have been the home of a wealthier family than the few finds would indicate.

147

148

Very close to Buckquoy was a house which is structurally related to and possibly contemporary with the late Pictish figure-of-eight house. It consisted of two conjoining circular rooms, one about 4.5m in diameter and the other slightly smaller, and there was some evidence to suggest a stone corbelled roof. Unlike the circular chamber of the Buckquoy house, the walls were built entirely of horizontal masonry with no use of upright slabs, although the floor of the house was below ground level.

The figure-of-eight type of house has also been found at Yarrows in Caithness in a post-broch settlement and at the Udal in North Uist, although in both cases the houses are smaller and less sophisticated in their construction than at Buckquoy. A larger social unit is implied by the presence of several houses at the Udal, though they may not all have been in use at one time, and a date within the seventh to early ninth centuries has been suggested. The identification of this distinctive type of house as Pictish should prove a useful cultural indicator for future excavations elsewhere.

By AD 800, the far north and west of Pictland was suffering the effects of Viking raiding expeditions, and the Northern Isles in particular were used by the Norsemen as a winter base from which to loot the wealth of Irish monasteries. They were not slow to recognize the rich potential of the Orkneys for permanent settlement, and it is clear that farms like Buckquoy were established early in the ninth century.

The attitude of the Picts towards these newcomers is unknown, but there is evidence to suggest that the two peoples existed side by side and that the Norsemen adopted several native traditions including Christianity. Nevertheless, Pictish culture was finally replaced by the Norse way of life, and the Orkneys became the political centre of a very powerful Norse earldom.

For southern Pictland, the loss of independence was rather more abrupt, and the end of the Pictish kingdom came around AD 843 with the establishment on the throne of a Dalriadan monarch. Many aspects of the take-over by the Scots are unclear; contemporary historical sources make no mention of the background to the event nor do they help to explain the political and linguistic eclipse of the Picts. Kenneth was by no means the first king to be of Scottish origin. His hold on the kingdom was, however, to be different from those of his predecessors, perhaps because of the general movement of Scots into the east at the same time, or perhaps there was already an important Scottish element in Pictland.

There was probably no place in the new Scotland for Pictish symbols and, although some production of sculpture continued, the quality of the designs declined. It is likely that the old, non-Indo-European language of the Picts was quickly lost, though it survived long enough for the place-names incorporating the term *pit* with Gaelic elements to be established. The identification of the *mormaer* and *toiseach* of later times as ranks belonging originally to Pictish government has shown that the Pictish contribution to the lifestyle of later medieval times may have been more extensive than previously supposed from records of the imposition of Scottish civil and ecclesiastical laws. It may well be that the Picts and the Scots together stood a better chance against Norse encroachment from the north and west, but it may be doubted whether the Picts relished the price.

Select Bibliography

Abbreviations

Proc. Soc. Antiq. Scot.	Proceedings of the Society of Antiquaries of Scotland
Scot. Archaeol. Forum	Scottish Archaeological Forum

General

EVANS, J. G., *The Environment of Early Man in the British Isles*, London, 1975

FEACHEM, R. W., *Guide to Prehistoric Scotland*, London, 2nd ed. 1977

FENTON, A., *Scottish Country Life*, London and Edinburgh, 1976

LAVELL, C. (ed.), *Archaeological Site Index to Radiocarbon Dates for Great Britain and Ireland*, Council for British Archaeology, London, 1971

MACKIE, E. W., *Scotland: An Archaeological Guide*, London, 1975

MCNEILL, P., and NICHOLSON, R. (eds), *An Historical Atlas of Scotland* c. *400*–c. *1600*, St Andrews, 1975

MEGAW, J. V. S., and SIMPSON, D. D. A., *Introduction to British Prehistory*, Leicester, 1979

MENZIES, G. (ed.), *Who Are the Scots?*, London, 1971

PIGGOTT, S. (ed.), *The Prehistoric Peoples of Scotland*, London, 1962

RENFREW, A. C. (ed.), *British Prehistory: A New Outline*, London, 1974

RITCHIE, A. and RITCHIE, J. N. G., *The Ancient Monuments of Orkney*, Edinburgh, 1978

RITCHIE, J. N. G. and RITCHIE, A., *Edinburgh and South-East Scotland*, London, 1972

Royal Commission on the Ancient and Historical Monuments of Scotland

Inventories of ancient and historical monuments have been prepared for the following counties: Argyll, vols 1–3 (1971, 1975 and 1980), Berwickshire (1909 and 1915), Caithness (1911), Clackmannan (1933), Dumfriesshire (1920), East Lothian (1924), Edinburgh (1951), Fife (1933), Kinross (1933), Kirkcudbright (1914), Lanarkshire: Prehistoric and Roman (1978), Midlothian (1929), Orkney (1946), Peeblesshire (1967), Roxburgh (1956), Selkirkshire (1957), Shetland (1946), Stirlingshire (1963), Sutherland (1911), Western Isles and Skye (1928), West Lothian (1929), Wigtownshire (1912)

SCOTT, J. G., *South-West Scotland*, London, 1967

SISSONS, J. B., *The Evolution of Scotland's Scenery*, Edinburgh and London, 1967

Chapter 1

CLARKE, D. L., 'Mesolithic Europe; the economic basis', in G. de G. Sieveking, I. H. Longworth and K. E. Wilson (eds), *Problems in Economic and Social Archaeology*, 449–81, London, 1976; also published separately, London, 1978

LACAILLE, A. D., *The Stone Age in Scotland*, Oxford, 1954

MELLARS, P. A., 'Excavation and Economic Analysis of Mesolithic Shell-Middens on the Island of Oronsay (Hebrides)', *Scot. Archaeol. Forum*, vol. 9 (1977), 43–61

MERCER, J., 'The Microlithic Succession in N Jura, Argyll, W Scotland', *Quaternaria*, vol. 13 (1970), 177–85; and a series of detailed papers on Jura sites in *Proc. Soc. Antiq. Scot.*

Chapter 2

BURGESS, C. and MIKET, R. (eds), *Settlement and Economy in the Third and Second Millennia BC*, Oxford, 1976. British Archaeological Reports, No. 33

CALDER, C. S. T., 'Report on the excavation of a neolithic temple at Stanydale in the Parish of Sandsting, Shetland', *Proc. Soc. Antiq. Scot.*, vol. 74 (1949–50), 185–205

—, 'Stone age house-sites in Shetland', *Proc. Soc. Antiq. Scot.*, vol. 79 (1955–6), 340–97

CHILDE, V. G., *Skara Brae, A Pictish Village in Orkney*, London, 1931

— and GRANT, W. G., 'A stone-age settlement at the Braes of Rinyo, Rousay, Orkney', *Proc. Soc. Antiq. Scot.*, vol. 63 (1938–9), 6–31, and vol. 71 (1946–7), 16–42

CLARKE, D. L., *Beaker Pottery in Great Britain and Ireland*, Cambridge, 1970

CLARKE, D. V., *The Neolithic Village at Skara Brae, Orkney: 1972–73 Excavations: an interim report*, Edinburgh, 1976

CORCORAN, J. X. W. P., 'The Excavation of Three Chambered Cairns at Loch Calder, Caithness', *Proc. Soc. Antiq. Scot.*, vol. 98 (1964–6), 1–75

—, 'Excavation of Two Chambered Cairns at Mid Gleniron Farm, Glenluce, Wigtownshire', *Transactions of the Dumfriesshire and Galloway Natural History and Antiquarian Society*, vol. 46 (1969), 29–90

HENSHALL, A. S., *The Chambered Tombs of Scotland*, Edinburgh, 1963 and 1972

LANTING, J. N. and VAN DER WAALS, J. D., 'British Beakers as seen from the Continent', *Helinium*, vol. 12 (1972), 20–46

MCINNES, I., 'A Scottish Neolithic Pottery Sequence', *Scot. Archaeol. Forum*, vol. 1 (1969), 19–30

MARSHALL, D. N., 'Carved stone balls', *Proc. Soc. Antiq. Scot.*, vol. 108 (1976–7), 40–72

MASTERS, L., 'The Lochhill long cairn', *Antiquity*, vol. 47 (1973), 43–5

PIGGOTT, S., 'Excavations in Passage-Graves and Ring-Cairns in the Clava Group, 1952–3', *Proc. Soc. Antiq. Scot.*, vol. 88 (1954–6), 171–207

—, 'Excavation of the Dalladies long barrow, Fettercairn, Kincardineshire', *Proc. Soc. Antiq. Scot.*, vol. 104 (1970–1), 23–47

—, 'Problems in the Interpretation of Chambered Tombs', in G. Daniel, and P. Kjaerum (eds), *Megalithic Graves and Ritual*, 9–15, Third Atlantic Conference, Mosegard, 1969 (published 1973)

POWELL, T. G. E. *et al.*, *Megalithic Enquiries in the West of Britain*, Liverpool, 1969

RENFREW, C., *Investigations in Orkney*, Society of Antiquaries of London Research Report, no. 38, London, 1979

RITCHIE, J. N. G., 'Excavation of the Chambered Cairn at Achnacreebeag', *Proc. Soc. Antiq. Scot.*, vol. 102 (1969–70), 31–55

RITCHIE, P. R., 'The stone implement trade in third millennium Scotland', in J. M. Coles and D. D. A. Simpson (eds), *Studies in Ancient Europe:* Essays presented to Stuart Piggott, 117–36, Leicester, 1968

SIMPSON, D. D. A. (ed.), *Economy and Settlement in Neolithic and Bronze Age Britain and Europe*, Leicester, 1971

Chapter 3

BURL, A., *The Stone Circles of the British Isles*, New Haven and London, 1976

MACKIE, E. W., *Science and Society in Prehistoric Britain*, London, 1977

PIGGOTT, S., 'The Excavations at Cairnpapple Hill, West Lothian, 1947–8', *Proc. Soc. Antiq. Soc.*, vol. 82 (1947–8), 68–123

—, and SIMPSON, D. D. A., 'Excavations of a Stone Circle at Croft Moraig, Perthshire, Scotland', *Proceedings of the Prehistoric Society*, vol. 37 (1971), 1–15

RITCHIE, J. N. G., 'Excavation of the Stone Circle and Cairn at Balbirnie, Fife', *Archaeological Journal*, vol. 131 (1974), 1–32

—, 'The Stones of Stenness, Orkney', *Proc. Soc. Antiq. Scot.*, vol. 107 (1975–6), 1–60

THOM, A., *Megalithic Sites in Britain*, Oxford, 1967

—, *Megalithic Lunar Observatories*, Oxford, 1971

Chapter 4

COLES, J. M., 'Scottish Late Bronze Age metalwork: typology, distributions and chronology', *Proc. Soc. Antiq. Scot.*, vol. 93 (1959–60), 16–134; 'Scottish Middle Bronze Age metalwork', *Proc. Soc. Antiq. Scot.*, vol. 97 (1963–4), 82–156; 'Scottish Early Bronze Age metalwork', *Proc. Soc. Antiq. Scot.*, vol. 101 (1968–9), 1–110

HEDGES, J., 'Excavation of two Orcadian Burnt Mounds at Liddle and Beaquoy', *Proc. Soc. Antiq. Scot.*, vol. 106 (1974–5), 39–98

MORRISON, A., 'Cinerary Urns and Pygmy Vessels in South-west Scotland', *Transactions of the Dumfriesshire and Galloway Natural History and Antiquarian Society*, vol. 45 (1968), 80–140

RITCHIE, J. N. G., 'Excavation of a Cairn at Strontoiller, Lorn, Argyll', *Glasgow Archaeological Journal*, vol. 2 (1971), 1–7

—, and MACLAREN, A., 'Ring Cairns and Related Monuments in Scotland', *Scot. Archaeol. Forum*, vol. 4 (1972), 1–17

SIMPSON, D. D. A. and THAWLEY, J. E., 'Single Grave Art in Britain', *Scot. Archaeol. Forum*, vol. 4 (1972), 81–104

Chapter 5

ATKINSON, R. J. C. and PIGGOTT, S., 'The Torrs Chamfrein', *Archaeologia*, vol. 96 (1955), 197–235

CHILDE, V. G., 'Excavation of the vitrified fort of Finavon, Angus', *Proc. Soc. Antiq. Scot.*, vol. 59 (1934–5), 49–80

CLARKE, D. V., 'Small Finds in the Atlantic Province: Problems of Approach', *Scot. Archaeol. Forum*, vol. 3 (1971), 22–54

CUNLIFFE, B., *Iron Age Communities in Britain*, London and Boston, 1974

FAIRHURST, H., 'The wheelhouse site at A Cheardach Bheag on Drimore Machair, South Uist', *Glasgow Archaeological Journal*, vol. 2 (1971), 72–106

HAMILTON, J. R. C., *Excavations at Jarlshof*, Edinburgh, 1956

—, *Excavations at Clickhimin, Shetland*, Edinburgh, 1968

HARDING, D. W. (ed.), *Hillforts, Later Prehistoric Earthworks in Great Britain and Ireland*, London, 1976

HILL, P., *Broxmouth Hillfort Excavations, 1977–78, an interim report*, University of Edinburgh, Department of Archaeology, Occasional Paper no. 2, 1979

JACKSON, K. H., *The Oldest Irish Tradition: A Window on the Iron Age*, Cambridge, 1964

JOBEY, G., 'Early Settlement and Topography in the Border Counties', *Scot. Archaeol. Forum*, vol. 2 (1970), 73–84

—, 'Excavations at Boonies, Westerkirk, and the nature of Romano – British Settlement in eastern Dumfriesshire', *Proc. Soc. Antiq. Scot.*, vol. 105 (1972–4), 119–40

—, 'Unenclosed Platforms and Settlements of the Later Second Millennium BC in Northern Britain', *Scot. Archaeol. Forum*, vol. 10 (1978), 12–26

MACGREGOR, M., *Early Celtic Art in North Britain*, Leicester, 1976

MACKIE, E. W., 'The origin and development of the broch and wheelhouse building cultures of the Scottish Iron Age', *Proceedings of the Prehistoric Society*, vol. 31 (1965), 93–146

—, 'Radiocarbon dates and the Scottish Iron Age', *Antiquity*, vol. 43 (1969), 15–26

—, 'English Migrants and Scottish Brochs', *Glasgow Archaeological Journal*, vol. 2 (1971), 39–71

—, *Dun Mor Vaul: An Iron Age Broch on Tiree*, Glasgow, 1974

—, 'The brochs of Scotland', in P. J. Fowler (ed.), *Recent Work in Rural Archaeology*, 72–92, Frome and London, 1975

MAXWELL, G., 'Duns and forts – a note on some iron

age monuments of the Atlantic Province', *Scot. Archaeol. Forum*, vol. 1 (1969), 41–52

MEGAW, J. V. S., *Art of the Iron Age: A study of the elusive image*, Bath, 1970

MUNRO, R., *Ancient Scottish Lake Dwellings*, Edinburgh, 1882

PIGGOTT, C. M., 'The excavations at Hownam Rings, Roxburghshire, 1948', *Proc. Soc. Antiq. Scot.*, vol. 72 (1947–8), 193–225

—, 'Milton Loch Crannog I: a native house of the 2nd century A.D. in Kirkcudbrightshire', *Proc. Soc. Antiq. Scot.*, vol. 77 (1952–3), 134–52

RITCHIE, A., 'Palisaded Sites in North Britain: their Context and Affinities', *Scot. Archaeol. Forum*, vol. 2 (1970), 48–67

RIVET, A. L. F. (ed.), *The Iron Age in Northern Britain*, Edinburgh, 1966

ROSS, A., *Everyday Life of the Pagan Celts*, London and New York, 1970

SCOTT, J. G., 'The Roman occupation of south-west Scotland from the recall of Agricola to the withdrawal under Trajan', *Glasgow Archaeological Journal*, vol. 4 (1976), 29–44

WAINWRIGHT, F. T., *The Souterrains of Southern Pictland*, London, 1963

Chapter 6

ALFOLDI, A., 'The moral barrier on Rhine and Danube', in E. Birley (ed.), *The Congress of Roman Frontier Studies, 1949*, 1–16, Durham, 1952

BREEZE, D. J., 'The Roman fortlet at Barburgh Mill, Dumfriesshire', *Britannia*, vol. 5 (1974), 130–62

—, *Roman Scotland: A Guide to the Visible Remains*, Newcastle-upon-Tyne, 1979

— and DOBSON, B., *Hadrian's Wall*, London, 1976

CURLE, J., *A Roman Frontier Post and Its People: the Fort of Newstead in the Parish of Melrose*, Glasgow, 1911

FRERE, S., *Britannia, A History of Roman Britain*, London, 1967 and 1974

HARTLEY, B. R., 'The Roman Occupation of Scotland: the evidence of samian ware', *Britannia*, vol. 3 (1972), 1–55

MACDONALD, G., *The Roman Wall in Scotland*, 2nd ed., Oxford, 1934

MANNING, W. H., 'Iron work hoards in Iron Age and Roman Britain', *Britannia*, vol. 3 (1972), 243–6

MANN, J. C., 'The Northern Frontier after A.D. 369', *Glasgow Archaeological Journal*, vol. 3 (1974), 34–42

MAXWELL, G. S., 'The Excavation of the Roman Fort at Crawford, Lanarkshire', *Proc. Soc. Antiq. Scot.*, vol. 104 (1971–2), 147–200

OGILVIE, R. M. and RICHMOND, I. A. (eds), *Cornelii Taciti de Vita Agricolae*, Oxford, 1967

ORDNANCE SURVEY, *The Antonine Wall*. 2½ Inch Map, Southampton, 1969

—, *Map of Roman Britain*, Southampton, 1978

PIGGOTT, S., 'Three Metal-work Hoards of the Roman Period in Scotland', *Proc. Soc. Antiq. Scot.*, vol. 87 (1952–3), 1–50

RICHMOND, I. A. (ed.), *Roman and Native in North Britain*, Edinburgh and London, 1958

— and STEER, K. A., '*Castellum Veluniate* and civilians on a Roman frontier', *Proc. Soc. Antiq. Scot.*, vol. 90 (1956–7), 1–6

ROBERTSON, A. S., 'Roman Finds from Non-Roman Sites in Scotland', *Britannia*, vol. 1 (1970), 198–226

—, 'Agricola's Campaigns in Scotland, and their Aftermath', *Scot. Archaeol. Forum*, vol. 7 (1975), 1–12

—, *Birrens (Blatobulgium)*, Edinburgh, 1975

—, *The Antonine Wall*, Glasgow, 1979

ROSS, A. and FEACHEM, R., 'Ritual Rubbish? The Newstead Pits', in Megaw, J. V. S. (ed.), *To Illustrate the Monuments*. Essays on Archaeology Presented to Stuart Piggott, 229–37. London, 1976

STEER, K. A., 'The Nature and Purpose of the Expansions on the Antonine Wall', *Proc. Soc. Antiq. Scot.*, vol. 90 (1956–7), 161–9

Chapter 7

ALCOCK, L., *Arthur's Britain. History and Archaeology AD 367–634*, London, 1971

—, 'A multi-disciplinary chronology for Alt Clut, Castle Rock, Dumbarton', *Proc. Soc. Antiq. Scot.*, vol. 107 (1975–6), 103–13

ANDERSON, A. O. and ANDERSON, M. O. (eds), *Adomnan's Life of St Columba*, Edinburgh, 1961

BANNERMAN, J., *Studies in the History of Dalriada*, Edinburgh and London, 1974

CRAMP, R., *Early Northumbrian Sculpture*, Jarrow Lecture, 1965

HOPE-TAYLOR, B., *Yeavering. An Anglo-British centre of early Northumbria*, London, 1977

HUGHES, K., *The Church in Early Irish Society*, London, 1966

— and HAMLIN, A., *The Modern Traveller to the Early Irish Church*, London, 1977

JACKSON, K. H., *Language and History in Early Britain*, Edinburgh, 1953

—, *The Gododdin: the Oldest Scottish Poem*, Edinburgh, 1969

LAMB, R. G., 'Coastal Settlements of the North', *Scot. Archaeol. Forum*, vol. 5 (1973), 76–98

MACQUEEN, J., *St. Nynia: a study of literary and linguistic evidence*, Edinburgh and London, 1961

MEGAW, J. V. S., 'Iona and Celtic Britain, with an Interim Account of the Russell Trust Excavations, 1958–1963', *The Journal of Religious History*, vol. 3 (1965), 212–42, Sydney University Press

RADFORD, C. A. R. and DONALDSON, G., *Whithorn and Kirkmadrine, Wigtownshire*, Edinburgh, 1957

REECE, R., 'Recent Work on Iona', *Scot. Archaeol. Forum*, vol. 5 (1973), 36–46

REYNOLDS, N., 'Dark Age Timber Halls and the Background to Excavation at Balbridie', *Scot. Archaeol. Forum*, 10 (1978), 41–60

RUTHERFORD, A. and RITCHIE, J. N. G., 'The Catstane', *Proc. Soc. Antiq. Scot.*, vol. 105 (1972–4), 183–8

STEVENSON, R. B. K., 'The Nuclear Fort of Dalmahoy, Midlothian, and other Dark Age Capitals', *Proc. Soc. Antiq. Scot.*, vol. 83 (1948–9), 186–98

THOMAS, A. C., 'Imported Pottery in Dark-Age

Western Britain', *Medieval Archaeology*, vol. 3 (1959), 89–111
—, 'An Early Christian Cemetery and Chapel on Ardwall Isle, Kirkcudbright', *Medieval Archaeology*, vol. 11 (1967), 127–88
—, *The Early Christian Archaeology of North Britain*, London, 1969
—, 'Imported Late-Roman Mediterranean Pottery in Ireland and Western Britain: Chronologies and Implications', *Proceedings of the Royal Irish Academy*, vol. 76, section C (1976), 245–55

Chapter 8

ALLEN, J. R. and ANDERSON, J., *The Early Christian Monuments of Scotland*, Edinburgh, 1903
ANDERSON, M. O., *Kings and Kingship in Early Scotland*, Edinburgh and London, 1973
CRAWFORD, I. A. and SWITSUR, R., 'Sandscaping and ^{14}C: the Udal, Uist', *Antiquity*, vol. 51 (1977), 124–36
CRUDEN, S. H., *The Early Christian and Pictish Monuments of Scotland*, Edinburgh, 1964
CURLE, C. L., 'The Chronology of the Early Christian Monuments of Scotland', *Proc. Soc. Antiq. Scot.*, vol. 74 (1939–40), 60–116
HENDERSON, I., 'The Origin Centre of the Pictish Symbol Stones', *Proc. Soc. Antiq. Scot.*, vol. 91 (1957–8), 44–60
—, *The Picts*, London, 1967
—, 'North Pictland' and 'The Meaning of the Pictish Symbol Stones', *The Dark Age in the Highlands*, Inverness Field Club, 1971, 37–52 and 53–67
—, 'Inverness, a Pictish Capital', *The Hub of the Highlands*, Inverness Field Club, Edinburgh, 1975, 91–108
—, 'Sculpture north of the Forth after the Take-over by the Scots', in J. Lang (ed.) *Anglo-Saxon and Viking-Age Sculpture and its Context*, 47–74, Oxford, 1978. British Archaeological Reports, British Series No. 49
—, 'The silver chain from Whitecleuch, Shieldholm, Crawfordjohn, Lanarkshire', *Transactions of the Dumfriesshire and Galloway Natural History and Antiquarian Society*, vol. 54 (1979), 20–8
HUGHES, K., *Early Christianity in Pictland*, Jarrow Lecture, 1970
JACKSON, A., 'Pictish Social Structure and Symbol-Stones. An anthropological assessment', *Scottish Studies*, vol. 15 (1971), 121–40
RITCHIE, A., 'Picts and Norsemen in Northern Scotland', *Scot. Archaeol. Forum*, vol. 6 (1974), 23–36
—, 'Excavation of Pictish and Viking-age farmsteads at Buckquoy, Orkney', *Proc. Soc. Antiq. Scot.*, vol. 108 (1976–7), 174–227
SMALL, A., 'Burghead', *Scot. Archaeol. Forum*, vol. 1 (1969), 31–40
—, THOMAS, A. C. and WILSON, D., *St Ninian's Isle and its Treasure*, Aberdeen, 1970
— and COTTAM, M. B., *Craig Phadrig: interim report on the 1971 excavation*, Dundee University, Department of Geography, 1972
STEVENSON, R. B. K., 'Sculpture in Scotland in the 6th–9th Centuries A.D.', *Kolloquium über spätantike und fruhmittelalterliche Skulptur Heidelberg 1970*, 65–74, Mainz, 1972
—, 'The Earlier Metalwork of Pictland', in J. V. S. Megaw (ed.) *To Illustrate the Monuments.* Essays on Archaeology Presented to Stuart Piggott, 245–51, London, 1976
THOMAS, A. C., 'The Animal Art of the Scottish Iron Age and its Origins', *Archaeological Journal*, vol. 118 (1961), 14–64
—, 'The Interpretation of the Pictish Symbol Stones', *Archaeological Journal*, vol. 120 (1963), 31–97
WAINWRIGHT, F. T. (ed.), *The Problem of the Picts*, Edinburgh, 1955
WILSON, D. M., *Reflections on the St. Ninian's Isle Treasure*, Jarrow Lecture, 1969

List of Illustrations

Permission to use photographs and drawings has been given as follows: Crown Copyright the Royal Commission on the Ancient and Historical Monuments of Scotland (nos 10, 12, 30–3, 39–40, 42, 47, 55–61, 67, 72, 82–4, 87, 90, 92, 95–7, 99–104, 106–7, 114, 116, 125, 128, 135); Crown Copyright the Scottish Development Department (nos 9, 11, 13–14, 19–21, 23–4, 34, 37, 48–9, 70, 74–6, 78, 80–1, 94, 98, 117–20, 122–4, 129–32, 134, 143–7) and the National Museum of Antiquities of Scotland (nos 26, 41, 54, 62, 64, 85–6, 88–9, 108–10, 112, 133, 136–42). A detailed list follows:

The Watch Stone and the Stone of Odin, with the Ring of Brodgar in the background, Orkney. After Elizabeth, Marchioness of Stafford, *Views in Orkney and on the North-Eastern Coast of Scotland*, 1807. Privately printed.

1 Map of Scotland showing administrative regions and districts.

2 Stone rings, Lussa Wood, Jura, Argyll. After J. Mercer, *Hebridean Islands: Colonsay, Gigha, Jura*, Glasgow and London, 1974, p. 54, fig. 6.

3 Flint microliths, Lussa Bay, Jura, Argyll. After J. Mercer, *Proc. Soc. Antiq. Scot.*, vol. 102, 1969–70, p. 10, fig. 6.

4 Left: three stone 'limpet-hammers', Caisteal-nan-Gillean, Oronsay, Argyll. Centre: two bone implements, MacArthur Cave, Oban, Argyll. Right: harpoons, Druimvargie Rock-shelter and MacArthur Cave, Oban, Argyll.
After H. Breuil, *Proc. Soc. Antiq. Scot.*, vol. 56, 1921–2, p. 268, fig. 4; p. 279, figs. 11 and 12; and A. D. Lacaille, *The Stone Age in Scotland*, Oxford, 1954, p. 205, fig. 81.

113 Iron spearhead, knives and point; antler cross-bow-nut, Buston Crannog, Ayrshire. After R. Munro, *Archaeological and Historical Collections relating to the counties of Ayrshire and Wigtownshire*, vol. 3, 1882, pp. 41–2, figs. 36, 37, 39, 42, 43; and A. MacGregor, *Proc. Soc. Antiq. Scot.*, vol. 107, 1975–6, p. 318, fig. 1.

114 Early Christian inscribed stone, Manor Water, Peeblesshire.

115 Cross-slab, Ardwall Island, Kirkcudbrightshire.

116 Catstane, Midlothian, view by James Drummond, 1849.

117 Catstane, Midlothian; part of the long-cist cemetry. Courtesy of Trevor Cowie.

118–19 Ruthwell Cross, Dumfriesshire, details of scroll ornament and Mary washing Christ's feet.

120 Dunadd, Argyll.

121 Iron ring, spearhead, knife, slotted object and inscribed stone disc, Dunadd, Argyll. After D. Christison and J. Anderson, *Proc. Soc. Antiq. Scot.*, vol. 39, 1904–5, pp. 312 and 319, figs. 32, 53–4, 57 and 59.

122 Abbey and *vallum*, Iona, Argyll.

123 Monastery complex, Brough of Deerness, Orkney.

124 Beehive cells, Eileach an Naoimh, Garvellachs, Argyll.

125 Symbol stone, Newton, Aberdeenshire; dumb-bell, serpent and Z-rod symbols.

126 Pictish symbols: a, mirror and comb; b, double-disc and Z-rod; c, crescent and V-rod; d, serpent and Z-rod; e, notched-rectangle and Z-rod; f, rectangle; g, tuning-fork; h, flower; i, 'dog's-head'; j, 'Pictish beast' or 'swimming elephant'.

127 Naturalistic symbols: a, serpent; b, eagle; c, fish; d, wolf; e, horse; f, stag; g, bull; h, boar.

128 Pictish symbol stone, Dunrobin, Sutherland; fish, tuning-fork and mirror and comb symbols.

129 Pictish cross-slab, Meigle no. 5, Perthshire; 'swimming elephant' and mirror symbols.

130 Pictish cross-slab, Glamis, Angus.

131–2 Pictish cross-slab, Aberlemno churchyard, Angus; front with cross, 'gripping beasts' and hippocamps, and back with military scenes, cauldron, and notched rectangle and Z-rod symbols.

133 Pictish slab, Invergowrie, Angus; horseman with drinking horn.

134 St Andrews tomb-shrine, Fife; detail showing David the hunter and David and the lion.

135 Pictish cross-slab, Nigg, Ross and Cromarty; detail of front showing Boss style.

136 Silver plaques, Norrie's Law, Fife.

137 Terminal ring from silver chain, Whitecleuch, Lanarkshire.

138 Silver chain, Hoardweel, Preston, Berwickshire. Courtesy Lord Home of the Hirsel K. T. and the Douglas & Angus Estates, The Hirsel, Coldstream.

139 Silver hoard, St Ninian's Isle, Shetland; bowl, sword chape, spoon and cones.

140–1 Silver hoard, St Ninian's Isle, Shetland; silver chape showing inscriptions on both sides.

142 Bronze pin with man's face, Golspie, Sutherland.

143 Pictish farmstead, Buckquoy, Orkney; cellular houses overlain by circular chamber of later house (scale in 50 cm divisions).

144 Pictish farmstead, Buckquoy, Orkney; figure-of-eight house (scale in 50 cm divisions).

145 Pictish farmstead, Buckquoy, Orkney; plan of figure-of-eight house. After A. Ritchie, *Proc. Soc. Antiq. Scot.*, vol. 108, 1976–7, p. 177, fig. 3.

146 Pictish farmstead, Buckquoy, Orkney; main hall of figure-of-eight house, showing hearth and kerbing (scale in 50 cm divisions).

147–8 Pictish farmstead, Buckquoy, Orkney; ogam-inscribed spindle-whorl and painted pebble. Whorl, Institute of Geological Sciences photograph published by permission of the Director; NERC copyright.

Index

Numerals in brackets following many entries indicate the modern administrative districts as shown on ill. 1. Numerals in italics refer to numbered illustrations.